Henry Wace, And Others

Christianity and Agnosticism

A Controversy

Henry Wace, And Others

Christianity and Agnosticism
A Controversy

ISBN/EAN: 9783337167370

Printed in Europe, USA, Canada, Australia, Japan

Cover: Foto ©ninafisch / pixelio.de

More available books at **www.hansebooks.com**

CHRISTIANITY AND AGNOSTICISM

A CONTROVERSY

CONSISTING OF PAPERS BY

HENRY WACE, D. D.,
PROF. THOMAS H. HUXLEY,
THE BISHOP OF PETERBOROUGH,
W. H. MALLOCK,
MRS. HUMPHRY WARD.

NEW YORK
D. APPLETON AND COMPANY
1889

The undisputed interest taken in the recent controversy between the Rev. Dr. Henry Wace, Principal of King's College, London, and Prof. Huxley, over the question of the true significance of agnosticism, and incidentally of the limits of natural knowledge; and the difficulty of getting at the complete discussion when scattered through different publications, have induced the publishers to bring the articles together in a single volume.

The opening paper, which led directly to those that follow, was read at the Church Congress in Manchester in 1888. The paper on "The Value of Witness to the Miraculous," though not strictly a part of the controversy, was published by Prof. Huxley while it was going on, and its direct bearing on the question at issue is a sufficient reason for its insertion. Mr. Mallock's paper on "Cowardly Agnosticism," and also that of Mrs. Humphry Ward, to which Dr. Wace makes reply in his second article, are included for the valuable side-lights they throw upon the general subject under discussion.

CONTENTS.

	PAGE
I.—ON AGNOSTICISM. By Henry Wace, D.D., Prebendary of St. Paul's Cathedral; Principal of King's College, London *(Read at the Manchester Church Congress, 1888.)*	5
II.—AGNOSTICISM. By Prof. Thomas H. Huxley *(From "The Nineteenth Century," February, 1889.)*	14
III.—AGNOSTICISM. A Reply to Prof. Huxley. By Henry Wace, D.D. *(From "The Nineteenth Century," March, 1889.)*	57
IV.—AGNOSTICISM. By W. C. Magee, D.D., Bishop of Peterborough *(From "The Nineteenth Century," March, 1889.)*	87
V.—AGNOSTICISM: A REJOINDER. By Prof. Thomas H. Huxley *(From "The Nineteenth Century," April, 1889.)*	91
VI.—CHRISTIANITY AND AGNOSTICISM. By Henry Wace, D.D. *(From "The Nineteenth Century," May, 1889.)*	130
VII.—AN EXPLANATION TO PROF. HUXLEY. By W. C. Magee, D.D., Bishop of Peterborough *(From "The Nineteenth Century," May, 1889.)*	166
VIII.—THE VALUE OF WITNESS TO THE MIRACULOUS. By Prof. Thomas H. Huxley *(From "The Nineteenth Century," March, 1889.)*	168
IX.—AGNOSTICISM AND CHRISTIANITY. By Prof. Thomas H. Huxley *(From "The Nineteenth Century," June, 1889.)*	194
X.—"COWARDLY AGNOSTICISM." A WORD WITH PROF. HUXLEY. By W. H. Mallock *(From "The Fortnightly Review," April, 1889.)*	241
XI.—THE NEW REFORMATION. By Mrs. Humphry Ward *(From "The Nineteenth Century," March, 1889.)*	284

I.

ON AGNOSTICISM.

A PAPER READ AT THE MANCHESTER CHURCH CONGRESS, 1888.

BY HENRY WACE, D. D.,
PREBENDARY OF ST. PAUL'S CATHEDRAL; PRINCIPAL OF KING'S COLLEGE, LONDON.

WHAT is agnosticism? In the new Oxford "Dictionary of the English Language," we are told that "an agnostic is one who holds that the existence of anything beyond and behind natural phenomena is unknown, and (so far as can be judged) unknowable, and especially that a First Cause and an unseen world are subjects of which we know nothing." The same authority quotes a letter from Mr. R. H. Hutton, stating that the word was suggested in his hearing, at a party held in 1869, by Prof. Huxley, who took it from St. Paul's mention of the altar at Athens to the Unknown God. "Agnostic," it is further said, in a passage quoted from the "Spectator" of June 11, 1876, "was the name demanded by Prof. Huxley for those who disclaimed atheism, and believed with him in an unknown and unknowable God, or, in other words, that the ultimate origin of all things must be some cause unknown and unknowable." Again, the late honored bishop of this diocese is quoted as saying, in the "Manchester Guardian" in 1880, that "the agnostic neither denied nor affirmed God. He simply put him on one side." The designation was suggested, therefore, for the purpose of avoiding a direct denial of beliefs respecting God such as are asserted by our faith. It proceeds, also, from a scientific source, and claims the scientific merit, or habit, of reserving opinion respecting matters not known or proved.

Now we are not here concerned with this doctrine as a mere question of abstract philosophy respecting the limits of our natural capacities. We have to consider it in relation to the Church and to Christianity, and the main consideration which it is the purpose of this paper to suggest is that, in this relation, the adoption of the term agnostic is only an attempt to shift the issue, and that it involves a mere evasion. A Christian Catechism says: "First, I learn to believe in God the Father, who hath made me, and all the world; secondly, in God the Son, who hath redeemed me, and all mankind; thirdly, in God the Holy Ghost, who sanctifieth me, and all the elect people of God." The agnostic says: "How do you know all that? I consider I have no means of knowing these things you assert respecting God. I do not know, and can not know, that God is a Father, and that he has a Son; and I do not and can not know that such a Father made me, or that such a Son redeemed me." But the Christian did not speak of what he knew, but of what he believed. The first word of a Christian is not "I know," but "I believe." He professes, not a science, but a faith; and at baptism he accepts, not a theory, but a creed.

Now it is true that in one common usage of the word, belief is practically equivalent to opinion. A man may say he believes in a scientific theory, meaning that he is strongly of opinion that it is true; or, in still looser language, he may say he believes it is going to be a fine day. I would observe, in passing, that even in this sense of the word, a man who refused to act upon what he could not know would be a very unpractical person. If you are suffering from an obscure disease, you go to a doctor to obtain, not his knowledge of your malady, but his opinion; and upon that opinion, in defiance of other opinions, even an emperor may have to stake his life. Similarly, from what is known of the proceedings in Parliament respecting the Manchester Ship-Canal, it may be presumed that engineers were not unanimous as to the possibilities and advantages of that undertaking; but Manchester men were content to act upon the best opinion, and to stake fortunes on their belief in it. However, it may be sufficient to have just alluded to the old and unanswered contention of Bishop Butler that, even if Christian belief and Christian duty were mere matters of probable opinion, a man who said in regard to them, "I do not know, and therefore I will not act," would be abandoning the first principle of human energy. He might be a philosopher; but he would not be a man—not at least, I fancy, according to the standard of Lancashire.

But there is another sense of the word "belief," which is of far more importance for our present subject. There is belief which is founded on the assurances of another person, and upon our trust in him. This sort of belief is not opinion, but faith; and it is this which has been the greatest force in creating religions, and through them in molding civilizations. What made the Mohammedan world? Trust and faith in the declarations and assurances of Mohammed. And what made the Christian world? Trust and faith in the declarations and assurances of Jesus

Christ and his apostles. This is not mere believing about things; it is believing a man and believing in a man. Now, the point of importance for the present argument is, that the chief articles of the Christian creed are directly dependent on personal assurances and personal declarations, and that our acceptance of them depends on personal trust. Why do we believe that Jesus Christ redeemed all mankind? Because he said so. There is no other ultimate ground for it. The matter is not one open to the observation of our faculties; and as a matter of science we are not in a position to know it. The case is the same with his divine Sonship and the office of his Spirit. He reveals himself by his words and acts; and in revealing himself he reveals his Father, and the Spirit who proceeds from both. His resurrection and his miracles afford us, as St. Paul says, assurance of his divine mission. But for our knowledge of his offices in relation to mankind, and of his nature in relation to God, we rest on his own words, confirmed and explained by those of his apostles. Who can dream of knowing, as a matter of science, that he is the Judge of quick and dead? But he speaks himself, in the Sermon on the Mount, of that day when men will plead before him, and when he will decide their fate; and Christians include in their creed a belief in that statement respecting the unseen and future world.

But if this be so, for a man to urge as an escape from this article of belief that he has no means of a scientific knowledge of the unseen world, or of the future, is irrelevant. His difference from Christians lies not in the fact that he has no knowledge of these things, but that he does not believe the authority on which they are stated. He may prefer to call himself an agnostic; but his real name is an older one—he is an infidel; that is to say, an unbeliever. The word infidel, perhaps, carries an unpleasant significance. Perhaps it is right that it should. It is, and it ought to be, an unpleasant thing for a man to have to say plainly that he does not believe Jesus Christ. It is, indeed, an awful thing to say. But even men who are not conscious of all it involves shrink from the ungraciousness, if from nothing more, of treating the beliefs inseparably associated with that sacred Person as an illusion. This, however, is what is really meant by agnosticism; and the time seems to have come when it is necessary to insist upon the fact.

Of course, there may be numberless attempts at respectful excuses or evasions, and there is one in particular which may require notice. It may be asked how far we can rely on the accounts we possess of our Lord's teaching on these subjects. Now it is unnecessary for the general argument before us to enter on those questions respecting the authenticity of the Gospel narratives, which ought to be regarded as settled by M. Renan's practical surrender of the adverse case. Apart from all disputed points of criticism, no one practically doubts that our Lord lived, and that he died on the cross, in the most intense sense of filial relation to his Father in heaven, and that he bore testimony to that Father's providence, love, and grace toward mankind. The Lord's Prayer affords sufficient evidence upon these points. If the Sermon on the Mount alone be added, the whole unseen world, of which the agnostic refuses to know anything, stands unveiled before us. There you see revealed the divine Father and Creator of all things, in personal relation to his creatures, hearing their prayers, witnessing their actions, caring for them and rewarding them. There you hear of a future judgment administered by Christ himself, and of a heaven to be hereafter revealed, in which those who live as the children of that Father, and who suffer in the cause and for the sake of Christ himself, will be abundantly rewarded. If Jesus Christ preached that sermon, made those promises, and taught that prayer, then any one who says that we know nothing of God, or of a future life, or of an unseen world, says that he does not believe Jesus Christ. Since the days when our Lord lived and taught, at all events, agnosticism has been impossible without infidelity.

Let it be observed, moreover, that to put the case in this way is not merely to make an appeal to authority. It goes further than that. It is in a vital respect an appeal to experience, and so far to science itself. It is an appeal to what I hope may be taken as, confessedly, the deepest and most sacred moral experience which has ever been known. No criticism worth mentioning doubts the story of the Passion; and that story involves the most solemn attestation, again and again, of truths of which an agnostic coolly says he knows nothing. An agnosticism which knows nothing of the relation of man to God must not only refuse belief to our Lord's most undoubted teaching, but must deny the reality of the spiritual convictions in which he lived and died. It must declare that his most intimate, most intense beliefs, and his dying aspirations, were an illusion. Is that supposition tolerable? It is because it is not tolerable, that men would fain avoid facing it, and would have themselves called agnostics rather than infidels; but I know not whether this cool and supercilious disregard of that solemn teaching, and of that sacred life and death, be not more offensive than the downright denials which look their responsibility boldly in the face, and say, not only that they do not know, but that they do not believe. This question of living faith in a living God and Saviour, with all it involves, is too urgent and momentous a thing to be put aside with a philosophical "I don't know." The best blood of the world has been shed over it; the deepest personal, social, and even political problems are still bound up with it. The intensest moral struggles of humanity have centered round this question, and it is really intolerable that all this bitter experience of men and women who have trusted and prayed, and suffered and died, in faith, should be set aside as not germane to a philosophical argument.

But, to say the least, from a purely scientific point of view, there is a portentous fallacy in the manner in which, in agnostic arguments, the testimony, not only of our Lord, but of psalmists, prophets, apostles, and saints, is disregarded. So far as the Christian faith can be treated as a scientific question, it is a question of experience; and what is to be said of a science which leaves out of account the most conspicuous and most influential experience in the matter? One thing may be said with confidence: that it defeats itself, by disregarding the greatest force with which it has to contend. While philosophers are arguing as to the abstract capacities of human thought, as though our Lord had never lived and died, he himself is still speaking; his words, as recorded by his apostles and evangelists, are still echoing over human hearts, touching their inmost affections, appealing to their deepest needs, commanding their profoundest trust, and awakening in them an apprehension of that divine relation and those unseen realities in which their spirits live. While agnostics are committing the enormous scientific as well as moral blunder of considering the relations of men to God and to an unseen world without taking his evidence into account, and then presuming to judge the faith he taught by their own partial knowledge, his word is still heard, in penetrating and comfortable words, bidding men believe in God and believe also in himself. He, after all, is the one sufficient answer to agnosticism, and—I will take the liberty of adding—to atheism and to pessimism also. Not merely his authority, though that would be enough, but his life, his soul, himself.

Accordingly, as our object here is to consider how to deal with these difficulties and objections, what these considerations would seem to point out is that we should take care to let Christ and Christ's own message be heard, and not to endure that they should be allowed to stand aside while a philosophical debate is proceeding. Philosophers are slow in these matters. They are still disputing, after some twenty-five hundred years of discussion, what is the true principle for determining moral right and wrong. Meanwhile men have been content to live by the Ten Commandments, and the main lines of duty are plain. In the same way religion has preceded the philosophy of religion, and men can be made sensible of their relation to God whether it can be philosophically explained or not. The Psalms, the Prophets, and, above all, the Gospels, are plain evidence, in matter of fact, that men are in relation to God and owe duties to him. Let men be made to attend to the facts; let them hear those simple, plain, and earnest witnesses; above all, let them hear the voice of Christ, and they will at least believe whatever may be the possibilities of knowledge. In a word, let us imitate St. Paul when his converts were perplexed by Greek philosophies at Corinth: "I, brethren, when I came to you, came not with excellency of speech or of wisdom, declaring unto you the testimony of God; for I determined not to know anything among you save Jesus Christ and him crucified."

II.

AGNOSTICISM.

By Prof. THOMAS H. HUXLEY.

Within the last few months the public has received much and varied information on the subject of agnostics, their tenets, and even their future. Agnosticism exercised the orators of the Church Congress at Manchester.* It has been furnished with a set of "articles" fewer, but not less rigid, and certainly not less consistent than the thirty-nine; its nature has been analyzed, and its future severely predicted by the most eloquent of that prophetical school whose Samuel is Auguste Comte. It may still be a question, however, whether the public is as much the wiser as might be expected, considering all the trouble that has been taken to enlighten it. Not only are the three accounts of the agnostic position sadly out of harmony with one another, but I propose to show cause for my belief that all three must be seriously questioned by any one who employs the term "agnostic" in the sense in which it was originally used. The learned principal of King's College, who brought the topic of agnosticism before the Church Congress, took a short and easy way of settling the business:

---

* See the "Official Report of the Church Congress held at Manchester," October, 1888, pp. 253, 254.

But if this be so, for a man to urge, as an escape from this article of belief, that he has no means of a scientific knowledge of the unseen world, or of the future, is irrelevant. His difference from Christians lies not in the fact that he has no knowledge of these things, but that he does not believe the authority on which they are stated. He may prefer to call himself an agnostic; but his real name is an older one—he is an infidel; that is to say, an unbeliever. The word infidel, perhaps, carries an unpleasant significance. Perhaps it is right that it should. It is, and it ought to be, an unpleasant thing for a man to have to say plainly that he does not believe in Jesus Christ.

And in the course of the discussion which followed, the Bishop of Peterborough departed so far from his customary courtesy and self-respect as to speak of "cowardly agnosticism" (p. 262).

So much of Dr. Wace's address either explicitly or implicitly concerns me, that I take upon myself to deal with it; but, in so doing, it must be understood that I speak for myself alone; I am not aware that there is any sect of Agnostics; and if there be, I am not its acknowledged prophet or pope. I desire to leave to the Comtists the entire monopoly of the manufacture of imitation ecclesiasticism.

Let us calmly and dispassionately consider Dr. Wace's appreciation of agnosticism. The agnostic, according to his view, is a person who says he has no means of attaining a scientific knowledge of the unseen world or of the future; by which somewhat loose phraseology Dr. Wace presumably means the theological unseen world and future. I can not think this description happy either in form or substance, but for the present it may pass. Dr. Wace continues, that is not "his difference from Christians." Are there, then, any Christians who say that they know nothing about the unseen world and the future? I was ignorant of the fact, but I am ready to accept it on the authority of a professional theologian, and I proceed to Dr. Wace's next proposition.

The real state of the case, then, is that the agnostic "does not believe the authority" on which "these things" are stated, which authority is Jesus Christ. He is simply an old-fashioned "infidel" who is afraid to own to his right name. As "Presbyter is priest writ large," so is "agnostic" the mere Greek equivalent for the Latin "infidel." There is an attractive simplicity about this solution of the problem; and it has that advantage of being somewhat offensive to the persons attacked, which is so dear to the less refined sort of controversialist. The agnostic says, "I can not find good evidence that so and so is true." "Ah," says his adversary, seizing his opportunity, "then you declare that Jesus Christ was untruthful, for he said so and so"; a very telling method of rousing prejudice. But suppose that the value of the evidence as to what Jesus may have said and done, and as to the exact nature and scope of his authority, is just that which the agnostic finds it most difficult to determine? If I venture to doubt that the Duke of Wellington gave the command, "Up, Guards, and at 'em!" at Waterloo, I do not think that even Dr. Wace would accuse me of disbelieving the duke. Yet it would be just as reasonable to do this as to accuse any one of denying what Jesus said before the preliminary question as to what he did say is settled.

Now, the question as to what Jesus really said and did is strictly a scientific problem, which is capable of solution by no other methods than those practiced by the historian and the literary critic. It is a problem of immense difficulty, which has occupied some of the best heads in Europe for the last century; and it is only of late years that their investigations have begun to converge toward one conclusion.*

That kind of faith which Dr. Wace describes and lauds is of no use here. Indeed, he himself takes pains to destroy its evidential value.

"What made the Mohammedan world? Trust and faith in the declarations and assurances of Mohammed. And what made the Christian world? Trust and faith in the declarations and assurances of Jesus Christ and his apostles" (*loc. cit.*, p. 253). The triumphant tone of this imaginary catechism leads me to suspect that its author has hardly appreciated its full import. Presumably, Dr. Wace regards Mohammed as an unbeliever, or, to use the term which he prefers, infidel; and considers that his assurances have given rise to a vast delusion, which has led, and is leading, millions of men straight to everlasting punishment. And this being so, the "trust and faith" which have "made the Mohammedan world," in just the same sense as they have "made the Christian world," must be trust and faith in falsehood. No man who has

---

* Dr. Wace tells us, "It may be asked how far we can rely on the accounts we possess of our Lord's teaching on these subjects." And he seems to think the question appropriately answered by the assertion that it "ought to be regarded as settled by M. Renan's practical surrender of the adverse case." I thought I knew M. Renan's works pretty well, but I have contrived to miss this "practical" (I wish Dr. Wace had defined the scope of that useful adjective) surrender. However, as Dr. Wace can find no difficulty in pointing out the passage of M. Renan's writings, by which he feels justified in making his statement, I shall wait for further enlightenment, contenting myself, for the present, with remarking that if M. Renan were to retract and do penance in Notre Dame to-morrow for any contributions to Biblical criticism that may be specially his property, the main results of that criticism as they are set forth in the works of Strauss, Baur, Reuss, and Volkmar, for example, would not be sensibly affected.

studied history, or even attended to the occurrences of every-day life, can doubt the enormous practical value of trust and faith; but as little will he be inclined to deny that this practical value has not the least relation to the reality of the objects of that trust and faith. In examples of patient constancy of faith and of unswerving trust, the "Acta Martyrum" do not excel the annals of Babism.

The discussion upon which we have now entered goes so thoroughly to the root of the whole matter; the question of the day is so completely, as the author of "Robert Elsmere" says, the value of testimony, that I shall offer no apology for following it out somewhat in detail; and, by way of giving substance to the argument, I shall base what I have to say upon a case, the consideration of which lies strictly within the province of natural science, and of that particular part of it known as the physiology and pathology of the nervous system.

I find, in the second Gospel (chap. v), a statement, to all appearance intended to have the same evidential value as any other contained in that history. It is the well-known story of the devils who were cast out of a man, and ordered, or permitted, to enter into a herd of swine, to the great loss and damage of the innocent Gerasene, or Gadarene, pig-owners. There can be no doubt that the narrator intends to convey to his readers his own conviction that this casting out and entering in were effected by the agency of Jesus of Nazareth; that, by speech and action, Jesus enforced this conviction; nor does any inkling of the legal and moral difficulties of the case manifest itself.

On the other hand, everything that I know of physiological and pathological science leads me to entertain a very strong conviction that the phenomena ascribed to possession are as purely natural as those which constitute small-pox; everything that I know of anthropology leads me to think that the belief in demons and demoniacal possession is a mere survival of a once universal superstition, and that its persistence at the present time is pretty much in the inverse ratio of the general instruction, intelligence, and sound judgment of the population among whom it prevails. Everything that I know of law and justice convinces me that the wanton destruction of other people's property is a misdemeanor of evil example. Again, the study of history, and especially of that of the fifteenth, sixteenth, and seventeenth centuries, leaves no shadow of doubt on my mind that the belief in the reality of possession and of witchcraft, justly based, alike by Catholics and Protestants, upon this and innumerable other passages in both the Old and New Testaments, gave rise, through the special influence of Christian ecclesiastics, to the most horrible persecutions and judicial murders of thousands upon thousands of innocent men, women, and children. And when I reflect that the record of a plain and simple declaration upon such an occasion as this, that the belief in witchcraft and possession is wicked nonsense, would have rendered the long agony of mediæval humanity impossible, I am prompted to reject, as dishonoring, the supposition that such declaration was withheld out of condescension to popular error.

"Come forth, thou unclean spirit, out of the man" (Mark v, 8),* are the words attributed to Jesus. If I declare, as I have no hesitation in doing, that I utterly disbelieve in the existence of "unclean spirits," and, conse-

---

* Here, as always, the revised version is cited.

quently, in the possibility of their "coming forth" out of a man, I suppose that Dr. Wace will tell me I am disregarding the "testimony of our Lord" (*loc. cit.*, p. 255). For if these words were really used, the most resourceful of reconcilers can hardly venture to affirm that they are compatible with a disbelief in "these things." As the learned and fair-minded, as well as orthodox, Dr. Alexander remarks, in an editorial note to the article "Demoniacs," in the "Biblical Cyclopædia" (vol. i, p. 664, note):

... On the lowest grounds on which our Lord and his apostles can be placed, they must, at least, be regarded as *honest* men. Now, though honest speech does not require that words should be used always and only in their etymological sense, it does require that they should not be used so as to affirm what the speaker knows to be false. While, therefore, our Lord and his apostles might use the word $\delta\alpha\iota\mu o\nu i\zeta\epsilon\sigma\theta\alpha\iota$, or the phrase $\delta\alpha\iota\mu\acute{o}\nu\iota o\nu$ $\H{\epsilon}\chi\epsilon\iota\nu$, as a popular description of certain diseases, without giving in to the belief which lay at the source of such a mode of expression, they could not speak of demons entering into a man, or being cast out of him, without pledging themselves to the belief of an actual possession of the man by the demons (Campbell, "Prel. Diss.," vi, 1, 10). If, consequently, they did not hold this belief, they spoke not as honest men.

The story which we are considering does not rest on the authority of the second Gospel alone. The third confirms the second, especially in the matter of commanding the unclean spirit to come out of the man (Luke viii, 29); and, although the first Gospel either gives a different version of the same story, or tells another of like kind, the essential point remains: "If thou cast us out, send us away into the herd of swine. And he said unto them, Go!" (Matthew viii, 31, 32).

If the concurrent testimony of the three synoptics, then, is really sufficient to do away with all rational doubt as to a matter of fact of the utmost practical and speculative importance—belief or disbelief in which may affect, and has affected, men's lives and their conduct toward other men in the most serious way—then I am bound to believe that Jesus implicitly affirmed himself to possess a "knowledge of the unseen world," which afforded full confirmation to the belief in demons and possession current among his contemporaries. If the story is true, the mediæval theory of the invisible world may be, and probably is, quite correct; and the witch-finders, from Sprenger to Hopkins and Mather, are much-maligned men.

On the other hand, humanity, noting the frightful consequences of this belief; common sense, observing the futility of the evidence on which it is based, in all cases that have been properly investigated; science, more and more seeing its way to inclose all the phenomena of so-called "possession" within the domain of pathology, so far as they are not to be relegated to that of the police—all these powerful influences concur in warning us, at our peril, against accepting the belief without the most careful scrutiny of the authority on which it rests.

I can discern no escape from this dilemma: either Jesus said what he is reported to have said, or he did not. In the former case, it is inevitable that his authority on matters connected with the "unseen world" should be roughly shaken; in the latter, the blow falls upon the authority of the synoptic gospels. If their report on a matter of such stupendous and far-reaching practical import as this is untrustworthy, how can we be sure of its trustworthiness in other cases? The favorite "earth," in which the hard-pressed reconciler takes refuge, that the Bible does not profess to teach science,* is stopped in this

---

* Does any one really mean to say that there is any internal or external criterion by which the reader of a biblical statement, in which scientific

instance. For the question of the existence of demons and of possession by them, though it lies strictly within the province of science, is also of the deepest moral and religious significance. If physical and mental disorders are caused by demons, Gregory of Tours and his contemporaries rightly considered that relics and exorcists were more useful than doctors; the gravest questions arise as to the legal and moral responsibilities of persons inspired by demoniacal impulses; and our whole conception of the universe and of our relations to it becomes totally different from what it would be on the contrary hypothesis.

The theory of life of an average mediæval Christian was as different from that of an average nineteenth-century Englishman as that of a West-African negro is now in these respects. The modern world is slowly, but surely, shaking off these and other monstrous survivals of savage delusions, and, whatever happens, it will not return to that wallowing in the mire. Until the contrary is proved, I venture to doubt whether, at this present moment, any Protestant theologian, who has a reputation to lose, will say that he believes the Gadarene story.

The choice then lies between discrediting those who

---

matter is contained, is enabled to judge whether it is to be taken *au sérieux* or not? Is the account of the Deluge, accepted as true in the New Testament, less precise and specific than that of the call of Abraham, also accepted as true therein? By what mark does the story of the feeding with manna in the wilderness, which involves some very curious scientific problems, show that it is meant merely for edification, while the story of the inscription of the law on stone by the hand of Jahveh is literally true? If the story of the Fall is not the true record of an historical occurrence, what becomes of Pauline theology? Yet the story of the Fall as directly conflicts with probability, and is as devoid of trustworthy evidence, as that of the Creation or that of the Deluge, with which it forms an harmoniously legendary series.

compiled the gospel biographies and disbelieving the Master, whom they, simple souls, thought to honor by preserving such traditions of the exercise of his authority over Satan's invisible world. This is the dilemma. No deep scholarship, nothing but a knowledge of the revised version (on which it is supposed all that mere scholarship can do has been done), with the application thereto of the commonest canons of common sense, is needful to enable us to make a choice between its horns. It is hardly doubtful that the story, as told in the first Gospel, is merely a version of that told in the second and third. Nevertheless, the discrepancies are serious and irreconcilable; and, on this ground alone, a suspension of judgment, at the least, is called for. But there is a great deal more to be said. From the dawn of scientific biblical criticism until the present day the evidence against the long-cherished notion that the three synoptic gospels are the works of three independent authors, each prompted by divine inspiration, has steadily accumulated, until, at the present time, there is no visible escape from the conclusion that each of the three is a compilation consisting of a groundwork common to all three—the threefold tradition; and of a superstructure, consisting, firstly, of matter common to it with one of the others, and, secondly, of matter special to each. The use of the terms "groundwork" and "superstructure" by no means implies that the latter must be of later date than the former. On the contrary, some parts of it may be, and probably are, older than some parts of the groundwork.*

---

* See, for an admirable discussion of the whole subject, Dr. Abbott's article on the Gospels in the "Encyclopædia Britannica"; and the remarkable monograph by Prof. Volkmar, "Jesus Nazarenus und die erste Christliche Zeit" (1882). Whether we agree with the conclusions of these writ-

The story of the Gadarenes-swine belongs to the groundwork; at least, the essential part of it, in which the belief in demoniac possession is expressed, does; and therefore the compilers of the first, second, and third Gospels, whoever they were, certainly accepted that belief (which, indeed, was universal among both Jews and pagans at that time), and attributed it to Jesus.

What then, do we know about the originator, or originators, of this groundwork — of that threefold edition which all three witnesses (in Paley's phrase) agree upon — that we should allow their mere statements to outweigh the counter-arguments of humanity, of common sense, of exact science, and to imperil the respect which all would be glad to be able to render to their Master?

Absolutely nothing.* There is no proof, nothing more than a fair presumption, that any one of the Gospels existed, in the state in which we find it in the authorized version of the Bible, before the second century, or, in other words, sixty or seventy years after the events recorded. And, between that time and the date of the oldest extant manuscripts of the Gospels, there is no telling what additions and alterations and interpolations may have been made. It may be said that this is all mere speculation, but it is a good deal more. As competent scholars and honest men, our revisers have felt compelled to point out that such things have happened even since the date of the oldest known manuscripts. The oldest two copies of the

---

ters or not, the method of critical investigation which they adopt is unimpeachable.

* Notwithstanding the hard words shot at me from behind the hedge of anonymity by a writer in a recent number of the "Quarterly Review," I repeat, without the slightest fear of refutation, that the four Gospels, as they have come to us, are the work of unknown writers.

second Gospel end with the eighth verse of the sixteenth chapter; the remaining twelve verses are spurious, and it is noteworthy that the maker of the addition has not hesitated to introduce a speech in which Jesus promises his disciples that "in my name shall they cast out devils."

The other passage "rejected to the margin" is still more instructive. It is that touching apologue, with its profound ethical sense, of the woman taken in adultery—which, if internal evidence were an infallible guide, might well be affirmed to be a typical example of the teachings of Jesus. Yet, say the revisers, pitilessly, "Most of the ancient authorities omit John vii, 53, viii 11." Now, let any reasonable man ask himself this question: If, after an approximative settlement of the canon of the New Testament, and even later than the fourth and fifth centuries, literary fabricators had the skill and the audacity to make such additions and interpolations as these, what may they have done when no one had thought of a canon; when oral tradition, still unfixed, was regarded as more valuable than such written records as may have existed in the latter portion of the first century? Or, to take the other alternative, if those who gradually settled the canon did not know of the existence of the oldest codices which have come down to us; or if, knowing them, they rejected their authority, what is to be thought of their competency as critics of the text?

People who object to free criticism of the Christian Scriptures forget that they are what they are in virtue of very free criticism; unless the advocates of inspiration are prepared to affirm that the majority of influential ecclesiastics during several centuries were safeguarded against error. For, even granting that some books of the period were inspired, they were certainly few among many; and those who selected the canonical books, unless they themselves were also inspired, must be regarded in the light of mere critics, and, from the evidence they have left of their intellectual habits, very uncritical critics. When one thinks that such delicate questions as those involved fell into the hands of men like Papias (who believed in the famous millenarian grape story); of Irenæus with his "reasons" for the existence of only four Gospels; and of such calm and dispassionate judges as Tertullian, with his "*Credo quia impossibile*," the marvel is that the selection which constitutes our New Testament is as free as it is from obviously objectionable matter. The apocryphal Gospels certainly deserve to be apocryphal; but one may suspect that a little more critical discrimination would have enlarged the Apocrypha not inconsiderably.

At this point a very obvious objection arises and deserves full and candid consideration. It may be said that critical skepticism carried to the length suggested is historical pyrrhonism; that if we are to altogether discredit an ancient or a modern historian, because he has assumed fabulous matter to be true, it will be as well to give up paying any attention to history. It may be said, and with great justice, that Eginhard's "Life of Charlemagne" is none the less trustworthy because of the astounding revelation of credulity, of lack of judgment, and even of respect for the eighth commandment, which he has unconsciously made in the "History of the Translation of the Blessed Martyrs Marcellinus and Paul." Or, to go no further back than the last number of this review, surely that excellent lady, Miss Strickland, is not to be refused all credence because of the myth about the second James's remains, which she seems to have unconsciously invented.

Of course this is perfectly true. I am afraid there is

no man alive whose witness could be accepted, if the condition precedent were proof that he had never invented and promulgated a myth. In the minds of all of us there are little places here and there, like the indistinguishable spots on a rock which give foothold to moss or stone-crop; on which, if the germ of a myth fall, it is certain to grow, without in the least degree affecting our accuracy or truthfulness elsewhere. Sir Walter Scott knew that he could not repeat a story without, as he said, "giving it a new hat and stick." Most of us differ from Sir Walter only in not knowing about this tendency of the mythopœic faculty to break out unnoticed. But it is also perfectly true that the mythopœic faculty is not equally active on all minds, nor in all regions and under all conditions of the same mind. David Hume was certainly not so liable to temptation as the Venerable Bede, or even as some recent historians who could be mentioned; and the most imaginative of debtors, if he owes five pounds, never makes an obligation to pay a hundred out of it. The rule of common sense is *prima facie* to trust a witness in all matters in which neither his self-interest, his passions, his prejudices, nor that love of the marvelous, which is inherent to a greater or less degree in all mankind, are strongly concerned; and, when they are involved, to require corroborative evidence in exact proportion to the contravention of probability by the thing testified.

Now, in the Gadarene affair, I do not think I am unreasonably skeptical if I say that the existence of demons who can be transferred from a man to a pig does thus contravene probability. Let me be perfectly candid. I admit I have no *a priori* objection to offer. There are physical things, such as *tæniæ* and *trichinæ*, which can be transferred from men to pigs, and *vice versa*, and which do undoubtedly produce most diabolical and deadly effects on both. For anything I can absolutely prove to the contrary, there may be spiritual things capable of the same transmigration, with like effects. Moreover, I am bound to add that perfectly truthful persons, for whom I have the greatest respect, believe in stories about spirits of the present day, quite as improbable as that we are considering.

So I declare, as plainly as I can, that I am unable to show cause why these transferable devils should not exist; nor can I deny that, not merely the whole Roman Church, but many Wacean "infidels" of no mean repute, do honestly and firmly believe that the activity of such-like demonic beings is in full swing in this year of grace 1889.

Nevertheless, as good Bishop Butler says, "probability is the guide of life," and it seems to me that this is just one of the cases in which the canon of credibility and testimony, which I have ventured to lay down, has full force. So that, with the most entire respect for many (by no means for all) of our witnesses for the truth of demonology, ancient and modern, I conceive their evidence on this particular matter to be ridiculously insufficient to warrant their conclusion.*

---

* Their arguments, in the long run, are always reducible to one form. Otherwise trustworthy witnesses affirm that such and such events took place. These events are inexplicable, except the agency of "spirits" is admitted. Therefore "spirits" were the cause of the phenomena.

And the heads of the reply are always the same. Remember Goethe's aphorism: "Alles factische ist schon Theorie." Trustworthy witnesses are constantly deceived, or deceive themselves, in their interpretation of sensible phenomena. No one can prove that the sensible phenomena, in these cases, could be caused only by the agency of spirits; and there is abundant ground for believing that they may be produced in other ways.

Therefore, the utmost that can be reasonably asked for, on the evidence

After what has been said I do not think that any sensible man, unless he happen to be angry, will accuse me of "contradicting the Lord and his apostles" if I reiterate my total disbelief in the whole Gadarene story. But, if that story is discredited, all the other stories of demoniac possession fall under suspicion. And if the belief in demons and demoniac possession, which forms the somber background of the whole picture of primitive Christianity presented to us in the New Testament, is shaken, what is to be said, in any case, of the uncorroborated testimony of the Gospels with respect to the "unseen world"?

I am not aware that I have been influenced by any more bias in regard to the Gadarene story than I have been in dealing with other cases of like kind the investigation of which has interested me. I was brought up in the strictest school of evangelical orthodoxy; and, when I was old enough to think for myself, I started upon my journey of inquiry with little doubt about the general truth of what I had been taught; and with that feeling of the unpleasantness of being called an "infidel" which, we are told, is so right and proper. Near my journey's end, I find myself in a condition of something more than mere doubt about these matters.

In the course of other inquiries, I have had to do with fossil remains which looked quite plain at a distance, and became more and more indistinct as I tried to define their outline by close inspection. There was something there —something which, if I could win assurance about it, might mark a new epoch in the history of the earth; but, study as long as I might, certainty eluded my

---

as it stands, is suspension of judgment. And, on the necessity for even that suspension, reasonable men may differ, according to their views of probability.

grasp. So has it been with me in my efforts to define the grand figure of Jesus as it lies in the primary strata of Christian literature. Is he the kindly, peaceful Christ depicted in the Catacombs? Or is he the stern judge who frowns above the altar of SS. Cosmas and Damianus? Or can he be rightly represented in the bleeding ascetic, broken down by physical pain, of too many mediæval pictures? Are we to accept the Jesus of the second, or the Jesus of the fourth Gospel, as the true Jesus? What did he really say and do; and how much that is attributed to him in speech and action is the embroidery of the various parties into which his followers tended to split themselves within twenty years of his death, when even the threefold tradition was only nascent?

If any one will answer these questions for me with something more to the point than feeble talk about the "cowardice of agnosticism," I shall be deeply his debtor. Unless and until they are satisfactorily answered, I say of agnosticism in this matter, "*J'y suis, et j'y reste.*"

But, as we have seen, it is asserted that I have no business to call myself an agnostic; that if I am not a Christian I am an infidel; and that I ought to call myself by that name of "unpleasant significance." Well, I do not care much what I am called by other people, and, if I had at my side all those who since the Christian era have been called infidels by other folks, I could not desire better company. If these are my ancestors, I prefer, with the old Frank, to be with them wherever they are. But there are several points in Dr. Wace's contention which must be eliminated before I can even think of undertaking to carry out his wishes. I must, for instance, know what a Christian is. Now what is a Christian? By whose authority is the signification of that term defined? Is there any doubt that the immediate followers of Jesus, the "sect of the Nazarenes," were strictly orthodox Jews, differing from other Jews not more than the Sadducees, the Pharisees, and the Essenes differed from one another; in fact, only in the belief that the Messiah, for whom the rest of their nation waited, had come? Was not their chief, "James, the brother of the Lord," reverenced alike by Sadducee, Pharisee, and Nazarene? At the famous conference which, according to the Acts, took place at Jerusalem, does not James declare that "myriads" of Jews, who, by that time had become Nazarenes, were "all zealous for the law"? Was not the name of "Christian" first used to denote the converts to the doctrine promulgated by Paul and Barnabas at Antioch? Does the subsequent history of Christianity leave any doubt that, from this time forth, the "little rift within the lute," caused by the new teaching developed, if not inaugurated, at Antioch, grew wider and wider, until the two types of doctrine irreconcilably diverged? Did not the primitive Nazarenism or Ebionism develop into the Nazarenism, and Ebionism, and Elkasaitism of later ages, and finally die out in obscurity and condemnation as damnable heresy; while the younger doctrine throve and pushed out its shoots into that endless variety of sects, of which the three strongest survivors are the Roman and Greek Churches and modern Protestantism?

Singular state of things! If I were to profess the doctrine which was held by "James, the brother of the Lord," and by every one of the "myriads" of his followers and co-religionists in Jerusalem up to twenty or thirty years after the crucifixion (and one knows not how much later at Pella), I should be condemned with unanimity as an ebionizing heretic by the Roman, Greek, and Protestant Churches! And, probably, this hearty and unanimous condemnation of the creed held by those who were in the closest personal relation with their Lord is almost the only point upon which they would be cordially of one mind. On the other hand—though I hardly dare imagine such a thing—I very much fear that the "pillars" of the primitive Hierosolymitan Church would have considered Dr. Wace an infidel. No one can read the famous second chapter of Galatians and the book of Revelation without seeing how narrow was even Paul's escape from a similar fate. And, if ecclesiastical history is to be trusted, the thirty-nine articles, be they right or wrong, diverge from the primitive doctrine of the Nazarenes vastly more than even Pauline Christianity did.

But, further than this, I have great difficulty in assuring myself that even James, "the brother of the Lord," and his "myriads" of Nazarenes, properly represented the doctrines of their Master. For it is constantly asserted by our modern "pillars" that one of the chief features of the work of Jesus was the instauration of religion by the abolition of what our sticklers for articles and liturgies, with unconscious humor, call the narrow restrictions of the law. Yet, if James knew this, how could the bitter controversy with Paul have arisen; and why did one or the other side not quote any of the various sayings of Jesus, recorded in the Gospels, which directly bear on the question — sometimes, apparently, in opposite directions?

So, if I am asked to call myself an "infidel," I reply, To what doctrine do you ask me to be faithful? Is it that contained in the Nicene and the Athanasian Creeds? My firm belief is that the Nazarenes, say of the year 40, headed by James, would have stopped their ears and thought worthy of stoning the audacious man who propounded it to them. Is it contained in the so-called Apostles' Creed? I am pretty sure that even that would have created a recalcitrant commotion at Pella in the year 70, among the Nazarenes of Jerusalem, who had fled from the soldiers of Titus. And yet if the unadulterated tradition of the teachings of "the Nazarene" were to be found anywhere, it surely should have been amid those not very aged disciples who may have heard them as they were delivered.

Therefore, however sorry I may be to be unable to demonstrate that, if necessary, I should not be afraid to call myself an "infidel," I can not do it, even to gratify the Bishop of Peterborough and Dr. Wace. And I would appeal to the bishop, whose native sense of humor is not the least marked of his many excellent gifts and virtues, whether asking a man to call himself an "infidel" is not rather a droll request. "Infidel" is a term of reproach, which Christians and Mohammedans, in their modesty, agree to apply to those who differ from them. If he had only thought of it, Dr. Wace might have used the term "miscreant," which, with the same etymological signification, has the advantage of being still more "unpleasant" to the persons to whom it is applied. But, in the name of all that is Hibernian, I ask the Bishop of Peterborough why should a man be expected to call himself a "miscreant" or an "infidel"? That St. Patrick "had two birthdays because he was a twin" is a reasonable and intelligible utterance beside that of the man who should declare himself to be an infidel on the ground of denying his own belief. It may be logically, if not ethically, defensible, that a Christian should call a Mohammedan an infidel, and *vice versa;* but, on Dr. Wace's principles, both ought to call themselves infidels, because each applies that term to the other.

Now I am afraid that all the Mohammedan world would agree in reciprocating that appellation to Dr. Wace himself. I once visited the Hazar Mosque, the great university of Mohammedanism, in Cairo, in ignorance of the fact that I was unprovided with proper authority. A swarm of angry undergraduates, as I suppose I ought to call them, came buzzing about me and my guide; and, if I had known Arabic, I suspect that "dog of an infidel" would have been by no means the most "unpleasant" of the epithets showered upon me, before I could explain and apologize for the mistake. If I had had the pleasure of Dr. Wace's company on that occasion, the undiscriminative followers of the Prophet would, I am afraid, have made no difference between us; not even if they had known that he was the head of an orthodox Christian seminary. And I have not the smallest doubt that even one of the learned mollahs, if his grave courtesy would have permitted him to say anything offensive to men of another mode of belief, would have told us that he wondered we did not find it "very unpleasant" to disbelieve in the Prophet of Islam.

From what precedes, I think it becomes sufficiently clear that Dr. Wace's account of the origin of the name of "Agnostic" is quite wrong. Indeed, I am bound to add that very slight effort to discover the truth would have convinced him that, as a matter of fact, the term arose otherwise. I am loath to go over an old story once more; but more than one object which I have in view will be served by telling it a little more fully than it has yet been told.

Looking back nearly fifty years, I see myself as a boy,

whose education had been interrupted, and who, intellectually, was left, for some years, altogether to his own devices. At that time I was a voracious and omnivorous reader; a dreamer and speculator of the first water, well endowed with that splendid courage in attacking any and every subject which is the blessed compensation of youth and inexperience. Among the books and essays, on all sorts of topics from metaphysics to heraldry, which I read at this time, two left indelible impressions on my mind. One was Guizot's "History of Civilization," the other was Sir William Hamilton's essay "On the Philosophy of the Unconditioned," which I came upon, by chance, in an odd volume of the "Edinburgh Review." The latter was certainly strange reading for a boy, and I could not possibly have understood a great deal of it;* nevertheless, I devoured it with avidity, and it stamped upon my mind the strong conviction that, on even the most solemn and important of questions, men are apt to take cunning phrases for answers; and that the limitation of our faculties, in a great number of cases, renders real answers to such questions not merely actually impossible, but theoretically inconceivable.

Philosophy and history having laid hold of me in this eccentric fashion, have never loosened their grip. I have no pretension to be an expert in either subject; but the turn for philosophical and historical reading, which rendered Hamilton and Guizot attractive to me, has not only filled many lawful leisure hours, and still more sleepless ones, with the repose of changed mental occupation,

---

* Yet I must somehow have laid hold of the pith of the matter, for, many years afterward, when Dean Mansell's Bampton lectures were published, it seemed to me I already knew all that this eminently agnostic thinker had to tell me.

but has not unfrequently disputed my proper work-time with my liege lady, Natural Science. In this way I have found it possible to cover a good deal of ground in the territory of philosophy; and all the more easily that I have never cared much about A's or B's opinions, but have rather sought to know what answer he had to give to the questions I had to put to him—that of the limitation of possible knowledge being the chief. The ordinary examiner, with his "State the views of So-and-so," would have floored me at any time. If he had said, "What do *you* think about any given problem?" I might have got on fairly well.

The reader who has had the patience to follow the enforced, but unwilling, egotism of this veritable history (especially if his studies have led him in the same direction), will now see why my mind steadily gravitated toward the conclusions of Hume and Kant, so well stated by the latter in a sentence, which I have quoted elsewhere:

"The greatest and perhaps the sole use of all philosophy of pure reason is, after all, merely negative, since it serves not as an organon for the enlargement [of knowledge], but as a discipline for its delimitation; and, instead of discovering truth, has only the modest merit of preventing error." *

When I reached intellectual maturity and began to ask myself whether I was an atheist, a theist, or a pantheist; a materialist or an idealist; a Christian or a freethinker—I found that the more I learned and reflected, the less ready was the answer; until, at last, I came to the conclusion that I had neither art nor part with any of these denominations, except the last. The one thing

---

* "Kritik der reinen Vernunft." Edit. Hartenstein, p. 256.

in which most of these good people were agreed was the one thing in which I differed from them. They were quite sure they had attained a certain "gnosis"—had, more or less successfully, solved the problem of existence; while I was quite sure I had not, and had a pretty strong conviction that the problem was insoluble. And, with Hume and Kant on my side, I could not think myself presumptuous in holding fast by that opinion. Like Dante—

"Nel mezzo del cammin di nostra vita
Mi ritrovai per una selva oscura," *

but, unlike Dante, I can not add—

" Che la diritta via era smarrita." †

On the contrary, I had, and have, the firmest conviction that I never left the *"verace via"*—the straight road; and that this road led nowhere else but into the dark depths of a wild and tangled forest. And though I have found leopards and lions in the path; though I have made abundant acquaintance with the hungry wolf, that with "privy paw devours apace and nothing said," as another great poet says of the ravening beast; and though no friendly specter has even yet offered his guidance, I was, and am, minded to go straight on, until I either come out on the other side of the wood, or find there is no other side to it—at least, none attainable by me.

This was my situation when I had the good fortune to find a place among the members of that remarkable confraternity of antagonists, long since deceased, but of green and pious memory, the Metaphysical Society.

---

* [In the midway of this our mortal life
I found me in a gloomy wood astray.]
† [Gone from the path direct.]

Every variety of philosophical and theological opinion was represented there, and expressed itself with entire openness; most of my colleagues were *ists* of one sort or another; and, however kind and friendly they might be, I, the man without a rag of a label to cover himself with, could not fail to have some of the uneasy feelings which must have beset the historical fox when, after leaving the trap in which his tail remained, he presented himself to his normally elongated companions. So I took thought, and invented what I conceived to be the appropriate title of "agnostic." It came into my head as suggestively antithetic to the "gnostic" of Church history, who professed to know so much about the very things of which I was ignorant; and I took the earliest opportunity of parading it at our society, to show that I, too, had a tail, like the other foxes. To my great satisfaction, the term took; and when the "Spectator" had stood godfather to it, any suspicion in the minds of respectable people, that a knowledge of its parentage might have awakened, was, of course, completely lulled.

That is the history of the origin of the terms "agnostic" and "agnosticism"; and it will be observed that it does not quite agree with the confident assertion of the reverend Principal of King's College, that "the adoption of the term agnostic is only an attempt to shift the issue, and that it involves a mere evasion" in relation to the Church and Christianity.*

The last objection (I rejoice, as much as my readers must do, that it is the last) which I have to take to Dr. Wace's deliverance before the Church Congress arises, I am sorry to say, on a question of morality.

---

* Page 6.

"It is, and it ought to be," authoritatively declares this official representative of Christian ethics, "an unpleasant thing for a man to have to say plainly that he does not believe in Jesus Christ" (*l. c.*, p. 254).

Whether it is so, depends, I imagine, a good deal on whether the man was brought up in a Christian household or not. I do not see why it should be "unpleasant" for a Mohammedan or a Buddhist to say so. But that "it ought to be" unpleasant for any man to say anything which he sincerely, and after due deliberation, believes, is, to my mind, a proposition of the most profoundly immoral character. I verily believe that the great good which has been effected in the world by Christianity has been largely counteracted by the pestilent doctrine on which all the churches have insisted, that honest disbelief in their more or less astonishing creeds is a moral offense, indeed a sin of the deepest dye, deserving and involving the same future retribution as murder and robbery. If we could only see, in one view, the torrents of hypocrisy and cruelty, the lies, the slaughter, the violations of every obligation of humanity, which have flowed from this source along the course of the history of Christian nations, our worst imaginations of hell would pale beside the vision.

A thousand times, no! It ought *not* to be unpleasant to say that which one honestly believes or disbelieves. That it so constantly is painful to do so, is quite enough obstacle to the progress of mankind in that most valuable of all qualities, honesty of word or of deed, without erecting a sad concomitant of human weakness into something to be admired and cherished. The bravest of soldiers often, and very naturally, "feel it unpleasant" to go into action; but a court-martial which did its duty would make short work of the officer who promulgated the doctrine that his men *ought* to feel their duty unpleasant.

I am very well aware, as I suppose most thoughtful people are in these times, that the process of breaking away from old beliefs is extremely unpleasant; and I am much disposed to think that the encouragement, the consolation, and the peace afforded to earnest believers in even the worst forms of Christianity are of great practical advantage to them. What deductions must be made from this gain on the score of the harm done to the citizen by the ascetic other-worldliness of logical Christianity; to the ruler, by the hatred, malice, and all uncharitableness of sectarian bigotry; to the legislator, by the spirit of exclusiveness and domination of those that count themselves pillars of orthodoxy; to the philosopher, by the restraints on the freedom of learning and teaching which every church exercises, when it is strong enough; to the conscientious soul, by the introspective hunting after sins of the mint and cummin type, the fear of theological error, and the overpowering terror of possible damnation, which have accompanied the churches like their shadow, I need not now consider; but they are assuredly not small. If agnostics lose heavily on the one side, they gain a good deal on the other. People who talk about the comforts of belief appear to forget its discomforts; they ignore the fact that the Christianity of the churches is something more than faith in the ideal personality of Jesus, which they create for themselves, *plus* so much as can be carried into practice, without disorganizing civil society, of the maxims of the Sermon on the Mount. Trip in morals or in doctrine (especially in doctrine), without due repentance or retractation, or fail to get properly baptized before you die, and a *plébiscite* of the Christians of Europe, if they were true to their creeds, would affirm your everlasting damnation by an immense majority.

Preachers, orthodox and heterodox, din into our ears that the world can not get on without faith of some sort. There is a sense in which that is as eminently as obviously true; there is another, in which, in my judgment, it is as eminently as obviously false, and it seems to me that the hortatory, or pulpit, mind is apt to oscillate between the false and the true meanings, without being aware of the fact.

It is quite true that the ground of every one of our actions, and the validity of all our reasonings, rest upon the great act of faith, which leads us to take the experience of the past as a safe guide in our dealings with the present and the future. From the nature of ratiocination it is obvious that the axioms on which it is based can not be demonstrated by ratiocination. It is also a trite observation that, in the business of life, we constantly take the most serious action upon evidence of an utterly insufficient character. But it is surely plain that faith is not necessarily entitled to dispense with ratiocination because ratiocination can not dispense with faith as a starting-point; and that because we are often obliged, by the pressure of events, to act on very bad evidence, it does not follow that it is proper to act on such evidence when the pressure is absent.

The writer of the epistle to the Hebrews tells us that "faith is the assurance of things hoped for, the proving of things not seen." In the authorized version "substance" stands for "assurance," and "evidence" for "the proving." The question of the exact meaning of the two words, ὑπόστασις and ἔλεγχος, affords a fine field of discussion for the scholar and the metaphysician. But I fancy we shall be not far from the mark if we take the writer to have had in his mind the profound psychological truth that men constantly feel certain about things for which they strongly hope, but have no evidence, in the legal or logical sense of the word; and he calls this feeling "faith." I may have the most absolute faith that a friend has not committed the crime of which he is accused. In the early days of English history, if my friend could have obtained a few more compurgators of like robust faith, he would have been acquitted. At the present day, if I tendered myself as a witness on that score, the judge would tell me to stand down, and the youngest barrister would smile at my simplicity. Miserable indeed is the man who has not such faith in some of his fellow-men—only less miserable than the man who allows himself to forget that such faith is not, strictly speaking, evidence; and when his faith is disappointed, as will happen now and again, turns Timon and blames the universe for his own blunders. And so, if a man can find a friend, the hypostasis of all his hopes, the mirror of his ethical ideal, in the Jesus of any, or all, of the Gospels, let him live by faith in that ideal. Who shall or can forbid him? But let him not delude himself with the notion that his faith is evidence of the objective reality of that in which he trusts. Such evidence is to be obtained only by the use of the methods of science, as applied to history and to literature, and it amounts at present to very little.

It appears that Mr. Gladstone, some time ago, asked Mr. Laing if he could draw up a short summary of the negative creed; a body of negative propositions, which have so far been adopted on the negative side as to be what the Apostles' and other accepted creeds are on the positive; and Mr. Laing at once kindly obliged Mr. Gladstone with the desired articles—eight of them.

If any one had preferred this request to me, I should have replied that, if he referred to agnostics, they have no creed; and, by the nature of the case, can not have any. Agnosticism, in fact, is not a creed, but a method, the essence of which lies in the rigorous application of a single principle. That principle is of great antiquity; it is as old as Socrates; as old as the writer who said, "Try all things, hold fast by that which is good"; it is the foundation of the Reformation, which simply illustrated the axiom that every man should be able to give a reason for the faith that is in him; it is the great principle of Descartes; it is the fundamental axiom of modern science. Positively the principle may be expressed: In matters of the intellect, follow your reason as far as it will take you, without regard to any other consideration. And negatively: In matters of the intellect, do not pretend that conclusions are certain which are not demonstrated or demonstrable. That I take to be the agnostic faith, which if a man keep whole and undefiled, he shall not be ashamed to look the universe in the face, whatever the future may have in store for him.

The results of the working out of the agnostic principle will vary according to individual knowledge and capacity, and according to the general condition of science. That which is unproved to-day may be proved, by the help of new discoveries, to-morrow. The only negative fixed points will be those negations which flow from the demonstrable limitation of our faculties. And the only obligation accepted is to have the mind always open to conviction. Agnostics who never fail in carrying out their principles are, I am afraid, as rare as other people of whom the same consistency can be truthfully predicated. But, if you were to meet with such a phœnix and to tell him that you had discovered that two and two make five, he would patiently ask you to state your reasons for that conviction, and express his readiness to agree with you if he found them satisfactory. The apostolic injunction to "suffer fools gladly," should be the rule of life of a true agnostic. I am deeply conscious how far I myself fall short of this ideal, but it is my personal conception of what agnostics ought to be.

However, as I began by stating, I speak only for myself; and I do not dream of anathematizing and excommunicating Mr. Laing. But, when I consider his creed and compare it with the Athanasian, I think I have, on the whole, a clearer conception of the meaning of the latter. "Polarity," in Article viii, for example, is a word about which I heard a good deal in my youth, when "Naturphilosophie" was in fashion, and greatly did I suffer from it. For many years past, whenever I have met with "polarity" anywhere but in a discussion of some purely physical topic, such as magnetism, I have shut the book. Mr. Laing must excuse me if the force of habit was too much for me when I read his eighth article.

And now, what is to be said to Mr. Harrison's remarkable deliverance "On the future of agnosticism"? * I would that it were not my business to say anything, for I am afraid that I can say nothing which shall manifest my great personal respect for this able writer, and for

---

* "Fortnightly Review," January, 1889.

the zeal and energy with which he ever and anon galvanizes the weakly frame of positivism until it looks more than ever like John Bunyan's Pope and Pagan rolled into one. There is a story often repeated, and I am afraid none the less mythical on that account, of a valiant and loud-voiced corporal, in command of two full privates, who, falling in with a regiment of the enemy in the dark, orders it to surrender under pain of instant annihilation by his force; and the enemy surrenders accordingly. I am always reminded of this tale when I read the positivist commands to the forces of Christianity and of Science; only the enemy show no more signs of intending to obey now than they have done any time these forty years.

The allocution under consideration has the papal flavor which is wont to hang about the utterances of the pontiffs of the Church of Comte. Mr. Harrison speaks with authority, and not as one of the common scribes of the period. He knows not only what agnosticism is and how it has come about, but what will become of it. The agnostic is to content himself with being the precursor of the positivist. In his place, as a sort of navvy leveling the ground and cleansing it of such poor stuff as Christianity, he is a useful creature who deserves patting on the back, on condition that he does not venture beyond his last. But let not these scientific Sanballats presume that they are good enough to take part in the building of the temple—they are mere Samaritans, doomed to die out in proportion as the Religion of Humanity is accepted by mankind. Well, if that is their fate, they have time to be cheerful. But let us hear Mr. Harrison's pronouncement of their doom:

"Agnosticism is a stage in the evolution of religion, an entirely negative stage, the point reached by physicists, a purely mental conclusion, with no relation to things social at all" (p. 154). I am quite dazed by this declaration. Are there, then, any "conclusions" that are not "purely mental"? Is there "no relation to things social" in "mental conclusions" which affect men's whole conception of life? Was that prince of agnostics, David Hume, particularly imbued with physical science? Supposing physical science to be non-existent, would not the agnostic principle, applied by the philologist and the historian, lead to exactly the same results? Is the modern more or less complete suspension of judgment as to the facts of the history of regal Rome, or the real origin of the Homeric poems, anything but agnosticism in history and in literature? And if so, how can agnosticism be the "mere negation of the physicist"?

"Agnosticism is a stage in the evolution of religion." No two people agree as to what is meant by the term "religion"; but if it means, as I think it ought to mean, simply the reverence and love for the ethical ideal, and the desire to realize that ideal in life, which every man ought to feel—then I say agnosticism has no more to do with it than it has to do with music or painting. If, on the other hand, Mr. Harrison, like most people, means by "religion" theology, then, in my judgment, agnosticism can be said to be a stage in its evolution, only as death may be said to be the final stage in the evolution of life.

When agnostic logic is simply one of the canons of thought, agnosticism, as a distinctive faith, will have spontaneously disappeared (p. 155).

I can but marvel that such sentences as this, and those already quoted, should have proceeded from Mr. Harrison's pen. Does he really mean to suggest that agnostics have a logic peculiar to themselves? Will he kindly help me out of my bewilderment when I try to think of "logic" being anything else than the canon (which, I believe means rule) of thought? As to agnosticism being a distinctive faith, I have already shown that it can not possibly be anything of the kind; unless perfect faith in logic is distinctive of agnostics, which, after all, it may be.

Agnosticism as a religious philosophy *per se* rests on an almost total ignoring of history and social evolution (p. 152).

But neither *per se* nor *per aliud* has agnosticism (if I know anything about it) the least pretension to be a religious philosophy; so far from resting on ignorance of history, and that social evolution of which history is the account, it is and has been the inevitable result of the strict adherence to scientific methods by historical investigators. Our forefathers were quite confident about the existence of Romulus and Remus, of King Arthur, and of Hengst and Horsa. Most of us have become agnostics in regard to the reality of these worthies. It is a matter of notoriety, of which Mr. Harrison, who accuses us all so freely of ignoring history, should not be ignorant, that the critical process which has shattered the foundations of orthodox Christian doctrine owes its origin, not to the devotees of physical science, but, before all, to Richard Simon, the learned French Oratorian, just two hundred years ago. I can not find evidence that either Simon, or any one of the great scholars and critics of the eighteenth and nineteenth centuries who have continued Simon's work, had any particular acquaintance with physical science. I have already pointed out that Hume was independent of it. And certainly one of the most potent influences in the same direction, upon history in the present century, that of Grote, did not come from the physical side. Physical science, in fact, has had nothing directly to do with the criticism of the Gospels; it is wholly incompetent to furnish demonstrative evidence that any statement made in these histories is untrue. Indeed, modern physiology can find parallels in nature for events of apparently the most eminently supernatural kind recounted in some of those histories.

It is a comfort to hear, upon Mr. Harrison's authority, that the laws of physical nature show no signs of becoming "less definite, less consistent, or less popular as time goes on" (p. 154). How a law of nature is to become indefinite, or "inconsistent," passes my poor powers of imagination. But with universal suffrage and the coach-dog theory of premiership in full view; the theory, I mean, that the whole duty of a political chief is to look sharp for the way the social coach is driving, and then run in front and bark loud—as if being the leading noise-maker and guiding were the same things—it is truly satisfactory to me to know that the laws of nature are increasing in popularity. Looking at recent developments of the policy which is said to express the great heart of the people, I have had my doubts of the fact; and my love for my fellow-countrymen has led me to reflect with dread on what will happen to them, if any of the laws of nature ever become so unpopular in their eyes as to be voted down by the transcendent authority of universal suffrage. If the legion of demons, before they set out on their journey in the swine, had had time to hold a meeting and to resolve unanimously, "That the law of gravitation is oppressive and ought to be repealed," I am afraid it would have made no sort of difference to the result, when their two thousand unwilling porters were once launched down the steep slopes of the fatal shore of Gennesaret.

The question of the place of religion as an element of human nature, as a force of human society, its origin, analysis, and functions, has never been considered at all from an agnostic point of view (p. 152).

I doubt not that Mr. Harrison knows vastly more about history than I do; in fact, he tells the public that some of my friends and I have had no opportunity of occupying ourselves with that subject. I do not like to contradict any statement which Mr. Harrison makes on his own authority; only, if I may be true to my agnostic principles, I humbly ask how he has obtained assurance on this head. I do not profess to know anything about the range of Mr. Harrison's studies; but as he has thought it fitting to start the subject, I may venture to point out that, on the evidence adduced, it might be equally permissible to draw the conclusion that Mr. Harrison's absorbing labors as the *pontifex maximus* of the positivist religion have not allowed him to acquire that acquaintance with the methods and results of physical science, or with the history of philosophy, or of philological and historical criticism, which is essential to any one who desires to obtain a right understanding of agnosticism. Incompetence in philosophy, and in all branches of science except mathematics, is the well-known mental characteristic of the founder of Positivism. Faithfulness in disciples is an admirable quality in itself; the pity is that it not unfrequently leads to the imitation of the weaknesses as well as of the strength of the master. It is only such over-faithfulness which can account for a "strong mind really saturated with the historical sense" (p. 153) exhibiting the extraordinary forgetfulness of the historical fact of the existence of David Hume implied by the assertion that

> it would be difficult to name a single known agnostic who has given to history anything like the amount of thought and study which he brings to a knowledge of the physical world (p. 153).

Whoso calls to mind, what I may venture to term, the bright side of Christianity; that ideal of manhood, with its strength and its patience; its justice and its pity for human frailty; its helpfulness, to the extremity of self-sacrifice; its ethical purity and nobility; which apostles have pictured, in which armies of martyrs have placed their unshakable faith, and whence obscure men and women, like Catherine of Sienna and John Knox, have derived the courage to rebuke popes and kings, is not likely to underrate the importance of the Christian faith as a factor in human history, or to doubt that if that faith should prove to be incompatible with our knowledge, or necessary want of knowledge, some other hypostasis of men's hopes, genuine enough and worthy enough to replace it, will arise. But that the incongruous mixture of bad science with eviscerated papistry, out of which Comte manufactured the positivist religion, will be the heir of the Christian ages, I have too much respect for the humanity of the future to believe. Charles II told his brother, "They will not kill me, James, to make you king." And if critical science is remorselessly destroying the historical foundations of the noblest ideal of humanity which mankind have yet worshiped, it is little likely to permit the pitiful reality to climb into the vacant shrine.

That a man should determine to devote himself to the service of humanity—including intellectual and moral self-culture under that name; that this should be, in the proper sense of the word, his religion—is not only an intelligible, but, I think, a laudable resolution. And I am greatly disposed to believe that it is the only religion which will prove itself to be unassailably acceptable so long as the human race endures. But when the positivist asks me to worship "Humanity"—that is to say, to adore the generalized conception of men as they ever have been and probably ever will be—I must reply that I could just as soon bow down and worship the generalized conception of a "wilderness of apes." Surely we are not going back to the days of paganism, when individual men were deified, and the hard good sense of a dying Vespasian could prompt the bitter jest, "*Ut puto Deus fio.*" No divinity doth hedge a modern man, be he even a sovereign ruler. Nor is there any one, except a municipal magistrate, who is officially declared worshipful. But if there is no spark of worship-worthy divinity in the individual twigs of humanity, whence comes that godlike splendor which the Moses of positivism fondly imagines to pervade the whole bush?

I know no study which is so unutterably saddening as that of the evolution of humanity, as it is set forth in the annals of history. Out of the darkness of prehistoric ages man emerges with the marks of his lowly origin strong upon him. He is a brute, only more intelligent than the other brutes; a blind prey to impulses, which as often as not lead him to destruction; a victim to endless illusions, which make his mental existence a terror and a burden, and fill his physical life with barren toil and battle. He attains a certain degree of physical comfort, and develops a more or less workable theory of life, in such favorable situations as the plains of Mesopotamia or of Egypt, and then, for thousands and thousands of years, struggles with varying fortunes, attended by infinite wickedness, bloodshed, and misery, to maintain himself at this point against the greed and the ambition of his fellow-men. He makes a point of killing and otherwise persecuting all those who first try to get him to move on; and when he has moved on a step, foolishly confers *post-mortem* deification on his victims. He exactly repeats the process with all who want to move a step yet farther. And the best men of the best epochs are simply those who make the fewest blunders and commit the fewest sins.

That one should rejoice in the good man; forgive the bad man; and pity and help all men to the best of one's ability, is surely indisputable. It is the glory of Judaism and of Christianity to have proclaimed this truth, through all their aberrations. But the worship of a God who needs forgiveness and help, and deserves pity every hour of his existence, is no better than that of any other voluntarily selected fetich. The Emperor Julian's project was hopeful, in comparison with the prospects of the new anthropolatry.

When the historian of religion in the twentieth century is writing about the nineteenth, I foresee he will say something of this kind:

The most curious and instructive events in the religious history of the preceding century are the rise and progress of two new sects, called Mormons and Positivists. To the student who has carefully considered these remarkable phenomena nothing in the records of religious self-delusion can appear improbable.

The Mormons arose in the midst of the great Republic, which, though comparatively insignificant at that time, in territory as in the number of its citizens, was (as we know from the fragments of the speeches of its orators which have come down to us) no less remarkable for the native intelligence of its population, than for the wide extent of their information, owing to the activity of their publishers in diffusing all that they could invent, beg, borrow, or steal. Nor were they less noted for their perfect freedom from all restraints in thought or speech or deed; except, to be sure, the beneficent and wise influence of the majority exerted, in case of need, through an institution known as "tarring and feathering," the exact nature of which is now disputed.

There is a complete consensus of testimony that the founder of Mormonism, one Joseph Smith, was a low-minded, ignorant scamp, and that he stole the "Scriptures" which he propounded; not being clever enough to forge even such contemptible stuff as they contain. Nevertheless he must have been a man of some force of character, for a considerable number of disciples soon gathered about him. In spite of repeated outbursts of popular hatred and violence—during one of which persecutions, Smith was brutally murdered—the Mormon body steadily increased, and became a flourishing community. But the Mormon practices being objectionable to the majority, they were, more than once, without any pretense of law, but by force of riot, arson, and murder, driven away from the land they had occupied. Harried by these persecutions, the Mormon body eventually committed itself to the tender mercies of a desert as barren as that of Sinai; and, after terrible sufferings and privations, reached the oasis of Utah. Here it grew and flourished, sending out missionaries to, and receiving converts from, all parts of Europe, sometimes to the number of 10,000 in a year; until in 1880, the rich and flourishing community numbered 110,000 souls in Utah alone, while there were probably 30,000 or 40,000 scattered abroad elsewhere. In the whole history of religions there is no more remarkable example of the power of faith; and, in this case, the founder of that faith was indubitably a most despicable creature. It is interesting to observe that the course taken by the great Republic and its citizens runs exactly parallel with that taken by the Roman Empire and its citizens toward the early Christians, except that the Romans had a certain legal excuse for their acts of violence, inasmuch as the Christian "sodalitia" were not licensed, and consequently were, *ipso facto*, illegal assemblages. Until, in the latter part of the nineteenth century, the United States Legislature decreed the illegality of polygamy, the Mormons were wholly within the law.

Nothing can present a greater contrast to all this than the history of the Positivists. This sect arose much about the same time as that of the Mormons, in the upper and most instructed stratum of the quick-witted, skeptical population of Paris. The founder, Auguste Comte, was a teacher of mathematics, but of no eminence in that department of knowledge, and with nothing but an amateur's acquaintance with physical, chemical, and biological science. His works are repulsive on account of the dull diffuseness of their style, and a certain air, as of a superior person, which characterizes them; but, nevertheless, they contain good things here and there. It would take too much space to reproduce in detail a system which proposes to regulate all human life by the promulgation of a gentile Leviticus. Suffice it to say that M. Comte may be described as a syncretic, who, like the gnostics of early Church history, attempted to combine the substance of imperfectly comprehended contemporary science with the form of Roman Christianity. It may be that this is the reason why his disciples were so very angry with some obscure people called Agnostics, whose views, if we may judge by the accounts left in the works of a great positivist controversial writer, were very absurd.

To put the matter briefly, M. Comte, finding Christianity and Science at daggers drawn, seems to have said to Science: "You find Christianity rotten at the core, do you? Well, I will scoop out the inside of it." And to Romanism: "You find Science mere dry light—cold and bare. Well, I will put your shell over it, and so, as schoolboys make a specter out of a turnip and a tallow candle, behold the new religion of Humanity complete!"

Unfortunately, neither the Romanists nor the people who were something more than amateurs in science could be got to worship M. Comte's new idol properly. In the native country of Positivism, one distinguished man of letters and one of science, for a time, helped to make up a roomful of the faithful, but their love soon grew cold. In England, on the other hand, there appears to be little doubt that, in the ninth decade of the century, the multitude of disciples reached the grand total of several score. They had the advantage of the advocacy of one or two most eloquent and learned apostles, and, at any rate, the sympathy of several persons of light and leading—and, if they were not seen, they were heard all over the world. On the other hand, as a sect, they labored under the prodigious disadvantage of being refined, estimable people, living in the midst of the worn-out civilization of the Old World; where any one who had tried to persecute them, as the Mormons were persecuted, would have been instantly hanged. But the majority never dreamed of persecuting them; on the contrary, they were rather given to scold, and otherwise try the patience of the majority.

The history of these sects in the closing years of the century is highly instructive. Mormonism . . . .

But I find I have suddenly slipped off Mr. Harrison's tripod, which I had borrowed for the occasion. The fact is, I am not equal to the prophetical business, and ought not to have undertaken it.

III.

AGNOSTICISM.

A REPLY TO PROFESSOR HUXLEY.

By HENRY WACE, D. D.

It would hardly be reasonable to complain of Prof. Huxley's delay in replying to the paper on "Agnosticism" which I read five months ago, when, at the urgent request of an old friend, I reluctantly consented to address the Church Congress at Manchester. I am obliged to him for doing it the honor to bring it to the notice of a wider circle than that to which it was directly addressed; and I fear that, for reasons which have been the occasion of universal regret, he may not have been equal to literary effort. But, at the same time, it is impossible not to notice that a writer is at a great advantage in attacking a fugitive essay a quarter of a year after it was made public. Such a lapse of time ought, indeed, to enable him to apprehend distinctly the argument with which he is dealing; and it might, at least, secure him from any such inaccuracy in quotation as greater haste might excuse. But if either his idiosyncrasy, or his sense of assured superiority, should lead him to pay no real attention to the argument he is attacking, or should betray him into material misquotation, he may at least be sure that scarcely any of his readers will care to refer to the original paper, or will have the opportunity of doing so. I can scarcely hope that Prof. Huxley's obliging reference to the "Official Report of the Church Congress" will induce many of those who are influenced by his answer to my paper to purchase that interesting volume, though they would be well repaid by some of its other contents; and I can hardly rely on their spending even twopence upon the reprint of the paper, published by the Society for Promoting Christian Knowledge. I have therefore felt obliged to ask the editor of this review to be kind enough to admit to his pages a brief restatement of the position which Prof. Huxley has assailed, with such notice of his arguments as is practicable within the comparatively brief space which can be afforded me. I could not, indeed, amid the pressing claims of a college like this in term time, besides the chairmanship of a hospital, a preachership, and other duties, attempt any reply which would deal as thoroughly as could be wished with an article of so much skill and finish. But it is a matter of justice to my cause and to myself to remove at once the unscientific and prejudiced representation of the case which Prof. Huxley has put forward; and fortunately there will be need of no elaborate argument for this purpose. There is no occasion to go beyond Prof. Huxley's own article and the language of my paper to exhibit his entire misapprehension of the point in dispute; while I am much more than content to rely for the invalidation of his own contentions upon the authorities he himself quotes.

What, then, is the position with which Prof. Huxley finds fault? He is good enough to say that what he calls my "description" of an agnostic may for the present pass, so that we are so far, at starting, on common ground.

The actual description of an agnostic, which is given in my paper, is indeed distinct from the words he quotes, and is taken from an authoritative source. But what I have said is that, as an escape from such an article of Christian belief as that we have a Father in heaven, or that Jesus Christ is the Judge of quick and dead, and will hereafter return to judge the world, an agnostic urges that "he has no means of a scientific knowledge of the unseen world or of the future"; and I maintain that this plea is irrelevant. Christians do not presume to say that they have a scientific knowledge of such articles of their creed. They say that they believe them, and they believe them mainly on the assurances of Jesus Christ. Consequently their characteristic difference from an agnostic consists in the fact that they believe those assurances, and that he does not. Prof. Huxley's observation, "Are there then any Christians who say that they know nothing about the unseen world and the future? I was ignorant of the fact, but I am ready to accept it on the authority of a professed theologian," is either a quibble, or one of many indications that he does not recognize the point at issue. I am speaking, as the sentence shows, of scientific knowledge—knowledge which can be obtained by our own reason and observation alone—and no one with Prof. Huxley's learning is justified in being ignorant that it is not upon such knowledge, but upon supernatural revelation, that Christian belief rests. However, as he goes on to say, my view of "the real state of the case is that the agnostic 'does not believe the authority' on which 'these things' are stated, which authority is Jesus Christ. He is simply an old-fashioned 'infidel' who is afraid to own to his right name." The argument has nothing to do with his motive, whether it is being afraid or not. It only concerns the fact that that by which he is distinctively separated from the Christian is that he does not believe the assurances of Jesus Christ.

Prof. Huxley thinks there is "an attractive simplicity about this solution of the problem"—he means, of course, this statement of the case—"and it has that advantage of being somewhat offensive to the persons attacked, which is so dear to the less refined sort of controversialist." I think Prof. Huxley must have forgotten himself and his own feelings in this observation. There can be no question, of course, of his belonging himself to the more refined sort of controversialist; but he has a characteristic fancy for solutions of problems, or statements of cases, which have the "advantage of being somewhat offensive to the persons attacked." Without taking this particular phrase into account, it certainly has "the advantage of being offensive to the persons attacked" that Prof. Huxley should speak in this article of "the pestilent doctrine on which all the churches have insisted, the honest disbelief"—the word honest is not a misquotation—"honest disbelief in their more or less astonishing creeds is a moral offense, indeed a sin of the deepest dye, deserving and involving the same future retribution as murder or robbery," or that he should say, "Trip in morals or in doctrine (especially in doctrine), without due repentance or retractation, or fail to get properly baptized before you die, and a *plébiscite* of the Christians of Europe, if they were true to their creeds, would affirm your everlasting damnation by an immense majority." We have fortunately nothing to do in this argument with *plébiscites;* and as statements of authoritative Christian teaching, the least that can be said of these allegations is that they are offensive exaggerations. It had "the advantage" again, of being "offensive to the persons attacked," when Prof. Huxley, in an article in this review on "Science and the Bishops," in November, 1887, said that "scientific ethics can and does declare that the profession of belief" in such narratives as that of the devils entering a herd of swine, or of the fig-tree that was blasted for bearing no figs, upon the evidence on which multitudes of Christians believe it, "is immoral"; and the observation which followed, that "theological apologists would do well to consider the fact that, in the matter of intellectual veracity, Science is already a long way ahead of the churches," has the same "advantage." I repeat that I can not but treat Prof. Huxley as an example of the more refined sort of controversialist; it must be supposed, therefore, that when he speaks of observations or insinuations which are somewhat offensive to the "persons attacked" being dear to the other sort of controversialist, he is unconscious of his own methods of controversy—or, shall I say, his own temptations?

But I desire as far as possible to avoid any rivalry with Prof. Huxley in these refinements—more or less—of controversy; and am, in fact, forced by pressure both of space and of time to keep as rigidly as possible to the points directly at issue. He proceeds to restate the case as follows: "The agnostic says, 'I can not find good evidence that so and so is true.' 'Ah,' says his adversary, seizing his opportunity, 'then you declare that Jesus Christ was untruthful, for he said so and so'—a very telling method of rousing prejudice." Now that superior scientific veracity to which, as we have seen, Prof. Huxley lays claim, should have prevented him putting such vulgar words into my mouth. There is not a word in my paper to charge agnostics with declaring that Jesus Christ was "untruthful." I believe it impossible in these days for any man who claims attention—I might say, for any man—to declare our Lord untruthful. What I said, and what I repeat, is that the position of an agnostic involves the conclusion that Jesus Christ was under an "illusion" in respect to the deepest beliefs of his life and teaching. The words of my paper are, "An agnosticism which knows nothing of the relation of man to God must not only refuse belief to our Lord's most undoubted teaching, but must deny the reality of the spiritual convictions in which he lived and died." The point is this—that there can, at least, be no reasonable doubt that Jesus Christ lived, and taught, and died, in the belief of certain great principles respecting the existence of God, our relation to God, and his own relation to us, which an agnostic says are beyond the possibilities of human knowledge; and of course an agnostic regards Jesus Christ as a man. If so, he must necessarily regard Jesus Christ as mistaken, since the notion of his being untruthful is a supposition which I could not conceive being suggested. The question I have put is not, as Prof. Huxley represents, what is the most unpleasant alternative to belief in the primary truths of the Christian religion, but what is the least unpleasant; and all I have maintained is that the least unpleasant alternative necessarily involved is, that Jesus Christ was under an illusion in his most vital convictions.

I content myself with thus rectifying the state of the case, without making the comments which I think would be justified on such a crude misrepresentation of my argument. But Prof. Huxley goes on to observe that "the value of the evidence as to what Jesus may have said and done, and as to the exact nature and scope of his authority, is just that which the agnostic finds it most difficult to determine." Undoubtedly, that is a primary question; but who would suppose from Prof. Huxley's statement of the case that the argument of the paper he is attacking proceeded to deal with this very point, and that he has totally ignored the chief consideration it alleged? Almost immediately after the words Prof. Huxley has quoted, the following passage occurs, which I must needs transfer to these pages, as containing the central point of the argument: "It may be asked how far we can rely on the accounts we possess of our Lord's teaching on these subjects. Now it is unnecessary for the general argument before us to enter on those questions respecting the authenticity of the gospel narratives, which ought to be regarded as settled by M. Renan's practical surrender of the adverse case. *Apart from all disputed points of criticism, no one practically doubts that our Lord lived, and that he died on the cross, in the most intense sense of filial relation to his Father in heaven, and that he bore testimony to that Father's providence, love, and grace toward mankind. The Lord's Prayer affords sufficient evidence upon these points. If the Sermon on the Mount alone be added, the whole unseen world, of which the agnostic refuses to know anything, stands unveiled before us. There you see revealed the divine Father and Creator of all things, in personal relation to his creatures, hearing their prayers, witnessing their actions, caring for them and rewarding them. There you hear of a future judgment administered by Christ himself, and of a heaven to be hereafter revealed, in which those who live as the children of that Father, and who suffer in the cause and for the sake of Christ himself, will be abundantly rewarded. If Jesus Christ preached that sermon, made those promises, and taught that prayer, then any one who says that we know nothing of God, or of a future life, or of an unseen world, says that he does not believe Jesus Christ."*

Prof. Huxley has not one word to say upon this argument, though the whole case is involved in it. Let us take as an example the illustration he proceeds to give. "If," he says, "I venture to doubt that the Duke of Wellington gave the command, 'Up, Guards, and at 'em!' at Waterloo, I do not think that even Dr. Wace would accuse me of disbelieving the duke." Certainly not. But if Prof. Huxley were to maintain that the pursuit of glory was the true motive of the soldier, and that it was an illusion to suppose that simple devotion to duty could be the supreme guide of military life, I should certainly charge him with contradicting the duke's teaching and disregarding his authority and example. A hundred stories like that of "Up, Guards, and at 'em!" might be doubted, or positively disproved, and it would still remain a fact beyond all reasonable doubt that the Duke of Wellington was essentially characterized by the sternest and most devoted sense of duty, and that he had inculcated duty as the very watchword of a soldier; and even Prof. Huxley would not suggest that Lord Tennyson's ode, which has embodied this characteristic in immortal verse, was an unfounded poetical romance.

The main question at issue, in a word, is one which Prof. Huxley has chosen to leave entirely on one side— whether, namely, allowing for the utmost uncertainty on other points of the criticism to which he appeals, there is any reasonable doubt that the Lord's Prayer and the Sermon on the Mount afford a true account of our Lord's essential belief and cardinal teaching. If they do—then I am not now contending that they involve the whole of the Christian creed; I am not arguing, as Prof. Huxley would represent, that he ought for that reason alone to be a Christian—I simply represent that, as an agnostic, he must regard those beliefs and that teaching as mistaken—the result of an illusion, to say the least. I am not going, therefore, to follow Prof. Huxley's example and go down a steep place with the Gadarene swine into a sea of uncertainties and possibilities, and stake the whole case of Christian belief as against agnosticism upon one of the most difficult and mysterious narratives in the New Testament. I will state my position on that question presently. But I am first and chiefly concerned to point out that Prof. Huxley has skillfully evaded the very point and edge of the argument he had to meet. Let him raise what difficulties he pleases, with the help of his favorite critics, about the Gadarene swine, or even about all the stories of demoniacs. He will find that his critics—and even critics more rationalistic than they—fail him when it comes to the Lord's Prayer and the Sermon on the Mount, and, I will add, the story of the Passion. He will find, or rather he must have found, that the very critics he relies upon recognize that in the Sermon on the Mount and the Lord's Prayer, allowing for variations in form and order, the substance of our Lord's essential teaching is preserved. On a point which, until Prof. Huxley shows cause to the contrary, can hardly want argument, the judgment of the most recent of his witnesses may suffice —Prof. Reuss, of Strasburg. In Prof. Huxley's article on the "Evolution of Theology" in the number of this review for March, 1886, he says, "As Reuss appears to me to be one of the most learned, acute, and fair-minded of those whose works I have studied, I have made most use of the commentary and dissertations in his splendid

French edition of the Bible." What, then, is the opinion of the critic for whom Prof. Huxley has this regard? In the volume of his work which treats of the first three Gospels, Reuss says at page 191–192, "If anywhere the tradition which has preserved to us the reminiscences of the life of Jesus upon earth carries with it certainty and the evidence of its fidelity, it is here"; and again: "In short, it must be acknowledged that the redactor, in thus concentrating the substance of the moral teaching of the Lord, has rendered a real service to the religious study of this portion of the tradition, and the reserves which historical criticism has a right to make with respect to the form will in no way diminish this advantage." It will be observed that Prof. Reuss thinks, as many good critics have thought, that the Sermon on the Mount combines various distinct utterances of our Lord, but he none the less recognizes that it embodies an unquestionable account of the substance of our Lord's teaching.

But it is surely superfluous to argue either this particular point, or the main conclusion which I have founded on it. Can there be any doubt whatever, in the mind of any reasonable man, that Jesus Christ had beliefs respecting God which an agnostic alleges there is no sufficient ground for? We know something at all events of what his disciples taught; we have authentic original documents, unquestioned by any of Prof. Huxley's authorities, as to what St. Paul taught and believed, and of what he taught and believed respecting his Master's teaching; and the central point of this teaching is a direct assertion of knowledge and revelation as against the very agnosticism from which Prof. Huxley manufactured that designation. "As I passed by," said St. Paul at Athens, "I found an altar with this inscription: 'To the unknown

God.' Whom therefore ye ignorantly—or in agnosticism—worship, Him I declare unto you." An agnostic withholds his assent from this primary article of the Christian creed; and though Prof. Huxley, in spite of the lack of information he alleges respecting early Christian teaching, knows enough on the subject to have a firm belief "that the Nazarenes, say of the year 40," headed by James, would have stoned any one who propounded the Nicene Creed to them, he will hardly contend that they denied that article, or doubted that Jesus Christ believed it. Let us again listen to the authority to whom Prof. Huxley himself refers. Reuss says at page 4 of the work already quoted:

Historical literature in the primitive church attaches itself in the most immediate manner to the reminiscences collected by the apostles and their friends, directly after their separation from their Master. The need of such a return to the past arose naturally from the profound impression which had been made upon them by the teaching, and still more by the individuality itself of Jesus, and on which both their hopes for the future and their convictions were founded. . . . It is in these facts, in this continuity of a tradition which could not but go back to the very morrow of the tragic scene of Golgotha that we have a strong guarantee for its authenticity. . . . We have direct historical proof that the thread of tradition was not interrupted. Not only does one of our evangelists furnish this truth in formal terms (Luke i, 2); but in many other places besides we perceive the idea, or the point of view, that all which the apostles know, think, and teach, is at bottom and essentially a reminiscence—a reflection of what they have seen and learned at another time, a reproduction of lessons and impressions received.

Now let it be allowed for argument's sake that the belief and teaching of the apostles are distinct from those of subsequent Christianity, yet it is surely a mere paradox to maintain that they did not assert, as taught by their Master, truths which an agnostic denies. They certainly spoke, as Paul did, of the love of God; they certainly spoke, as Paul did, of Jesus having been raised from the dead by God the Father (Gal. i, 1); they certainly spoke, as Paul did, of Jesus Christ returning to judge the world; they certainly spoke, as Paul did, of "the God and Father of our Lord Jesus Christ" (2 Cor. xi, 31). That they could have done this without Jesus Christ having taught God's love, or having said that God was his Father, or having declared that he would judge the world, is a supposition which will certainly be regarded by an overwhelming majority of reasonable men as a mere paradox; and I can not conceive, until he says so, that Prof. Huxley would maintain it. But if so, then all Prof. Huxley's argumentation about the Gadarene swine is mere irrelevance to the argument he undertakes to answer. The Gospels might be obliterated as evidence to-morrow, and it would remain indisputable that Jesus Christ taught certain truths respecting God, and man's relation to God, from which an agnostic withholds his assent. If so, he does not believe Jesus Christ's teaching; he is so far an unbeliever, and "unbeliever," Dr. Johnson says, is an equivalent of "infidel."

This consideration will indicate another irrelevance in Prof. Huxley's argument. He asks for a definition of what a Christian is, before he will allow that he can be justly called an infidel. But without being able to give an accurate definition of a crayfish, which perhaps only Prof. Huxley could do, I may be very well able to say that some creatures are not crayfish; and it is not necessary to frame a definition of a Christian in order to say confidently that a person who does not believe the broad and unquestionable elements of Christ's teachings and convictions is not a Christian. "Infidel" or "unbeliever" is of course, as Prof. Huxley says, a relative and not a positive term. He makes a great deal of play out what he seems to suppose will be a very painful and surprising consideration to myself, that to a Mohammedan I am an infidel. Of course I am; and I should never expect a Mohammedan, if he were called upon, as I was, to argue before an assembly of his own fellow-believers, to call me anything else. Prof. Huxley is good enough to imagine me in his company on a visit to the Hazar Mosque at Cairo. When he entered that mosque without due credentials, he suspects that, had he understood Arabic, "dog of an infidel" would have been by no means the most "unpleasant" of the epithets showered upon him, before he could explain and apologize for the mistake. If, he says, "I had had the pleasure of Dr. Wace's company on that occasion, the undiscriminative followers of the Prophet would, I am afraid, have made no difference between us; not even if they had known that he was the head of an orthodox Christian seminary." Probably not; and I will add that I should have felt very little confidence in any attempts which Prof. Huxley might have made, in the style of his present article, to protect me, by repudiating for himself the unpleasant epithets which he deprecates. It would, I suspect, have been of very little avail to attempt a subtle explanation, to one of the learned mollahs of whom he speaks, that he really did not mean to deny that there was one God, but only that he did not know anything on the subject, and that he desired to avoid expressing any opinion respecting the claims of Mohammed. It would be plain to the learned mollah that Prof. Huxley did not believe either of the articles of the Mohammedan creed—in other words that, for all his fine distinctions, he was at bottom a downright infidel, such as I confessed myself, and that there was an end of the matter. There is no fair way of avoiding the plain matter of fact in either case. A Mohammedan believes and asserts that there is no God but God, and that Mohammed is the prophet of God. I don't believe Mohammed. In the plain, blunt, sensible phrase people used to use on such subjects I believe he was a false prophet, and I am a downright infidel about him. The Christian creed might almost be summed up in the assertion that there is one, and but one God, and that Jesus Christ is his prophet; and whoever denies that creed says that he does not believe Jesus Christ, by whom it was undoubtedly asserted. It is better to look facts in the face, especially from a scientific point of view. Whether Prof. Huxley is justified in his denial of that creed is a further question, which demands separate consideration, but which was not, and is not now, at issue. All I say is that his position involves that disbelief or infidelity, and that this is a responsibility which must be faced by agnosticism.

But I am forced to conclude that Prof. Huxley can not have taken the pains to understand the point I raised, not only by the irrelevance of his argument on these considerations, but by a misquotation which the superior accuracy of a man of science ought to have rendered impossible. Twice over in the article he quotes me as saying that "it is, and it ought to be, an unpleasant thing for a man to have to say plainly that he does not believe in Jesus Christ." As he winds up his attack upon my paper by bringing against this statement his rather favorite charge of "immorality"—and even "most profound immorality"—he was the more bound to accuracy in his quotation of my words. But neither in the official report of the congress to which he refers, nor in any report that I have seen, is this the statement attributed to me. What I said, and what I meant to say, was that it ought to be an unpleasant thing for a man to have to say plainly "that he does not believe Jesus Christ." By inserting the little word "in," Prof. Huxley has, by an unconscious ingenuity, shifted the import of the statement. He goes on to denounce "the pestilent doctrine on which all the churches have insisted, that honest disbelief in their more or less astonishing creeds is a moral offense, indeed a sin of the deepest dye." * His interpretation exhibits, in fact, the idea in his own mind, which he has doubtless conveyed to his readers, that I said it ought to be unpleasant to a man to have to say that he does not believe in the Christian creed. I certainly think it ought, for reasons I will mention; but that is not what I said. I spoke, deliberately, not of the Christian creed as a whole, but of Jesus Christ as a person, and regarded as a witness to certain primary truths which an agnostic will not acknowledge. It was a personal consideration to which I appealed, and not a dogmatic one; and I am sorry, for that reason, that Prof. Huxley will not allow me to leave it in the reserve with which I hoped it had been sufficiently indicated. I said that "no criticism worth mentioning doubts the story of the Passion; and that story involves the most solemn attestation, again and again, of truths of which an agnostic coolly says he knows nothing. An agnosticism which knows nothing of the relation of man to God must not only refuse belief to our Lord's most undoubted teaching, but must deny the reality of the spiritual convictions in which he lived and died. It must declare that his most intimate, most intense beliefs,

---

* Page 39.

and his dying aspirations were an illusion. Is that supposition tolerable?" I do not think this deserves to be called "a proposition of the most profoundly immoral character." I think it ought to be unpleasant, and I am sure it always will be unpleasant, for a man to listen to the Saviour on the cross uttering such words as "Father, into thy hands I commend my spirit," and to say that they are not to be trusted as revealing a real relation between the Saviour and God. In spite of all doubts as to the accuracy of the Gospels, Jesus Christ—I trust I may be forgiven, under the stress of controversy, for mentioning his sacred name in this too familiar manner—is a tender and sacred figure to all thoughtful minds, and it is, it ought to be, and it always will be, a very painful thing, to say that he lived and died under a mistake in respect to the words which were first and last on his lips. I think, as I have admitted, that it should be unpleasant for a man who has as much appreciation of Christianity, and of its work in the world, as Prof. Huxley sometimes shows, to have to say that its belief was founded on no objective reality. The unpleasantness, however, of denying one system of thought may be balanced by the pleasantness, as Prof. Huxley suggests, of asserting another and a better one. But nothing, to all time, can do away with the unpleasantness, not only of repudiating sympathy with the most sacred figure of humanity in his deepest beliefs and feelings, but of pronouncing him under an illusion in his last agony. If it be the truth, let it by all means be said; but if we are to talk of "immorality" in such matters, I think there must be a lack of moral sensibility in any man who could say it without pain.

The plain fact is that this misquotation would have been as impossible as a good deal else of Prof. Huxley's argument, had he, in any degree, appreciated the real strength of the hold which Christianity has over men's hearts and minds. The strength of the Christian Church, in spite of its faults, errors, and omissions, is not in its creed, but in its Lord and Master. In spite of all the critics, the Gospels have conveyed to the minds of millions of men a living image of Christ. They see him there; they hear his voice; they listen, and they believe him. It is not so much that they accept certain doctrines as taught by him, as that they accept him, himself, as their Lord and their God. The sacred fire of trust in him descended upon the apostles, and has from them been handed on from generation to generation. It is with that living personal figure that agnosticism has to deal; and as long as the Gospels practically produce the effect of making that figure a reality to human hearts, so long will the Christian faith, and the Christian Church, in their main characteristics, be vital and permanent forces in the world. Prof. Huxley tells us, in a melancholy passage, that he can not define "the grand figure of Jesus." Who shall dare to "define" it? But saints have both written and lived an *imitatio Christi*, and men and women can feel and know what they can not define. Prof. Huxley, it would seem, would have us all wait coolly until we have solved all critical difficulties, before acting on such a belief. "Because," he says, "we are often obliged, by the pressure of events, to act on very bad evidence, it does not follow that it is proper to act on such evidence when the pressure is absent." Certainly not; but it is strange ignorance of human nature for Prof. Huxley to imagine that there is no "pressure" in this matter. It was a voice which understood the human heart better which said, "Come unto me, all ye that labor and are heavy laden, and I will give you rest"; and the attraction of that voice outweighs many a critical difficulty under the pressure of the burdens and the sins of life.

Prof. Huxley, indeed, admits, in one sentence of his article, the force of this influence on individuals.

> If (he says) a man can find a friend, the hypostasis of all his hopes, the mirror of his ethical ideal, in the pages of any, or of all, of the Gospels, let him live by faith in that ideal. Who shall, or can, forbid him? But let him not delude himself with the notion that his faith is evidence of the objective reality of that in which he trusts. Such evidence is to be obtained only by the use of the methods of science, as applied to history and to literature, and it amounts at present to very little.

Well, a single man's belief in an ideal may be very little evidence of its objective reality. But the conviction of millions of men, generation after generation, of the veracity of the four evangelical witnesses, and of the human and divine reality of the figure they describe, has at least something of the weight of the verdict of a jury. *Securus judicat orbis terrarum.* Practically the figure of Christ lives. The Gospels have created it; and it subsists as a personal fact in life, alike among believers and unbelievers. Prof. Huxley himself, in spite of all his skepticism, appears to have his own type of this character. The apologue of the woman taken in adultery might, he says, "if internal evidence were an infallible guide, well be affirmed to be a typical example of the teachings of Jesus." Internal evidence may not be an infallible guide; but it certainly carries great weight, and no one has relied more upon it in these questions than the critics whom Prof. Huxley quotes.

But as I should be sorry to imitate Prof. Huxley, on so momentous a subject, by evading the arguments and facts he alleges, I will consider the question of external evidence on which he dwells. I must repeat that the argument of my paper is independent of this controversy. The fact that our Lord taught and believed what agnostics ignore is not dependent on the criticism of the four Gospels. In addition to the general evidence to which I have alluded, there is a further consideration which Prof. Huxley feels it necessary to mention, but which he evades by an extraordinary inconsequence. He alleges that the story of the Gadarene swine involves fabulous matter, and that this discredits the trustworthiness of the whole Gospel record. But he says:

> At this point a very obvious objection arises and deserves full and candid consideration. It may be said that critical skepticism carried to the length suggested is historical pyrrhonism; that if we are to altogether discredit an ancient or a modern historian because he has assumed fabulous matter to be true, it will be as well to give up paying any attention to history. . . . Of course (he acknowledges) this is perfectly true. I am afraid there is no man alive whose witness could be accepted, if the condition precedent were proof that he had never invented and promulgated a myth.

The question, then, which Prof. Huxley himself raises, and which he had to answer, was this: Why is the general evidence of the Gospels, on the main facts of our Lord's life and teaching, to be discredited, even if it be true that they have invented or promulgated a myth about the Gadarene swine? What is his answer to that simple and broad question? Strange to say, absolutely none at all! He leaves this vital question without any answer, and goes back to the Gadarene swine. The question he raises is whether the supposed incredibility of the story of the Gadarene swine involves the general untrustworthiness of the story of the Gospels; and his conclusion is that it involves the incredibility of the story of the Gadarene swine. A more complete evasion of his own question it would be difficult to imagine. As Prof. Huxley almost challenges me to state what I think of that story, I have only to say that I fully believe it, and moreover that Prof. Huxley, in this very article, has removed the only consideration which would have been a serious obstacle to my belief. If he were prepared to say, on his high scientific authority, that the narrative involves a contradiction of established scientific truth, I could not but defer to such a decision, and I might be driven to consider those possibilities of interpolation in the narrative, which Prof. Huxley is good enough to suggest to all who feel the improbability of the story too much for them. But Prof. Huxley expressly says:

> I admit I have no *a priori* objection to offer. . . . For anything I can absolutely prove to the contrary, there may be spiritual things capable of the same transmigration, with like effects. . . . So I declare, as plainly as I can, that I am unable to show cause why these transferable devils should not exist.

Very well, then, as the highest science of the day is unable to show cause against the possibility of the narrative, and as I regard the Gospels as containing the evidence of trustworthy persons who were contemporary with the events narrated, and as their general veracity carries to my mind the greatest possible weight, I accept their statement in this as in other instances. Prof. Huxley ventures "to doubt whether at this present moment any Protestant theologian, who has a reputation to lose, will say that he believes the Gadarene story." He will judge whether I fall under his description; but I repeat that I believe it, and that he has removed the only objection to my believing it.

However, to turn finally to the important fact of external evidence. Prof. Huxley reiterates, again and again, that the verdict of scientific criticism is decisive against the supposition that we possess in the four Gospels the authentic and contemporary evidence of known writers. He repeats, "without the slightest fear of refutation, that the four Gospels, as they have come to us, are the work of unknown writers." In particular, he challenges my allegation of "M. Renan's practical surrender of the adverse case"; and he adds the following observations, to which I beg the reader's particular attention:

I thought (he says) I knew M. Renan's works pretty well, but I have contrived to miss this "practical"—(I wish Dr. Wace had defined the scope of that useful adjective)—surrender. However, as Dr. Wace can find no difficulty in pointing out the passage of M. Renan's writings, by which he feels justified in making his statement, I shall wait for further enlightenment, contenting myself, for the present, with remarking that if M. Renan were to retract and do penance in Notre Dame to-morrow for any contributions to biblical criticism that may be specially his property, the main results of that criticism, as they are set forth in the works of Strauss, Baur, Reuss, and Volkmar, for example, would not be sensibly affected.

Let me begin then, by enlightening Prof. Huxley about M. Renan's surrender. I have the less difficulty in doing so as the passages he has contrived to miss have been collected by me already in a little tract on the "Authenticity of the Gospels," * and in some lectures on the "Gospel and its Witnesses"; † and I shall take the liberty, for convenience' sake, of repeating some of the observations there made.

I beg first to refer to the preface to M. Renan's "Vie de Jésus." ‡ There M. Renan says:

---

* Religious Tract Society.   † John Murray, 1883.
‡ Fifteenth edition, p. xlix.

As to Luke, doubt is scarcely possible. The Gospel of St. Luke is a regular composition, founded upon earlier documents. It is the work of an author who chooses, curtails, combines. The author of this Gospel is certainly the same as the author of the Acts of the Apostles. Now, the author of the Acts seems to be a companion of St. Paul—a character which accords completely with St. Luke. I know that more than one objection may be opposed to this reasoning; but one thing at all events is beyond doubt, namely, that the author of the third Gospel and of the Acts is a man who belonged to the second apostolic generation; and this suffices for our purpose. The date of this Gospel, moreover, may be determined with sufficient precision by considerations drawn from the book itself. The twenty-first chapter of St. Luke, which is inseparable from the rest of the work, was certainly written after the siege of Jerusalem, but not long after. We are, therefore, here on solid ground, for we are dealing with a work proceeding entirely from the same hand, and possessing the most complete unity.

It may be important to observe that this admission has been supported by M. Renan's further investigations, as expressed in his subsequent volume on "The Apostles." In the preface to that volume he discusses fully the nature and value of the narrative contained in the Acts of the Apostles, and he pronounces the following decided opinions as to the authorship of that book, and its connection with the Gospel of St. Luke (page x *sq.*):

One point which is beyond question is that the Acts are by the same author as the third Gospel, and are a continuation of that Gospel. One need not stop to prove this proposition, which has never been seriously contested. The prefaces at the commencement of each work, the dedication of each to Theophilus, the perfect resemblance of style and of ideas, furnish on this point abundant demonstrations.

A second proposition, which has not the same certainty, but which may, however, be regarded as extremely probable, is that the author of the Acts is a disciple of Paul, who accompanied him for a considerable part of his travels.

At a first glance, M. Renan observes, this proposition appears indubitable, from the fact that the author, on so many occasions, uses the pronoun "we," indicating that on those occasions he was one of the apostolic band by whom St. Paul was accompanied. "One may even be astonished that a proposition apparently so evident should have found persons to contest it." He notices, however, the difficulties which have been raised on the point, and then proceeds as follows (page 14):

> Must we be checked by these objections? I think not; and I persist in believing that the person who finally prepared the Acts is really the disciple of Paul, who says "we" in the last chapters. All difficulties, however insoluble they may appear, ought to be, if not dismissed, at least held in suspense, by an argument so decisive as that which results from the use of this word "we."

He then observes that MSS. and tradition combine in assigning the third Gospel to a certain Luke, and that it is scarcely conceivable that a name in other respects obscure should have been attributed to so important a work for any other reason than that it was the name of the real author. Luke, he says, had no place in tradition, in legend, or in history, when these two treatises were ascribed to him. M. Renan concludes in the following words: "We think, therefore, that the author of the third Gospel and of the Acts is in all reality Luke, the disciple of Paul."

Now let the import of these expressions of opinion be duly weighed. Of course, M. Renan's judgments are not to be regarded as affording in themselves any adequate basis for our acceptance of the authenticity of the chief books of the New Testament. The Acts of the Apostles and the four Gospels bear on their face certain positive claims, on the faith of which they have been accepted in all ages of the Church ; and they do not rest, in the first instance, on the authority of any modern critic. But though M. Renan would be a very unsatisfactory witness to rely upon for the purpose of positive testimony to the Gospels, his estimates of the value of modern critical objections to those sacred books have all the weight of the admissions of a hostile witness. No one doubts his familiarity with the whole range of the criticism represented by such names as Strauss and Baur, and no one questions his disposition to give full weight to every objection which that criticism can urge. Even without assuming that he is prejudiced on either one side or the other, it will be admitted on all hands that he is more favorably disposed than otherwise to such criticism as Prof. Huxley relies on. When, therefore, with this full knowledge of the literature of the subjects, such a writer comes to the conclusion that the criticism in question has entirely failed to make good its case on a point like that of the authorship of St. Luke's Gospel, we are at least justified in concluding that critical objections do not possess the weight which unbelievers or skeptics are wont to assign to them. M. Renan, in a word, is no adequate witness to the Gospels ; but he is a very significant witness as to the value of modern critical objections to them.

Let us pass to the two other so-called "synoptical" Gospels. With respect to St. Matthew, M. Renan says in the same preface ("Vie de Jésus," p. lxxxi):

> To sum up, I admit the four canonical Gospels as serious documents. All go back to the age which followed the death of Jesus; but their historical value is very diverse. St. Matthew evidently deserves peculiar confidence for the discourses. Here are "the oracles," the very notes taken while the memory of the instruction of Jesus was living and definite. A kind of flashing brightness at once sweet and terrible, a divine force, if I may so say, underlies

these words, detaches them from the context, and renders them easily recognizable by the critic.

In respect again to St. Mark, he says (p. lxxxii):

> The Gospel of St. Mark is the one of the three synoptics which has remained the most ancient, the most original, and to which the least of later additions have been made. The details of fact possess in St. Mark a definiteness which we seek in vain in the other evangelists. He is fond of reporting certain sayings of our Lord in Syro-Chaldaic. He is full of minute observations, proceeding, beyond doubt, from an eye-witness. There is nothing to conflict with the supposition that this eye-witness, who had evidently followed Jesus, who had loved him and watched him in close intimacy, and who had preserved a vivid image of him, was the apostle Peter himself, as Papias has it.

I call these admissions a "practical surrender" of the adverse case, as stated by critics like Strauss and Baur, who denied that we had in the Gospels contemporary evidence, and I do not think it necessary to define the adjective, in order to please Prof. Huxley's appetite for definitions. At the very least it is a direct contradiction of Prof. Huxley's statement [*] that we know "absolutely nothing" of "the originator or originators" of the narratives in the first three Gospels; and it is an equally direct contradiction of the case, on which his main reply to my paper is based, that we have no trustworthy evidence of what our Lord taught and believed.

But Prof. Huxley seems to have been apprehensive that M. Renan would fail him, for he proceeds, in the passage I have quoted, to throw him over and to take refuge behind "the main results of biblical criticism, as they are set forth in the works of Strauss, Baur, Reuss, and Volkmar, for example." It is scarcely comprehen-

---

[*] Page 24.

sible how a writer, who has acquaintance enough with this subject to venture on Prof. Huxley's sweeping assertions, can have ventured to couple together those four names for such a purpose. "Strauss, Baur, Reuss, and Volkmar"! Why, they are absolutely destructive of one another! Baur rejected Strauss's theory and set up one of his own; while Reuss and Volkmar in their turn have each dealt fatal blows at Baur's. As to Strauss, I need not spend more time on him than to quote the sentence in which Baur himself puts him out of court on this particular controversy. He says,* "The chief peculiarity of Strauss's work is, that it is a criticism of the Gospel history without a criticism of the Gospels." Strauss, in fact, explained the miraculous stories in the Gospels by resolving them into myths, and it was of no importance to his theory how the documents originated. But Baur endeavored, by a minute criticism of the Gospels themselves, to investigate the historical circumstances of their origin; and he maintained that they were *Tendenz-Schriften*, compiled in the second century, with polemical purposes. Volkmar, however, is in direct conflict with Baur on this point, and in the very work to which Prof. Huxley refers,† he enumerates (p. 18) among "the written testimonies of the first century"—besides St. Paul's epistles to the Galatians, Corinthians, and Romans, and the apocalypse of St. John—"the Gospel of Jesus Christ, the Son of God, according to John Mark of Jerusalem, written a few years after the destruction of Jerusalem, between the years 70 and 80 of our reckoning—about 75 probably; to be precise, about 73," and he proceeds to give a detailed account

---

* "Kritische Untersuchungen über die kanonischen Evangelien," 1847, p. 41.

† "Jesus Nazarenus und die erste christliche Zeit," 1882.

AGNOSTICISM.

of it, "according to the oldest text, and particularly the Vatican text," as indispensable to his account of Jesus of Nazareth. He treats it as written (p. 172) either by John Mark of Jerusalem himself, or by a younger friend of his. Baur, therefore, having upset Strauss, Volkmar proceeds to upset Baur; and what does Reuss do? I quote again from that splendid French edition of the Bible, on which Prof. Huxley so much relies. On page 88 of Reuss's introduction to the synoptic Gospels, he sums up "the results he believes to have been obtained by critical analysis," under thirteen heads; and the following are some of them:

2. Of the three synoptic Gospels one only, that which ecclesiastical tradition agrees in attributing to Luke, has reached us in its primitive form.

3. Luke could draw his knowledge of the Gospel history partly from oral information; he was able, in Palestine itself, to receive direct communications from immediate witnesses. . . . We may think especially here of the history of the passion and the resurrection, and perhaps also of some other passages of which he is the sole narrator.

4. A book, which an ancient and respectable testimony attributes to Mark, the disciple of Peter, was certainly used by St. Luke as the principal source of the portion of his Gospel between chapter iv, 31, and ix, 50; and between xviii, 15, and xxi, 38.

5. According to all probability, the book of Mark, consulted by Luke, comprised in its primitive form what we read in the present day from Mark i, 21, to xiii, 37.

It seems unnecessary, for the purpose of estimating the value of Prof. Huxley's appeal to these critics, to quote any more. It appears from these statements of Reuss that if "the results of biblical criticism," as represented by him, are to be trusted, we have the whole third Gospel in its primitive form, as it was written by St. Luke; and in this, as we have seen, Reuss is in entire agreement with Renan. But besides this, a previous book written by Mark, St. Peter's disciple, was certainly in existence before Luke's Gospel, and was used by Luke; and in all probability this book was, in its primitive form, the greater part of our present Gospel of St. Mark.

Such are those "results of biblical criticism" to which Prof. Huxley has appealed; and we may fairly judge by these not only of the value of his special contention in reply to my paper, but of the worth of the sweeping assertions he, and writers like him, are given to making about modern critical science. Prof. Huxley says that we know "absolutely nothing" about the originators of the Gospel narratives, and he appeals to criticism in the persons of Volkmar and Reuss. Volkmar says that the second Gospel is really either by St. Mark or by one of his friends, and was written about the year 75. Reuss says that the third Gospel, as we now have it, was really by St. Luke. Now Prof. Huxley is, of course, entitled to his own opinion; but he is not entitled to quote authorities in support of his opinion when they are in direct opposition to it. He asserts, without the slightest fear of refutation, that "the four Gospels, as they have come to us, are the work of unknown writers." His arguments in defense of such a position will be listened to with great respect; but let it be borne in mind that the opposite arguments he has got to meet are not only those of orthodox critics like myself, but those of Renan, of Volkmar, and of Reuss—I may add of Pfleiderer, well known in this country by his Hibbert Lectures, who, in his recent work on original Christianity, attributes most positively the second Gospel in its present form to St. Mark, and declares that there is no ground whatever for that supposition of an *Ur-Marcus*—that is an original groundwork—from which Prof. Huxley alleges that "at the present time there is no visible escape." If I were such an authority on morality as Prof. Huxley, I might perhaps use some unpleasant language respecting this vague assumption of criticism being all on his side, when it, in fact, directly contradicts him; and his case is not the only one to which such strictures might be applied. In "Robert Elsmere," for example, there is some vaporing about the "great critical operation of the present century" having destroyed the historical basis of the Gospel narrative. As a matter of fact, as we have seen, the great critical operation has resulted, according to the testimony of the critics whom Prof. Huxley himself selects, in establishing the fact that we possess contemporary records of our Lord's life from persons who were either eye-witnesses, or who were in direct communication with eye-witnesses, on the very scene in which it was passed. Either Prof. Huxley's own witnesses are not to be trusted, or Prof. Huxley's allegations are rash and unfounded. Conclusions which are denied by Volkmar, denied by Renan, denied by Reuss, are not to be thrown at our heads with a superior air, as if they could not be reasonably doubted. The great result of the critical operation of this century has, in fact, been to prove that the contention with which it started in the persons of Strauss and Baur, that we have no contemporary records of Christ's life, is wholly untenable. It has not convinced any of the living critics to whom Prof. Huxley appeals; and if he, or any similar writer, still maintains such an assertion let it be understood that he stands alone against the leading critics of Europe in the present day.

Perhaps I need say no more for the present in reply to Prof. Huxley. I have, I think, shown that he has evaded my point; he has evaded his own points; he has misquoted my words; he has misrepresented the results of the very criticism to which he appeals; and he rests his case on assumptions which his own authorities repudiate. The questions he touches are very grave ones, not to be adequately treated in a review article. But I should have supposed it a point of scientific morality to treat them, if they are to be treated, with accuracy of reference and strictness of argument.

IV.

AGNOSTICISM.

A REPLY TO PROFESSOR HUXLEY.

By W. C. MAGEE,
BISHOP OF PETERBOROUGH.

I SHOULD be wanting in the respect which I sincerely entertain for Prof. Huxley if I were not to answer his "appeal" to me in the last number of this review for my opinion on a point in controversy between him and Dr. Wace. Prof. Huxley asks me, "in the name of all that is Hibernian, why a man should be expected to call himself a miscreant or an infidel"? I might reply to this after the alleged fashion of my countrymen by asking him another question, namely—When or where did I ever say that I expected him to call himself by either of these names? I can not remember having said anything that even remotely implied this, and I do not therefore exactly see why he should appeal to my confused "Hibernian" judgment to decide such a question.

As he has done so, however, I reply that I think it unreasonable to expect a man to call himself anything unless and until good and sufficient reason has been given him why he should do so. We are all of us bad judges as to what we are and as to what we should therefore be called. Other persons classify us according to what they know, or think they know, of our characters or opinions, sometimes correctly, sometimes incorrectly. And were I to find myself apparently incorrectly classified, as I very often do, I should be quite content with asking the person who had so classified me, first to define his terms, and next to show that these, as defined, were correctly applied to me. If he succeeded in doing this, I should accept his designation of me without hesitation, inasmuch as I should be sorry to call myself by a false name.

In this case, accordingly, if I might venture a suggestion to Prof. Huxley, it would be that the term "infidel" is capable of definition, and that when Dr. Wace has defined it, if the professor accept his definition, it would remain for them to decide between them whether Prof. Huxley's utterances do or do not bring him under the category of infidels, as so defined. Then, if it could be clearly proved that they do, from what I know of Prof. Huxley's love of scientific accuracy and his courage and candor, I certainly should expect that he would call himself an infidel—and a miscreant too, in the original and etymological sense of that unfortunate term, and that he would even glory in those titles. If they should not be so proved to be applicable, then I should hold it to be as unreasonable to expect him to call himself by such names as he, I suppose, would hold it to be to expect us Christians to admit, without better reason than he has yet given us, that Christianity is "the sorry stuff" which, with his "profoundly" moral readiness to say "unpleasant" things, he is pleased to say that it is.

There is another reference to myself, however, in the professor's article as to which I feel that he has a better right to appeal to me—or, rather, against me, to the readers of this review—and that is, as to my use, in my speech at the Manchester Congress, of the expression "cowardly agnosticism." I have not the report of my speech before me, and am writing, therefore, from memory; but my memory or the report must have played me sadly false if I am made to describe all agnostics as cowardly. A much slighter knowledge than I possess of Prof. Huxley's writings would have certainly prevented my applying to all agnosticism or agnostics such an epithet.

What I intended to express, and what I think I did express by this phrase was, that there is an agnosticism which is cowardly. And this I am convinced that there is, and that there is a great deal of it too, just now. There is an agnosticism which is simply the cowardly escaping from the pain and difficulty of contemplating and trying to solve the terrible problems of life by the help of the convenient phrase, "I don't know," which very often means "I don't care." "We don't know anything, don't you know, about these things. Prof. Huxley, don't you know, says that we do not, and I agree with him. Let us split a B. and S."

There is, I fear, a very large amount of this kind of agnosticism among the more youthful professors of that philosophy, and indeed among a large number of easy-going, comfortable men of the world, as they call themselves, who find agnosticism a pleasant shelter from the trouble of thought and the pain of effort and self-denial. And if I remember rightly it was of such agnostics I was speaking when I described them as "chatterers in our clubs and drawing-rooms," and as "freethinkers who had yet to learn to think."

There is therefore in my opinion *a* cowardly agnosticism just as there is also *a* cowardly Christianity. A Christian who spends his whole life in the selfish aim of saving his own soul, and never troubles himself with trying to help to save other men, either from destruction in the next world or from pain and suffering here, is a cowardly Christian. The eremites of the early days of Christianity, who fled away from their place in the world where God had put them, to spend solitary and, as they thought, safer lives in the wilderness, were typical examples of such cowardice. But in saying that there is such a thing as *a* cowardly Christianity, I do not thereby allege that there is no Christianity which is not cowardly. Similarly, when I speak of *a* cowardly agnosticism, I do not thereby allege that there is no agnosticism which is not cowardly, or which may not be as fearless as Prof. Huxley has always shown himself to be.

I hope that I have now satisfied the professor on the two points on which he has appealed to me. There is much in the other parts of his article which tempts me to reply. But I have a dislike to thrusting myself into other men's disputes, more especially when a combatant like Dr. Wace, so much more competent than myself, is in the field. I leave the professor in his hands, with the anticipation that he will succeed in showing him that a scientist dealing with questions of theology or biblical criticism may go quite as far astray as theologians often do in dealing with questions of science.

My reply to Prof. Huxley is accordingly confined to the strictly personal questions raised by his references to myself. I hope that, after making due allowance for Hibernicisms and for imperfect acquaintance with English modes of thought and expression, he will accept my explanation as sufficient.

AGNOSTICISM: A REJOINDER.

By Prof. THOMAS H. HUXLEY.

The concluding paragraph of the Bishop of Peterborough's reply to the appeal which I addressed to him in the penultimate number of this review, leads me to think that he has seen a personal reference where none was intended. I had ventured to suggest that the demand that a man should call himself an infidel, savored very much of the flavor of a "bull"; and, even had the Right Reverend prelate been as stolid an Englishman as I am, I should have entertained the hope, that the oddity of talking of the cowardice of persons who object to call themselves by a nickname, which must in their eyes be as inappropriate as, in the intention of the users, it is offensive, would have struck him. But, to my surprise, the bishop has not even yet got sight of that absurdity. He thinks, that if I accept Dr. Wace's definition of his much-loved epithet, I am logically bound not only to adopt the titles of infidel and miscreant, but that I shall "even glory in those titles." As I have shown, "infidel" merely means somebody who does not believe what you believe yourself, and therefore Dr. Wace has a perfect right to call, say, my old Egyptian donkey-driver, Nooleh, and myself, infidels, just as Nooleh and I have a right to call him an infidel. The ludicrous aspect of the thing comes in only when either of us demands that the two others should so label themselves. It is a terrible business to have to explain a mild jest, and I pledge myself not to run the risk of offending in this way again. I see how wrong I was in trusting to the bishop's sense of the ludicrous, and I beg leave unreservedly to withdraw my misplaced confidence. And I take this course the more readily as there is something about which I am obliged again to trouble the Bishop of Peterborough, which is certainly no jesting matter. Referring to my question, the bishop says that if they (the terms "infidel" and "miscreant")

should not be so proved to be applicable, then I should hold it to be as unreasonable to expect him to call himself by such names as he, I suppose, would hold it to be to expect us Christians to admit, without better reason than he has yet given us, that Christianity is "the sorry stuff" which, with his "profoundly" moral readiness to say "unpleasant" things, he is pleased to say that it is.*

According to those "English modes of thought and expression," of which the bishop seems to have but a poor opinion, this is a deliberate assertion that I had said that Christianity is "sorry stuff." And, according to the same standard of fair dealing, it is, I think, absolutely necessary for the Bishop of Peterborough to produce the evidence on which this positive statement is based. I shall be unfeignedly surprised if he is successful in proving it; but it is proper for me to wait and see.

Those who passed from Dr. Wace's article in the last number of this review to the anticipatory confutation of it which followed in "The New Reformation," must have enjoyed the pleasure of a dramatic surprise—just as when

---

* Page 88.

the fifth act of a new play proves unexpectedly bright and interesting. Mrs. Ward will, I hope, pardon the comparison, if I say that her effective clearing away of antiquated incumbrances from the lists of the controversy reminds me of nothing so much as of the action of some neat-handed, but strong-wristed, Phyllis, who, gracefully wielding her long-handled "Turk's head," sweeps away the accumulated results of the toil of generations of spiders. I am the more indebted to this luminous sketch of the results of critical investigation, as it is carried out among those theologians who are men of science and not mere counsel for creeds, since it has relieved me from the necessity of dealing with the greater part of Dr. Wace's polemic, and enables me to devote more space to the really important issues which have been raised.†

Perhaps, however, it may be well for me to observe that approbation of the manner in which a great biblical scholar, for instance Reuss, does his work does not commit me to the adoption of all, or indeed of any of his views; and further, that the disagreements of a series of investigators do not in any way interfere with the fact that each of them has made important contributions to the body of truth ultimately established. If I cite Buffon, Linnæus, Lamarck, and Cuvier, as having each and all taken a leading share in building up modern biology, the statement that every one of these great naturalists disagreed with, and even more or less contradicted, all the rest is quite true; but the supposition that the latter assertion is in any way inconsistent with the former, would betray a strange

---

† I may perhaps return to the question of the authorship of the Gospels. For the present I must content myself with warning my readers against any reliance upon Dr. Wace's statements as to the results arrived at by modern criticism. They are as gravely as surprisingly erroneous.

ignorance of the manner in which all true science advances.

Dr. Wace takes a great deal of trouble to make it appear that I have desired to evade the real questions raised by his attack upon me at the Church Congress. I assure the reverend principal that in this, as in some other respects, he has entertained a very erroneous conception of my intentions. Things would assume more accurate proportions in Dr. Wace's mind if he would kindly remember that it is just thirty years since ecclesiastical thunderbolts began to fly about my ears. I have had the "Lion and the Bear" to deal with, and it is long since I got quite used to the threatenings of episcopal Goliaths, whose crosiers were like unto a weaver's beam. So that I almost think I might not have noticed Dr. Wace's attack, personal as it was; and although, as he is good enough to tell us, separate copies are to be had for the modest equivalent of twopence, as a matter of fact, it did not come under my notice for a long time after it was made. May I further venture to point out that (reckoning postage) the expenditure of twopence-halfpenny, or, at the most, threepence, would have enabled Dr. Wace so far to comply with ordinary conventions as to direct my attention to the fact that he had attacked me before a meeting at which I was not present? I really am not responsible for the five months' neglect of which Dr. Wace complains. Singularly enough, the Englishry who swarmed about the Engadine, during the three months that I was being brought back to life by the glorious air and perfect comfort of the Maloja, did not, in my hearing, say anything about the important events which had taken place at the Church Congress; and I think I can venture to affirm that there was not a single copy of Dr. Wace's pamphlet in any of the hotel libraries which I rummaged in search of something more edifying than dull English or questionable French novels.

And now, having, as I hope, set myself right with the public as regards the sins of commission and omission with which I have been charged, I feel free to deal with matters to which time and type may be more profitably devoted.

The Bishop of Peterborough indulges in the anticipation that Dr. Wace will succeed in showing me "that a scientist dealing with questions of theology or biblical criticism may go quite as far astray as theologians often do in dealing with questions of science." * I have already admitted that vaticination is not in my line; and I can not so much as hazard a guess whether the spirit of prophecy which has descended on the bishop comes from the one or the other of the two possible sources recognized by the highest authorities. But I think it desirable to warn those who may be misled by phraseology of this kind, that the antagonists in the present debate are not quite rightly represented by it. Undoubtedly, Dr. Wace is a theologian; and I should be the last person to question that his whole cast of thought and style of argumentation are pre-eminently and typically theological. And, if I must accept the hideous term "scientist" (to which I object even more than I do to "infidel"), I am ready to admit that I am one of the people so denoted.

But I hope and believe that there is not a solitary argument I have used, or that I am about to use, which is original, or has anything to do with the fact that I have been chiefly occupied with natural science. They are all, facts and reasoning alike, either identical with, or conse-

---

* Page 90.

quential upon, propositions which are to be found in the works of scholars and theologians of the highest repute in the only two countries, Holland and Germany,* in which, at the present time, professors of theology are to be found whose tenure of their posts does not depend upon the results to which their inquiries lead them. †

It is true that, to the best of my ability, I have satisfied myself of the soundness of the foundations on which my arguments are built, and I desire to be held fully responsible for everything I say. But, nevertheless, my position is really no more than that of an expositor; and my justification for undertaking it is simply that conviction of the supremacy of private judgment (indeed, of the impossibility of escaping it) which is the foundation of the Protestant Reformation, and which was the doctrine accepted by the vast majority of the Anglicans of my youth, before that backsliding toward the "beggarly rudiments" of an effete and idolatrous sacerdotalism which has, even now, provided us with the saddest spectacle which has been offered to the eyes of Englishmen in this

---

* The United States ought, perhaps, to be added, but I am not sure.

† Imagine that all our chairs of Astronomy had been founded in the fourteenth century, and that their incumbents were bound to sign Ptolemaic articles. In that case, with every respect for the efforts of persons thus hampered to attain and expound the truth, I think men of common sense would go elsewhere to learn astronomy. Zeller's "Vorträge und Abhandlungen" were published and came into my hands a quarter of a century ago. The writer's rank, as a theologian to begin with, and subsequently as a historian of Greek philosophy, is of the highest. Among these essays are two—"Das Urchristenthum" and "Die Tübinger historische Schule"— which are likely to be of more use to those who wish to know the real state of the case than all that the official "apologists," with their one eye on truth and the other on the tenets of their sect, have written. For the opinion of a scientific theologian about theologians of this stamp see pp. 225 and 227 of the "Vorträge."

generation. A high court of ecclesiastical jurisdiction, with a host of great lawyers in battle array, is, and, for Heaven knows how long, will be occupied with these very questions of "washings of cups and pots and brazen vessels," which the Master, whose professed representatives are rending the Church over these squabbles, had in his mind when, as we are told, he uttered the scathing rebuke:

> Well did Isaiah prophesy of you hypocrites, as it is written:
> This people honoreth me with their lips,
> But their heart is far from me:
> But in vain do they worship me,
> Teaching as their doctrines the precepts of men (Mark vii, 6, 7).

Men who can be absorbed in bickerings over miserable disputes of this kind can have but little sympathy with the old evangelical doctrine of the "open Bible," or anything but a grave misgiving of the results of diligent reading of the Bible, without the help of ecclesiastical spectacles, by the mass of the people. Greatly to the surprise of many of my friends, I have always advocated the reading of the Bible, and the diffusion of the study of that most remarkable collection of books among the people. Its teachings are so infinitely superior to those of the sects, who are just as busy now as the Pharisees were eighteen hundred years ago, in smothering them under "the precepts of men"; it is so certain, to my mind, that the Bible contains within itself the refutation of nine tenths of the mixture of sophistical metaphysics and old-world superstition which has been piled round it by the so-called Christians of later times; it is so clear that the only immediate and ready antidote to the poison which has been mixed with Christianity, to the intoxication and delusion of mankind, lies in copious draughts from the undefiled spring, that I exercise the right and duty of free judgment on the part of every man, mainly for the purpose of inducing other laymen to follow my example. If the New Testament is translated into Zulu by Protestant missionaries, it must be assumed that a Zulu convert is competent to draw from its contents all the truths which it is necessary for him to believe. I trust that I may, without immodesty, claim to be put on the same footing as the Zulu.

The most constant reproach which is launched against persons of my way of thinking is, that it is all very well for us to talk about the deductions of scientific thought, but what are the poor and the uneducated to do? Has it ever occurred to those who talk in this fashion that the creeds and articles of their several confessions; their determination of the exact nature and extent of the teachings of Jesus; their expositions of the real meaning of that which is written in the Epistles (to leave aside all questions concerning the Old Testament) are nothing more than deductions, which, at any rate, profess to be the result of strictly scientific thinking, and which are not worth attending to unless they really possess that character? If it is not historically true that such and such things happened in Palestine eighteen centuries ago, what becomes of Christianity? And what is historical truth but that of which the evidence bears strict scientific investigation? I do not call to mind any problem of natural science which has come under my notice, which is more difficult, or more curiously interesting as a mere problem, than that of the origin of the synoptic Gospels and that of the historical value of the narratives which they contain. The Christianity of the churches stands or falls by the results of the purely scientific investigation of these questions. They were first taken up in a purely scientific spirit just about a century ago; they have been studied, over and over again, by men of vast knowledge and critical acumen; but he would be a rash man who should assert that any solution of these problems, as yet formulated, is exhaustive. The most that can be said is that certain prevalent solutions are certainly false, while others are more or less probably true.

If I am doing my best to rouse my countrymen out of their dogmatic slumbers, it is not that they may be amused by seeing who gets the best of it, in a contest between a "scientist" and a theologian. The serious question is whether theological men of science, or theological special pleaders, are to have the confidence of the general public; it is the question whether a country in which it is possible for a body of excellent clerical and lay gentlemen to discuss, in public meeting assembled, how much it is desirable to let the congregations of the faithful know of the results of biblical criticism, is likely to wake up with anything short of the grasp of a rough lay hand upon its shoulder; it is the question whether the New Testament books, being as I believe they were, written and compiled by people who, according to their lights, were perfectly sincere, will not, when properly studied as ordinary historical documents, afford us the means of self-criticism. And it must be remembered that the New Testament books are not responsible for the doctrine invented by the churches that they are anything but ordinary historical documents. The author of the third Gospel tells us as straightforwardly as a man can that he has no claim to any other character than that of an ordinary compiler and editor, who had before him the works of many and variously qualified predecessors.

In my former papers, according to Dr. Wace, I have evaded giving an answer to his main proposition, which he states as follows:

> Apart from all disputed points of criticism, no one practically doubts that our Lord lived and that he died on the cross, in the most intense sense of filial relation to his Father in heaven, and that he bore testimony to that Father's providence, love, and grace toward mankind. The Lord's Prayer affords a sufficient evidence on these points. If the Sermon on the Mount alone be added, the whole unseen world, of which the agnostic refuses to know anything, stands unveiled before us. . . . If Jesus Christ preached that sermon, made those promises, and taught that prayer, then any one who says that we know nothing of God, or of a future life, or of an unseen world, says that he does not believe Jesus Christ.*

Again—

> The main question at issue, in a word, is one which Prof. Huxley has chosen to leave entirely on one side—whether, namely, allowing for the utmost uncertainty on other points of the criticism to which he appeals, there is any reasonable doubt that the Lord's Prayer and the Sermon on the Mount afford a true account of our Lord's essential belief and cardinal teaching.†

I certainly was not aware that I had evaded the questions here stated; indeed, I should say that I have indicated my reply to them pretty clearly; but, as Dr. Wace wants a plainer answer, he shall certainly be gratified. If, as Dr. Wace declares it is, his "whole case is involved in" the argument as stated in the latter of these two extracts, so much the worse for his whole case. For I am of opinion that there is the gravest reason for doubting whether the "Sermon on the Mount" was ever preached, and whether the so-called "Lord's Prayer" was ever prayed by Jesus of Nazareth. My reasons for this opinion are, among others, these: There is now no

---

* Page 63.   † Page 64.

doubt that the three synoptic Gospels, so far from being the work of three independent writers, are closely interdependent,* and that in one of two ways. Either all three contain, as their foundation, versions, to a large extent verbally identical, of one and the same tradition; or two of them are thus closely dependent on the third; and the opinion of the majority of the best critics has, of late years, more and more converged toward the conviction that our canonical second Gospel (the so-called "Mark's" Gospel) is that which most closely represents the primitive groundwork of the three.† That I take to be one of the most valid results of New Testament criticism, of immeasurably greater importance than the discussion about dates and authorship.

But if, as I believe to be the case, beyond any rational doubt or dispute, the second Gospel is the nearest extant representative of the oldest tradition, whether written or

---

* I suppose this is what Dr. Wace is thinking about when he says that I allege that there "is no visible escape" from the supposition of an "Ur-Marcus" (p. 82). That a "theologian of repute" should confound an indisputable fact with one of the modes of explaining that fact, is not so singular as those who are unaccustomed to the ways of theologians might imagine.

† Any examiner whose duty it has been to examine into a case of "copying" will be particularly well prepared to appreciate the force of the case stated in that most excellent little book, "The Common Tradition of the Synoptic Gospels," by Dr. Abbott and Mr. Rushbrooke (Macmillan, 1884). To those who have not passed through such painful experiences I may recommend the brief discussion of the genuineness of the "Casket Letters" in my friend Mr. Skelton's interesting book, "Maitland of Lethington." The second edition of Holtzmann's "Lehrbuch," published in 1886, gives a remarkably fair and full account of the present results of criticism. At page 366 he writes that the present burning question is whether the "relatively primitive narration and the root of the other synoptic texts is contained in Matthew or in Mark. It is only on this point that properly informed (*sachkundige*) critics differ," and he decides in favor of Mark.

oral, how comes it that it contains neither the "Sermon on the Mount" nor the "Lord's Prayer," those typical embodiments, according to Dr. Wace, of the "essential belief and cardinal teaching" of Jesus? Not only does "Mark's" Gospel fail to contain the "Sermon on the Mount," or anything but a very few of the sayings contained in that collection; but, at the point of the history of Jesus where the "Sermon" occurs in "Matthew," there is in "Mark" an apparently unbroken narrative, from the calling of James and John to the healing of Simon's wife's mother. Thus the oldest tradition not only ignores the "Sermon on the Mount," but, by implication, raises a probability against its being delivered when and where the later "Matthew" inserts it in his compilation.

And still more weighty is the fact that the third Gospel, the author of which tells us that he wrote after "many" others had "taken in hand" the same enterprise; who should therefore have known the first Gospel (if it existed), and was bound to pay to it the deference due to the work of an apostolic eye-witness (if he had any reason for thinking it was so)—this writer, who exhibits far more literary competence than the other two, ignores any "Sermon on the Mount," such as that reported by "Matthew," just as much as the oldest authority does. Yet "Luke" has a great many passages identical, or parallel, with those in "Matthew's" "Sermon on the Mount," which are, for the most part, scattered about in a totally different connection.

Interposed, however, between the nomination of the apostles and a visit to Capernaum; occupying, therefore, a place which answers to that of the "Sermon on the Mount" in the first Gospel, there is, in the third Gospel, a discourse which is as closely similar to the "Sermon on the Mount" in some particulars, as it is widely unlike it in others.

This discourse is said to have been delivered in a "plain" or "level place" (Luke vi, 17), and by way of distinction we may call it the "Sermon on the Plain."

I see no reason to doubt that the two evangelists are dealing, to a considerable extent, with the same traditional material; and a comparison of the two "sermons" suggests very strongly that "Luke's" version is the earlier. The correspondences between the two forbid the notion that they are independent. They both begin with a series of blessings, some of which are almost verbally identical. In the middle of each (Luke vi, 27-38, Matthew v, 43-48) there is a striking exposition of the ethical spirit of the command given in Leviticus xix, 18. And each ends with a passage containing the declaration that a tree is to be known by its fruit, and the parable of the house built on the sand. But while there are only twenty-nine verses in the "Sermon on the Plain," there are one hundred and seven in the "Sermon on the Mount"; the excess in length of the latter being chiefly due to the long interpolations, one of thirty verses before, and one of thirty-four verses after, the middlemost parallelism with Luke. Under these circumstances, it is quite impossible to admit that there is more probability that "Matthew's" version of the sermon is historically accurate than there is that Luke's version is so; and they can not both be accurate.

"Luke" either knew the collection of loosely connected and aphoristic utterances which appear under the name of the "Sermon on the Mount" in "Matthew," or he did not. If he did not, he must have been ignorant of the existence of such a document as our canonical "Matthew," a fact which does not make for the genuineness or the authority of that book. If he did, he has shown that he does not care for its authority on a matter of fact of no small importance; and that does not permit us to conceive that he believed the first Gospel to be the work of an authority to whom he ought to defer, let alone that of an apostolic eye-witness.

The tradition of the Church about the second Gospel, which I believe to be quite worthless, but which is all the evidence there is for "Mark's" authorship, would have us believe that "Mark" was little more than the mouth-piece of the apostle Peter. Consequently, we are to suppose that Peter either did not know, or did not care very much for, that account of the "essential belief and cardinal teaching" of Jesus which is contained in the Sermon on the Mount; and, certainly, he could not have shared Dr. Wace's view of its importance.*

I thought that all fairly attentive and intelligent students of the Gospels, to say nothing of theologians of reputation, knew these things. But how can any one who does know them have the conscience to ask whether there is "any reasonable doubt" that the Sermon on the Mount was preached by Jesus of Nazareth? If conjecture is permissible, where nothing else is possible, the most probable conjecture seems to be that "Matthew," having

---

* Holtzmann ("Die synoptischen Evangelien," 1863, p. 75), following Ewald, argues that the "Source A" (= the threefold tradition, more or less) contained something that answered to the "Sermon on the Plain" immediately after the words of our present Mark, "And he cometh into a house" (iii, 19). But what conceivable motive could "Mark" have for omitting it? Holtzmann has no doubt, however, that the "Sermon on the Mount" is a compilation, or, as he calls it in his recently published "Lehrbuch" (p. 372), "an artificial mosaic work."

a *cento* of sayings attributed—rightly or wrongly it is impossible to say—to Jesus, among his materials, thought they were, or might be, records of a continuous discourse, and put them in at the place he thought likeliest. Ancient historians of the highest character saw no harm in composing long speeches which never were spoken, and putting them into the mouths of statesmen and warriors; and I presume that whoever is represented by "Matthew" would have been grievously astonished to find that any one objected to his following the example of the best models accessible to him.

So with the "Lord's Prayer." Absent in our representative of the oldest tradition, it appears in both "Matthew" and "Luke." There is reason to believe that every pious Jew, at the commencement of our era, prayed three times a day, according to a formula which is embodied in the present *Schmone-Esre* * of the Jewish prayer-book. Jesus, who was assuredly, in all respects, a pious Jew, whatever else he may have been, doubtless did the same. Whether he modified the current formula, or whether the so-called "Lord's Prayer" is the prayer substituted for the *Schmone-Esre* in the congregations of the Gentiles, who knew nothing of the Jewish practice, is a question which can hardly be answered.

In a subsequent passage of Dr. Wace's article † he adds to the list of the verities which he imagines to be unassailable, " The story of the Passion." I am not quite sure what he means by this—I am not aware that any one (with the exception of certain ancient heretics) has propounded doubts as to the reality of the crucifixion; and

---

* See Schürer, "Geschichte des jüdischen Volkes," Zweiter Theil, p. 384.

† Page 65.

certainly I have no inclination to argue about the precise accuracy of every detail of that pathetic story of suffering and wrong. But, if Dr. Wace means, as I suppose he does, that that which, according to the orthodox view, happened after the crucifixion, and which is, in a dogmatic sense, the most important part of the story, is founded on solid historical proofs, I must beg leave to express a diametrically opposite conviction.

What do we find when the accounts of the events in question, contained in the three synoptic Gospels, are compared together? In the oldest, there is a simple, straightforward statement which, for anything that I have to urge to the contrary, may be exactly true. In the other two, there is, round this possible and probable nucleus, a mass of accretions of the most questionable character.

The cruelty of death by crucifixion depended very much upon its lingering character. If there were a support for the weight of the body, as not unfrequently was the case, the pain during the first hours of the infliction was not, necessarily, extreme; nor need any serious physical symptoms at once arise from the wounds made by the nails in the hands and feet, supposing they were nailed, which was not invariably the case. When exhaustion set in, and hunger, thirst, and nervous irritation had done their work, the agony of the sufferer must have been terrible; and the more terrible that, in the absence of any effectual disturbance of the machinery of physical life, it might be prolonged for many hours, or even days. Temperate, strong men, such as the ordinary Galilean peasants were, might live for several days on the cross. It is necessary to bear these facts in mind when we read the account contained in the fifteenth chapter of the second Gospel.

Jesus was crucified at the third hour (xv, 25), and the narrative seems to imply that he died immediately after the ninth hour (v. 34). In this case he would have been crucified only six hours; and the time spent on the cross can not have been much longer, because Joseph of Arimathea must have gone to Pilate, made his preparations, and deposited the body in the rock-cut tomb before sunset, which, at that time of the year, was about the twelfth hour. That any one should die after only six hours' crucifixion could not have been at all in accordance with Pilate's large experience in the effects of that method of punishment. It, therefore, quite agrees with what might be expected if Pilate "marveled if he were already dead," and required to be satisfied on this point by the testimony of the Roman officer who was in command of the execution party. Those who have paid attention to the extraordinarily difficult question, What are the indisputable signs of death?—will be able to estimate the value of the opinion of a rough soldier on such a subject; even if his report to the procurator were in no wise affected by the fact that the friend of Jesus, who anxiously awaited his answer, was a man of influence and of wealth.

The inanimate body, wrapped in linen, was deposited in a spacious,* cool, rock chamber, the entrance of which was closed, not by a well-fitting door, but by a stone rolled against the opening, which would of course allow free passage of air. A little more than thirty-six hours afterward (Friday 6 P. M., to Sunday 6 A. M., or a little after) three women visit the tomb and find it empty. And they are told by a young man "arrayed in a white robe" that Jesus is gone to his native country of Gali-

---

* Spacious, because a young man could sit in it "on the right side" (xv, 5), and therefore with plenty of room to spare.

lee, and that the disciples and Peter will find him there.

Thus it stands, plainly recorded, in the oldest tradition that, for any evidence to the contrary, the sepulchre may have been vacated at any time during the Friday or Saturday nights. If it is said that no Jew would have violated the Sabbath by taking the former course, it is to be recollected that Joseph of Arimathea might well be familiar with that wise and liberal interpretation of the fourth commandment, which permitted works of mercy to men—nay even the drawing of an ox or an ass out of a pit—on the Sabbath. At any rate, the Saturday night was free to the most scrupulous observers of the law.

These are the facts of the case as stated by the oldest extant narrative of them. I do not see why any one should have a word to say against the inherent probability of that narrative; and, for my part, I am quite ready to accept it as an historical fact, that so much and no more is positively known of the end of Jesus of Nazareth. On what grounds can a reasonable man be asked to believe any more? So far as the narrative in the first Gospel, on the one hand, and those in the third Gospel and the Acts, on the other go beyond what is stated in the second Gospel, they are hopelessly discrepant with one another. And this is the more significant because the pregnant phrase "some doubted," in the first Gospel, is ignored in the third.

But it is said that we have the witness Paul speaking to us directly in the Epistles. There is little doubt that we have, and a very singular witness he is. According to his own showing, Paul, in the vigor of his manhood, with every means of becoming acquainted, at first hand, with the evidence of eye-witnesses, not merely refused to credit them, but "persecuted the church of God and made havoc of it." The reasoning of Stephen fell dead upon the acute intellect of this zealot for the traditions of his fathers: his eyes were blind to the ecstatic illumination of the martyr's countenance "as it had been the face of an angel"; and when, at the words "Behold, I see the heavens opened and the Son of man standing on the right hand of God," the murderous mob rushed upon and stoned the rapt disciple of Jesus, Paul ostentatiously made himself their official accomplice.

Yet this strange man, because he has a vision one day, at once, and with equally headlong zeal, flies to the opposite pole of opinion. And he is most careful to tell us that he abstained from any re-examination of the facts.

> Immediately I conferred not with flesh and blood; neither went I up to Jerusalem to them which were apostles before me; but I went away into Arabia. (Galatians i, 16, 17.)

I do not presume to quarrel with Paul's procedure. If it satisfied him, that was his affair; and, if it satisfies any one else, I am not called upon to dispute the right of that person to be satisfied. But I certainly have the right to say that it would not satisfy me in like case; that I should be very much ashamed to pretend that it could, or ought to, satisfy me; and that I can entertain but a very low estimate of the value of the evidence of people who are to be satisfied in this fashion, when questions of objective fact, in which their faith is interested, are concerned. So that, when I am called upon to believe a great deal more than the oldest Gospel tells me about the final events of the history of Jesus on the authority of Paul (1 Corinthians xv, 5–8), I must pause. Did he think it, at any subsequent time, worth while "to confer with flesh and blood," or, in modern phrase, to re-examine the facts for himself?

or was he ready to accept anything that fitted in with his preconceived ideas? Does he mean, when he speaks of all the appearances of Jesus after the crucifixion as if they were of the same kind, that they were all visions, like the manifestation to himself? And, finally, how is this account to be reconciled with those in the first and the third Gospels—which, as we have seen, disagree with one another?

Until these questions are satisfactorily answered, I am afraid that, so far as I am concerned, Paul's testimony can not be seriously regarded, except as it may afford evidence of the state of traditional opinion at the time at which he wrote, say between 55 and 60 A. D.; that is, more than twenty years after the event; a period much more than sufficient for the development of any amount of mythology about matters of which nothing was really known. A few years later, among the contemporaries and neighbors of the Jews, and, if the most probable interpretation of the Apocalypse can be trusted, among the followers of Jesus also, it was fully believed, in spite of all evidence to the contrary, that the Emperor Nero was not really dead, but that he was hidden away somewhere in the East, and would speedily come again at the head of a great army, to be revenged upon his enemies.

Thus, I conceive that I have shown cause for the opinion that Dr. Wace's challenge touching the Sermon on the Mount, the Lord's Prayer, and the Passion, was more valorous than discreet. After all this discussion I am still at the agnostic point. Tell me, first, what Jesus can be proved to have been, said, and done, and I will tell you whether I believe him, or in him,* or not! As Dr.

---

* I am very sorry for the interpolated "in," because citation ought to be accurate in small things as in great. But what difference it makes

Wace admits that I have dissipated his lingering shade of unbelief about the bedevilment of the Gadarene pigs, he might have done something to help mine. Instead of that, he manifests a total want of conception of the nature of the obstacles which impede the conversion of his "infidels."

The truth I believe to be, that the difficulties in the way of arriving at a sure conclusion as to these matters, from the Sermon on the Mount, the Lord's Prayer, or any other data offered by the synoptic Gospels (and *a fortiori* from the fourth Gospel) are insuperable. Every one of these records is colored by the prepossessions of those among whom the primitive traditions arose and of those by whom they were collected and edited; and the difficulty of making allowance for these prepossessions is enhanced by our ignorance of the exact dates at which the documents were first put together; of the extent to which they have been subsequently worked over and interpolated; and of the historical sense, or want of sense, and the dogmatic tendencies, of their compilers and editors. Let us see if there is any other road which will take us into something better than negation.

There is a wide-spread notion that the "primitive Church," while under the guidance of the apostles and their immediate successors, was a sort of dogmatic dovecote, pervaded by the most loving unity and doctrinal harmony. Protestants, especially, are fond of attributing to themselves the merit of being nearer "the Church of the apostles" than their neighbors; and they are the less to be excused for their strange delusion because they are great

---

whether one "believes Jesus" or "believes in Jesus" much thought has not enabled me to discover. If you "believe him" you must believe him to be what he professed to be—that is, "believe in him"; and if you "believe in him" you must necessarily "believe him."

readers of the documents which prove the exact contrary. The fact is that, in the course of the first three centuries of its existence, the Church rapidly underwent a process of evolution of the most remarkable character, the final stage of which is far more different from the first than Anglicanism is from Quakerism. The key to the comprehension of the problem of the origin of that which is now called "Christianity," and its relation to Jesus of Nazareth, lies here. Nor can we arrive at any sound conclusion as to what it is probable that Jesus actually said and did without being clear on this head. By far the most important and subsequently influential steps in the evolution of Christianity took place in the course of the century, more or less, which followed upon the crucifixion. It is almost the darkest period of Church history, but, most fortunately, the beginning and the end of the period are brightly illuminated by the contemporary evidence of two writers of whose historical existence there is no doubt,* and against the genuineness of whose most important works there is no widely admitted objection. These are Justin, the philosopher and martyr, and Paul, the Apostle to the Gentiles. I shall call upon these witnesses only to testify to the condition of opinion among those who called themselves disciples of Jesus in their time.

Justin, in his dialogue with Trypho the Jew, which was written somewhere about the middle of the second century, enumerates certain categories of persons who, in his opinion, will, or will not, be saved.† These are:

---

* True for Justin; but there is a school of theological critics, who more or less question the historical reality of Paul and the genuineness of even the four cardinal epistles.

† See "Dial. cum Tryphone," sections 47 and 35. It is to be understood that Justin does not arrange these categories in order as I have done.

1. Orthodox Jews who refuse to believe that Jesus is the Christ. *Not saved.*

2. Jews who observe the law; believe Jesus to be the Christ; but who insist on the observance of the law by Gentile converts. *Not saved.*

3. Jews who observe the law; believe Jesus to be the Christ, and hold that Gentile converts need not observe the law. *Saved* (in Justin's opinion; but some of his fellow-Christians think the contrary).

4. Gentile converts to the belief in Jesus as the Christ, who observe the law. *Saved* (possibly).

5. Gentile believers in Jesus as the Christ, who do not observe the law themselves (except so far as the refusal of idol sacrifices), but do not consider those who do observe it heretics. *Saved* (this is Justin's own view).

6. Gentile believers who do not observe the law except in refusing idol sacrifices, and hold those who do observe it to be heretics. *Saved.*

7. Gentiles who believe Jesus to be the Christ and call themselves Christians, but who eat meats sacrificed to idols. *Not saved.*

8. Gentiles who disbelieve in Jesus as the Christ. *Not saved.*

Justin does not consider Christians who believe in the natural birth of Jesus, of whom he implies that there is a respectable minority, to be heretics, though he himself strongly holds the preternatural birth of Jesus and his pre-existence as the "Logos" or "Word." He conceives the Logos to be a second God, inferior to the first, unknowable, God, with respect to whom Justin, like Philo, is a complete agnostic. The Holy Spirit is not regarded by Justin as a separate personality, and is often mixed up with the "Logos." The doctrine of the natural immortality of the soul is, for Justin, a heresy; and he is as firm a believer in the resurrection of the body as in the speedy second coming and the establishment of the millennium.

This pillar of the Church in the middle of the second century—a much-traveled native of Samaria—was certainly well acquainted with Rome, probably with Alexandria, and it is likely that he knew the state of opinion throughout the length and breadth of the Christian world as well as any man of his time. If the various categories above enumerated are arranged in a series thus—

		Justin's Christianity.		
Orthodox Judaism.	Judæo-Christianity.		Idolothytic Christianity.	Paganism.
I	II III IV	V VI	VII	VIII

it is obvious that they form a gradational series from orthodox Judaism, on the extreme left, to paganism, whether philosophic or popular, on the extreme right; and it will further be observed that, while Justin's conception of Christianity is very broad, he rigorously excludes two classes of persons who, in his time, called themselves Christians; namely, those who insist on circumcision and other observances of the law on the part of Gentile converts; that is to say, the strict Judæo-Christians (II), and on the other hand, those who assert the lawfulness of eating meat offered to idols—whether they are gnostics or not (VII). These last I have called "idolothytic" Christians, because I can not devise a better name, not because it is strictly defensible etymologically.

At the present moment I do not suppose there is an English missionary in any heathen land who would trouble himself whether the materials of his dinner had been previously offered to idols or not. On the other hand, I suppose there is no Protestant sect within the pale of orthodoxy, to say nothing of the Roman and Greek Churches, which would hesitate to declare the practice of circumcision and the observance of the Jewish Sabbath and dietary rules, shockingly heretical.

Modern Christianity has, in fact, not only shifted far to the right of Justin's position, but it is of much narrower compass.

```
                         Justin.
          Judæo-Christianity.      Modern Christianity.  Paganism.
Judaism.  ⌒⌒⌒⌒⌒⌒⌒⌒⌒⌒⌒⌒⌒⌒⌒⌒⌒        ⌒⌒⌒⌒⌒⌒⌒⌒⌒⌒⌒⌒⌒⌒⌒       ⌒⌒⌒⌒⌒
   I      II    III    IV     V     VI        VII          VIII
```

For, though it includes VII, and even, in saint and relic worship, cuts a "monstrous cantle" out of paganism, it excludes, not only all Judæo-Christians, but all who doubt that such are heretics. Ever since the thirteenth century, the Inquisition would have cheerfully burned, and in Spain did abundantly burn, all persons who came under the categories II, III, IV, V. And the wolf would play the same havoc now if it could only get its blood-stained jaws free from the muzzle imposed by the secular arm.

Further, there is not a Protestant body except the Unitarian, which would not declare Justin himself a heretic, on account of his doctrine of the inferior godship of the Logos; while I am very much afraid that, in strict logic, Dr. Wace would be under the necessity, so painful to him, of calling him an "infidel," on the same and on other grounds.

Now let us turn to our other authority. If there is any result of critical investigations of the sources of Christianity which is certain,* it is that Paul of Tarsus

---

* I guard myself against being supposed to affirm that even the four cardinal epistles of Paul may not have been seriously tampered with. See note on page 112.

wrote the Epistle to the Galatians somewhere between the years 55 and 60 A. D., that is to say, roughly, twenty, or five-and-twenty, years after the crucifixion. If this is so, the Epistle to the Galatians is one of the oldest, if not the very oldest, of extant documentary evidences of the state of the primitive Church. And, be it observed, if it is Paul's writing, it unquestionably furnishes us with the evidence of a participator in the transactions narrated. With the exception of two or three of the other Pauline epistles, there is not one solitary book in the New Testament of the authorship and authority of which we have such good evidence.

And what is the state of things we find disclosed? A bitter quarrel, in his account of which Paul by no means minces matters or hesitates to hurl defiant sarcasms against those who were "reputed to be pillars": James, "the brother of the Lord," Peter, the rock on whom Jesus is said to have built his Church, and John, "the beloved disciple." And no deference toward "the rock" withholds Paul from charging Peter to his face with "dissimulation."

The subject of the hot dispute was simply this: Were Gentile converts bound to obey the law or not? Paul answered in the negative; and, acting upon his opinion, had created at Antioch (and elsewhere) a specifically "Christian" community, the sole qualifications for admission into which were the confession of the belief that Jesus was the Messiah, and baptism upon that confession. In the epistle in question, Paul puts this—his "gospel," as he calls it—in its most extreme form. Not only does he deny the necessity of conformity with the law, but he declares such conformity to have a negative value. "Behold, I, Paul, say unto you, that if ye receive circumcision, Christ will profit you nothing" (Galatians v, 2). He calls the legal observances "beggarly rudiments," and anathematizes every one who preaches to the Galatians any other gospel than his own—that is to say, by direct consequence, he anathematizes the Jerusalem Nazarenes whose zeal for the law is testified by James in a passage of the Acts cited further on. In the first Epistle to the Corinthians, dealing with the question of eating meat offered to idols, it is clear that Paul himself thinks it a matter of indifference; but he advises that it should not be done, for the sake of the weaker brethren. On the other hand, the Nazarenes of Jerusalem most strenuously opposed Paul's "gospel," insisting on every convert becoming a regular Jewish proselyte, and consequently on his observance of the whole law; and this party was led by James and Peter and John (Galatians ii, 9). Paul does not suggest that the question of principle was settled by the discussion referred to in Galatians. All he says is that it ended in the practical agreement that he and Barnabas should do as they had been doing in respect of the Gentiles; while James and Peter and John should deal in their own fashion with Jewish converts. Afterward he complains bitterly of Peter, because, when on a visit to Antioch, he at first inclined to Paul's view, and ate with the Gentile converts; but when "certain came from James," "drew back, and separated himself, fearing them that were of the circumcision. And the rest of the Jews dissembled likewise with him; insomuch that even Barnabas was carried away with their dissimulation" (Galatians ii, 12, 13).

There is but one conclusion to be drawn from Paul's account of this famous dispute, the settlement of which determined the fortunes of the nascent religion. It is that the disciples at Jerusalem, headed by "James, the Lord's brother," and by the leading apostles, Peter and John, were strict Jews, who objected to admit any converts to their body, unless these, either by birth or by becoming proselytes, were also strict Jews. In fact, the sole difference between James and Peter and John, with the body of disciples whom they led, and the Jews by whom they were surrounded, and with whom they for many years shared the religious observances of the Temple, was that they believed that the Messiah, whom the leaders of the nation yet looked for, had already come in the person of Jesus of Nazareth.

The Acts of the Apostles is hardly a very trustworthy history; it is certainly of later date than the Pauline epistles, supposing them to be genuine. And the writer's version of the conference of which Paul gives so graphic a description, if that is correct, is unmistakably colored with all the art of a reconciler, anxious to cover up a scandal. But it is none the less instructive on this account. The judgment of the "council" delivered by James is that the Gentile converts shall merely "abstain from things sacrificed to idols, and from blood and from things strangled, and from fornication." But notwithstanding the accommodation in which the writer of the Acts would have us believe, the Jerusalem church held to its endeavor to retain the observance of the law. Long after the conference, some time after the writing of the Epistles to the Galatians and Corinthians, and immediately after the dispatch of that to the Romans, Paul makes his last visit to Jerusalem, and presents himself to James and all the elders. And this is what the Acts tells us of the interview:

And they said unto him, Thou seest, brother, how many thousands (or myriads) there are among the Jews of them which have believed; and they are all zealous for the law: and they have been informed concerning thee, that thou teachest all the Jews which are among the Gentiles to forsake Moses, telling them not to circumcise their children, neither to walk after the customs (Acts xxi, 20, 21).

They therefore request that he should perform a certain public religious act in the Temple, in order that

all shall know that there is no truth in the things whereof they have been informed concerning thee; but that thou thyself walkest orderly, keeping the law (ibid., 24).

How far Paul could do what he is here requested to do, and which the writer of the Acts goes on to say he did, with a clear conscience, if he wrote the epistles to the Galatians and Corinthians, I may leave any candid reader of those epistles to decide. The point to which I wish to direct attention is the declaration that the Jerusalem church, led by the brother of Jesus and by his personal disciples and friends, twenty years and more after his death, consisted of strict and zealous Jews.

Tertullus, the orator, caring very little about the internal dissensions of the followers of Jesus, speaks of Paul as a "ringleader of the sect of the Nazarenes" (Acts xxiv, 5), which must have affected James much in the same way as it would have moved the Archbishop of Canterbury, in George Fox's day, to hear the latter called a "ringleader of the sect of Anglicans." In fact, "Nazarene" was, as is well known, the distinctive appellation applied to Jesus; his immediate followers were known as Nazarenes, while the congregation of the disciples, and, later, of converts at Jerusalem—the Jerusalem church—was emphatically the "sect of the Nazarenes," no more in itself to be regarded as anything outside Judaism than the sect of the Sadducees or of the Essenes.* In fact, the tenets of both the Sadducees and the Essenes diverged much more widely from the Pharisaic standard of orthodoxy than Nazarenism did.

Let us consider the position of affairs now (A. D. 50–60) in relation to that which obtained in Justin's time, a century later. It is plain that the Nazarenes—presided over by James "the brother of the Lord," and comprising within their body all the twelve apostles—belonged to Justin's second category of "Jews who observe the law, believe Jesus to be the Christ, but who insist on the observance of the law by Gentile converts," up till the time at which the controversy reported by Paul arose. They then, according to Paul, simply allowed him to form his congregation of non-legal Gentile converts at Antioch and elsewhere; and it would seem that it was to these converts, who would come under Justin's fifth category, that the title of "Christian" was first applied. If any of these Christians had acted upon the more than half-permission given by Paul, and had eaten meats offered to idols, they would have belonged to Justin's seventh category.

Hence, it appears that, if Justin's opinion, which was doubtless that of the Church generally in the middle of the second century, was correct, James and Peter and John and their followers could not be saved; neither could Paul, if he carried into practice his views as to the indifference of eating meats offered to idols. Or, to put the matter another way, the center of gravity of orthodoxy, which is at the extreme right of the series in the nineteenth century, was at the extreme left, just before

---

* All this was quite clearly pointed out by Ritschl nearly forty years ago. See "Die Entstehung der alt-katholischen Kirche" (1850), p. 108.

the middle of the first century, when the "sect of the Nazarenes" constituted the whole church founded by Jesus and the apostles; while, in the time of Justin, it lay midway between the two. It is therefore a profound mistake to imagine that the Judæo-Christians (Nazarenes and Ebionites) of later times were heretical outgrowths from a primitive, universalist "Christianity." On the contrary, the universalist "Christianity" is an outgrowth from the primitive, purely Jewish, Nazarenism; which, gradually eliminating all the ceremonial and dietary parts of the Jewish law, has thrust aside its parent, and all the intermediate stages of its development, into the position of damnable heresies.

Such being the case, we are in a position to form a safe judgment of the limits within which the teaching of Jesus of Nazareth must have been confined. Ecclesiastical authority would have us believe that the words which are given at the end of the first Gospel, "Go ye, therefore, and makes disciples of all the nations, baptizing them in the name of the Father and of the Son and of the Holy Ghost," are part of the last commands of Jesus, issued at the moment of his parting with the eleven. If so, Peter and John must have heard these words; they are too plain to be misunderstood; and the occasion is too solemn for them to be ever forgotten. Yet the "Acts" tells us that Peter needed a vision to enable him so much as to baptize Cornelius; and Paul, in the Galatians, knows nothing of words which would have completely borne him out as against those whö, though they heard, must be supposed to have either forgotten or ignored them. On the other hand, Peter and John, who are supposed to have heard the "Sermon on the Mount," know nothing of the saying that Jesus had not come to destroy the law, but that every jot and tittle of the law must be fulfilled, which surely would have been pretty good evidence for their view of the question.

We are sometimes told that the personal friends and daily companions of Jesus remained zealous Jews and opposed Paul's innovations, because they were hard of heart and dull of comprehension. This hypothesis is hardly in accordance with the concomitant faith of those who adopt it, in the miraculous insight and superhuman sagacity of their Master; nor do I see any way of getting it to harmonize with the other orthodox postulate; namely, that Matthew was the author of the first Gospel and John of the fourth. If that is so, then, most assuredly, Matthew was no dullard; and as for the fourth Gospel— a theosophic romance of the first order—it could have been written by none but a man of remarkable literary capacity, who had drunk deep of Alexandrian philosophy. Moreover, the doctrine of the writer of the fourth Gospel is more remote from that of the "sect of the Nazarenes" than is that of Paul himself. I am quite aware that orthodox critics have been capable of maintaining that John, the Nazarene, who was probably well past fifty years of age when he is supposed to have written the most thoroughly Judaizing book in the New Testament—the Apocalypse—in the roughest of Greek, underwent an astounding metamorphosis of both doctrine and style by the time he reached the ripe age of ninety or so, and provided the world with a history in which the acutest critic can not make out where the speeches of Jesus end and the text of the narrative begins; while that narrative is utterly irreconcilable in regard to matters of fact with that of his fellow-apostle, Matthew.

The end of the whole matter is this: The "sect of the Nazarenes," the brother and the immediate followers of Jesus, commissioned by him as apostles, and those who were taught by them up to the year 50 A. D., were not "Christians" in the sense in which that term has been understood ever since its asserted origin at Antioch, but Jews—strict orthodox Jews—whose belief in the Messiahship of Jesus never led to their exclusion from the Temple services, nor would have shut them out from the wide embrace of Judaism.* The open proclamation of their special view about the Messiah was doubtless offensive to the Pharisees, just as rampant Low Churchism is offensive to bigoted High Churchism in our own country; or as any kind of dissent is offensive to fervid religionists of all creeds. To the Sadducees, no doubt, the political danger of any Messianic movement was serious, and they would have been glad to put down Nazarenism, lest it should end in useless rebellion against their Roman masters, like that other Galilean movement headed by Judas, a generation earlier. Galilee was always a hot-bed of seditious enthusiasm against the rule of Rome; and high priest and procurator alike had need to keep a sharp eye upon natives of that district. On the whole, however, the Nazarenes were but little troubled for the first twenty years of their existence; and the undying hatred of the Jews against those later converts whom they regarded as apostates and fautors of a sham Judaism was awakened by Paul. From their point of view, he was a mere renegade Jew, opposed alike to orthodox Judaism and to orthodox Nazarenism, and whose teachings threatened Judaism

---

* "If every one was baptized as soon as he acknowledged Jesus to be the Messiah, the first Christians can have been aware of no other essential differences from the Jews."—Zeller, "Vorträge" (1865), p. 216.

with destruction. And, from their point of view, they were quite right. In the course of a century, Pauline influences had a large share in driving primitive Nararenism from being the very heart of the new faith into the position of scouted error; and the spirit of Paul's doctrine continued its work of driving Christianity further and further away from Judaism, until "meats offered to idols" might be eaten without scruple, while the Nazarene methods of observing even the Sabbath or the Passover were branded with the mark of Judaizing heresy.

But if the primitive Nazarenes of whom the Acts speaks were orthodox Jews, what sort of probability can there be that Jesus was anything else? How can he have founded the universal religion which was not heard of till twenty years after his death?* That Jesus possessed in a rare degree the gift of attaching men to his person and to his fortunes; that he was the author of many a striking saying, and the advocate of equity, of love, and of humility; that he may have disregarded the subtleties of the bigots for legal observance, and appealed rather to those noble conceptions of religion which constituted the pith and kernel of the teaching of the great prophets of his nation seven hundred years earlier; and that, in the last scenes of his career, he may have embodied the ideal sufferer of Isaiah—may be, as I think it is, extremely probable. But all this involves not a step beyond the borders of orthodox Judaism. Again, who is to say whether Jesus proclaimed himself the veritable Messiah, expected by his

---

* Dr. Harnack, in the lately published second edition of his "Dogmengeschichte," says (p. 39), "Jesus Christ brought forward no new doctrine"; and again (p. 65), "It is not difficult to set against every portion of the utterances of Jesus an observation which deprives him of originality." See also Zusatz 4, on the same page.

nation since the appearance of the pseudo-prophetic work of Daniel, a century and a half before his time; or whether the enthusiasm of his followers gradually forced him to assume that position?

But one thing is quite certain: if that belief in the speedy second coming of the Messiah which was shared by all parties in the primitive Church, whether Nazarene or Pauline; which Jesus is made to prophesy, over and over again, in the synoptic Gospels; and which dominated the life of Christians during the first century after the crucifixion—if he believed and taught that, then assuredly he was under an illusion, and he is responsible for that which the mere efluxion of time has demonstrated to be a prodigious error.

When I ventured to doubt "whether any Protestant theologian who has a reputation to lose will say that he believes the Gadarene story," it appears that I reckoned without Dr. Wace, who, referring to this passage in my paper, says:

He will judge whether I fall under his description; but I repeat that I believe it, and that he has removed the only objection to my believing it.*

Far be it from me to set myself up as a judge of any such delicate question as that put before me; but I think I may venture to express the conviction that, in the matter of courage, Dr. Wace has raised for himself a monument *ære perennius*. For, really, in my poor judgment, a certain splendid intrepidity, such as one admires in the leader of a forlorn hope, is manifested by Dr. Wace, when he solemnly affirms that he believes the Gadarene story

---

* Page 76.

on the evidence offered. I feel less complimented perhaps than I ought to do, when I am told that I have been an accomplice in extinguishing in Dr. Wace's mind the last glimmer of doubt which common sense may have suggested. In fact, I must disclaim all responsibility for the use to which the information I supplied has been put. I formally decline to admit that the expression of my ignorance whether devils, in the existence of which I do not believe, if they did exist, might or might not be made to go out of men into pigs, can, as a matter of logic, have been of any use whatever to a person who already believed in devils and in the historical accuracy of the Gospels.

Of the Gadarene story, Dr. Wace, with all solemnity and twice over, affirms that he "believes it." I am sorry to trouble him further, but what does he mean by "it"? Because there are two stories, one in "Mark" and "Luke," and the other in "Matthew." In the former, which I quoted in my previous paper, there is one possessed man; in the latter there are two. The story is told fully, with the vigorous, homely diction and the picturesque details of a piece of folk-lore, in the second Gospel. The immediately antecedent event is the storm on the Lake of Gennesareth. The immediately consequent events are the message from the ruler of the synagogue and the healing of the woman with an issue of blood. In the third Gospel, the order of events is exactly the same, and there is an extremely close general and verbal correspondence between the narratives of the miracle. Both agree in stating that there was only one possessed man, and that he was the residence of many devils, whose name was "Legion."

In the first Gospel, the event which immediately precedes the Gadarene affair is, as before, the storm; the message from the ruler and the healing of the issue are separated from it by the accounts of the healing of a paralytic, of the calling of Matthew, and of a discussion with some Pharisees. Again, while the second Gospel speaks of the country of the "Gerasenes" as the locality of the event, the third Gospel has "Gerasenes," "Gergesenes," and "Gadarenes" in different ancient MSS.; while the first has "Gadarenes."

The really important points to be noticed, however, in the narrative of the first Gospel, are these—that there are two possessed men instead of one; and that while the story is abbreviated by omissions, what there is of it is often verbally identical with the corresponding passages in the other two Gospels. The most unabashed of reconcilers can not well say that one man is the same as two, or two as one; and, though the suggestion really has been made, that two different miracles, agreeing in all essential particulars, except the number of the possessed, were effected immediately after the storm on the lake, I should be sorry to accuse any one of seriously adopting it. Nor will it be pretended that the allegory refuge is accessible in this particular case.

So, when Dr. Wace says that he believes in the synoptic evangelists' account of the miraculous bedevilment of swine, I may fairly ask which of them does he believe? Does he hold by the one evangelist's story, or by that of the two evangelists? And having made his election, what reasons has he to give for his choice? If it is suggested that the witness of two is to be taken against that of one, not only is the testimony dealt with in that common-sense fashion against which theologians of his school protest so warmly; not only is all question of inspiration at an end, but the further inquiry arises, after all, is it the testimony of two against one? Are the authors of the versions in the second and the third Gospels really independent witnesses? In order to answer this question, it is only needful to place the English versions of the two side by side, and compare them carefully. It will then be seen that the coincidences between them, not merely in substance, but in arrangement, and in the use of identical words in the same order, are such, that only two alternatives are conceivable: either one evangelist freely copied from the other, or both based themselves upon a common source, which may either have been a written document, or a definite oral tradition learned by heart. Assuredly these two testimonies are not those of independent witnesses. Further, when the narrative in the first Gospel is compared with that in the other two, the same fact comes out.

Supposing, then, that Dr. Wace is right in his assumption that Matthew, Mark, and Luke wrote the works which we find attributed to them by tradition, what is the value of their agreement, even that something more or less like this particular miracle occurred, since it is demonstrable, either that all depend on some antecedent statement, of the authorship of which nothing is known, or that two are dependent upon the third?

Dr. Wace says he believes the Gadarene story; whichever version of it he accepts, therefore, he believes that Jesus said what he is stated in all the versions to have said, and thereby virtually declared that the theory of the nature of the spiritual world involved in the story is true. Now I hold that this theory is false, that it is a monstrous and mischievous fiction; and I unhesitatingly express my disbelief in any assertion that it is true, by whomsoever made. So that, if Dr. Wace is right in his belief, he is also quite right in classing me among the people he calls "infidels"; and although I can not fulfill the eccentric expectation of the Bishop of Peterborough, that I shall glory in a title which, from my point of view, it would be simply silly to adopt, I certainly shall rejoice not to be reckoned among the bishop's "us Christians" so long as the profession of belief in such stories as the Gadarene pig affair, on the strength of a tradition of unknown origin, of which two discrepant reports, also of unknown origin, alone remain, forms any part of the Christian faith. And, although I have, more than once, repudiated the gift of prophecy, yet I think I may venture to express the anticipation, that if "Christians" generally are going to follow the line taken by the Bishop of Peterborough and Dr. Wace, it will not be long before all men of common sense qualify for a place among the "infidels."

VI.

CHRISTIANITY AND AGNOSTICISM.

By HENRY WACE, D. D.

READERS who may be willing to look at this further reply on my part to Prof. Huxley need not be apprehensive of being entangled in any such obscure points of church history as those with which the professor has found it necessary to perplex them in support of his contentions; still less of being troubled with any personal explanations. The tone which Prof. Huxley has thought fit to adopt, not only toward myself, but toward English theologians in general, excuses me from taking further notice of any personal considerations in the matter. I endeavored to treat him with the respect due to his great scientific position, and he replies by sneering at "theologians who are mere counsel for creeds," saying that the serious question at issue "is whether theological men of science, or theological special pleaders, are to have the confidence of the general public," observing that Holland and Germany are "the only two countries in which, at the present time, professors of theology are to be found whose tenure of their posts does not depend upon the result to which their inquiries lead them," and thus insinuating that English theologians are debarred by selfish interests from candid inquiry. I shall presently have something to say on the grave misrepresentation of German theology which these insinuations involve; but for myself and for English theologians I shall not condescend to reply to them. I content myself with calling the reader's attention to the fact that, in this controversy, it is Prof. Huxley who finds it requisite for his argument to insinuate that his opponents are biased by sordid motives; and I shall for the future leave him and his sneers out of account, and simply consider his arguments for as much, or as little, as they may be worth. For a similar reason I shall confine myself as far as possible to the issue which I raised at the Church Congress, and for which I then made myself responsible. I do not care, nor would it be of any avail, to follow over the wide and sacred field of Christian evidences an antagonist who resorts to the imputation of mean motives, and who, as I shall show, will not face the witnesses to whom he himself appeals. The manner in which Prof. Huxley has met the particular issue he challenged will be a sufficient illustration to impartial minds of the value which is to be attached to any further assaults which he may make upon the Christian position.

Let me then briefly remind the reader of the simple question which is at issue between us. What I alleged was that "an agnosticism which knows nothing of the relation of man to God must not only refuse belief to our Lord's most undoubted teaching, but must deny the reality of the spiritual convictions in which he lived and died." As evidence of that teaching and of those convictions I appealed to three testimonies—the Sermon on the Mount, the Lord's Prayer, and the story of the Passion—and I urged that whatever critical opinion might be held respecting the origin and structure of the four Gospels, there could not be any reasonable doubt that those testimonies "afford a true account of our Lord's essential belief and cardinal teaching." In his original reply, instead of meeting this appeal to three specific testimonies, Prof. Huxley shifted the argument to the question of the general credibility of the Gospels, and appealed to "the main results of biblical criticism, as they are set forth in the works of Strauss, Baur, Reuss, and Volkmar." He referred to these supposed "results" in support of his assertion that we know "absolutely nothing" of the authorship or genuineness of the four Gospels, and he challenged my reference to Renan as a witness to the fact that criticism has established no such results. In answer, I quoted passage after passage from Renan and from Reuss showing that the results at which they had arrived were directly contradictory of Prof. Huxley's assertions. How does he meet this evidence? He simply says, in a foot-note, "For the present I must content myself with warning my readers against any reliance upon Dr. Wace's statements as to the results arrived at by modern criticism. They are as gravely as surprisingly erroneous." I might ask by what right Prof. Huxley thus presumes to pronounce, as it were *ex cathedra*, without adducing any evidence, that the statements of another writer are "surprisingly erroneous"? But I in my turn content myself with pointing out that, if my quotations from Renan and Reuss had been incorrect, he could not only have said so, but could have produced the correct quotations. But he does not deny, as of course he can not, that Reuss, for example, really states, as the mature result of his investigations, what I quoted from him respecting St. Luke's Gospel, namely, that it was written by St. Luke and has reached us in its primitive form, and, further, that St. Luke used a book written by St. Mark, the disciple of St. Peter, and that this book in all probability comprised in its primitive form what we read in the present day from Mark i, 21, to xiii, 37. These are the results of modern criticism as stated by a biblical critic in whom Prof. Huxley expressed special confidence. It was not therefore my statements of the results of biblical criticism with which Prof. Huxley was confronted, but Reuss's statements; and, unless he can show that my quotation was a false one, he ought to have had the candor to acknowledge that Reuss, at least, is on these vital points dead against him. Instead of any such frank admission, he endeavors to explain away the force of his reference to Reuss. It may, he says, be well for him

to observe that approbation of the manner in which a great biblical scholar—for instance, Reuss—does his work does not commit me to the adoption of all, or indeed of any, of his views; and, further, that the disagreements of a series of investigators do not in any way interfere with the fact that each of them has made important contributions to the body of truth ultimately established.

But I beg to observe that Prof. Huxley did not appeal to Reuss's methods, but to Reuss's results. He said that no retractation by M. Renan would sensibly affect "the *main results of biblical criticism as they are set forth in the works of* Strauss, Baur, Reuss, and Volkmar." I have given him the results as set forth by Reuss in Reuss's own words, and all he has to offer in reply is an *ipse dixit* in a foot-note and an evasion in the text of his article.

But, as I said, this general discussion respecting the authenticity and credibility of the Gospels was an evasion of my argument, which rested upon the specific testimony of the Sermon on the Mount, the Lord's Prayer, and the narrative of the Passion; and, accordingly, in his present rejoinder Prof. Huxley, with much protestation that he made no evasion, addressed himself to these three points. And what is his answer? I feel obliged to characterize it as another evasion, and in one particular an evasion of a flagrant kind. The main point of his argument is that from various circumstances, which I will presently notice more particularly, there is much reason to doubt whether the Sermon on the Mount was ever actually delivered in the form in which it is recorded in St. Matthew. He notices, for instance, the combined similarity and difference between St. Matthew's Sermon on the Mount and St. Luke's so-called "Sermon on the Plain," and then he adds:

I thought that all fairly attentive and intelligent students of the Gospels, to say nothing of theologians of reputation, knew these things. But how can any one who does know them have the conscience to ask whether there is "any reasonable doubt" that the Sermon on the Mount was preached by Jesus of Nazareth?

It is a pity that Prof. Huxley seems as incapable of accuracy in his quotations of an opponent's words as in his references to the authorities to whom he appeals. I did not ask "whether there is any reasonable doubt that the Sermon on the Mount was preached by Jesus of Nazareth," and I expressly observed, in the article to which Prof. Huxley is replying, that "Prof. Reuss thinks, as many good critics have thought, that the Sermon on the Mount combines various distinct utterances of our Lord." What I did ask, in words which Prof. Huxley quotes, and therefore had before his eyes, was "whether there is any reasonable doubt that the Lord's Prayer and the Sermon on the Mount afford a true account of our Lord's essential belief and cardinal teaching." That is an absolutely distinct question from the one which Prof. Huxley dissects, and a confusion of the two is peculiarly inexcusable in a person who holds that purely human view of the Gospel narratives which he represents. If a long report of a speech appears in the "Times" and a shortened report appears in the "Standard," every one knows that we are none the less made acquainted—perhaps made still better acquainted—with the essential purport and cardinal meaning of the speaker. On the supposition, similarly, that St. Matthew and St. Luke are simply giving two distinct accounts of the same address, with such omissions and variations of order as suited the purposes of their respective narratives, we are in at least as good a position for knowing what was the main burden of the address as if we had only one account, and perhaps in a better position, as we see what were the points which both reporters deemed essential. As Prof. Huxley himself observes, we have reports of speeches in ancient historians which are certainly not in the very words of the speakers; yet no one doubts that we know the main purport of the speeches of Pericles which Thucydides records.

This attempt, therefore, to answer my appeal to the substance of the teaching of the Sermon on the Mount is a palpable evasion, and it is aggravated by the manner in which Prof. Huxley quotes a high German authority in support of his contention. I am much obliged to him for appealing to Holtzmann; for, though Holtzmann's own conclusions respecting the books of the New Testament seem to me often extravagantly skeptical and far-fetched, and though I can not, therefore, quite agree with Prof. Huxley that his "Lehrbuch" gives "a remarkably full and fair account of the present results of criticism," yet I agree that it gives on the whole a full and fair account of the course of criticism and of the opinions of its chief representatives. Instead, therefore, of imitating Prof. Huxley, and pronouncing an *ipse dixit* as to the state of criticism or the opinions of critics, I am very glad to be able to refer to a book of which the authority is recognized by him, and which will save both my readers and myself from embarking on the wide and waste ocean of the German criticism of the last fifty years. "Holtzmann, then," says Prof. Huxley in a note on page 104, "has no doubt that the Sermon on the Mount is a compilation, or, as he calls it in his recently published 'Lehrbuch' (p. 372), 'an artificial mosaic work.'" Now, let the reader attend to what Holtzmann really says in the passage referred to. His words are: "In the so-called Sermon on the Mount (Matt. v–vii) we find constructed, on the basis of a real discourse of fundamental significance, a skillfully articulated mosaic work."* The phrase was not so long a one that Prof. Huxley need have omitted the important words by which those he quotes are qualified. Holtzmann recognizes, as will be seen, that a real discourse of fundamental significance underlies the Sermon on the Mount. That is enough for my purpose; for no reasonable person will suppose that the fundamental significance of the real discourse has been entirely obliterated, especially as the main purport of the sermon in St. Luke is of the same character. But Prof. Huxley must know perfectly well, as every one else does, that he would be maintaining a paradox, in which every critic of repute,

---

* "In der sog. Bergpredigt, Mt. 5–7, gibt sich eine, auf Grund einer wirklichen Rede von fundamentaler Bedeutung sich erhebende, kunstreich gegliederte Mosaikarbeit."

to say nothing of every man of common sense, would be against him, if he were to maintain that the Sermon on the Mount does not give a substantially correct idea of our Lord's teaching. But to admit this is to admit my point, so he rides off on a side issue as to the question of the precise form in which the sermon was delivered.

I must, however, take some notice of Prof. Huxley's argument on this irrelevant issue, as it affords a striking illustration of that superior method of ratiocination in these matters on which he prides himself. I need not trouble the reader much on the questions he raises as to the relations of the first three Gospels. Any one who cares to see a full and thorough discussion of that difficult question, conducted with a complete knowledge of foreign criticism on the subject, and at the same time marked by the greatest lucidity and interest, may be referred to the admirable "Introduction to the New Testament," by Dr. Salmon, who, like Prof. Huxley, is a Fellow of the Royal Society, and who became eminent as one of the first mathematicians of Europe before he became similarly eminent as a theologian. I am content here to let Prof. Huxley's assumptions pass, as I am only concerned to illustrate the fallacious character of the reasoning he founds upon them. He tells us, then, that—

there is now no doubt that the three synoptic Gospels, so far from being the work of three independent writers, are closely interdependent, and that in one of two ways. Either all three contain, as their foundation, versions, to a large extent, verbally identical, of one and the same tradition; or two of them are thus closely dependent on the third; and the opinion of the majority of the best critics has, of late years, more and more converged toward the conviction that our canonical second Gospel (the so-called "Mark's" Gospel) is that which most closely represents the primitive groundwork of the three. That I take to be one of the most valid results of New Testament criticism, of immeasurably greater importance than the discussion about dates and authorship. But if, as I believe to be the case beyond any rational doubt or dispute, the second Gospel is the nearest extant representative of the oldest tradition, whether written or oral, how comes it that it contains neither the "Sermon on the Mount" nor the "Lord's Prayer," those typical embodiments, according to Dr. Wace, of the "essential belief and cardinal teaching" of Jesus?

I have quoted every word of this passage because I am anxious for the reader to estimate the value of Prof. Huxley's own statement of his case. It is, as he says, the opinion of many critics of authority that a certain fixed tradition, written or oral, was used by the writers of the first three Gospels. In the first place, why this should prevent those three Gospels from being the work of "three independent writers" I am at a loss to conceive. If Mr. Froude, the late Prof. Brewer, and the late Mr. Green each use the Rolls Calendars of the reign of Henry VIII, I do not see that this abolishes their individuality. Any historian who describes the Peloponnesian War uses the memoirs of that war written by Thucydides; but Bishop Thirlwall and Mr. Grote were, I presume, independent writers. But to pass to a more important point, that which is assumed is that the alleged tradition, written or oral, was the groundwork of our first three Gospels, and it is, therefore, older than they are. Let it be granted, for the sake of argument. But how does this prove that the tradition in question is "the oldest," so that anything which was not in it is thereby discredited? It was, let us allow, an old tradition used by the writers of the first three Gospels. But how does this fact raise the slightest presumption against the probability that there were other traditions equally old which they might use with equal justification so far as their scope required? Prof. Huxley alleges, and I do not care to dispute the allegation, that the first three Gospels embody a certain record older than themselves. But by what right does he ask me to accept this as evidence, or as affording even the slightest presumption, that there was no other? Between his allegation in one sentence that the second Gospel "most closely represents the primitive groundwork of the three," and his allegation, in the next sentence but one, that "the second Gospel is the nearest extant representative of the oldest tradition," there is an absolute and palpable *non sequitur.* It is a mere juggle of phrases, and upon this juggle the whole of his subsequent argument on this point depends. St. Mark's Gospel may very well represent the oldest tradition *relative to the common matter of the three,* without, therefore, necessarily representing "the oldest tradition" in such a sense as to be a touchstone for all other reports of our Lord's life. Prof. Huxley must know very well that from the time of Schleiermacher many critics have believed in the existence of another document containing a collection of our Lord's discourses. Holtzmann concludes ("Lehrbuch," page 376) that "under all the circumstances the hypothesis of two sources offers the most probable solution of the synoptical problem"; and it is surely incredible that no old traditions of our Lord's teaching should have existed beyond those which are common to the three Gospels. St. Luke, in fact, in that preface which Prof. Huxley has no hesitation in using for his own purposes, says that "many had taken in hand to set forth in order a declaration of those things which are most surely believed among us"; but Prof. Huxley asks us to assume that none of these records were old, and none trustworthy, but that particular one which furnishes a sort of skeleton to the first three Gospels. There is no evidence whatever, beyond Prof. Huxley's private judgment, for such an assumption. Nay, he himself tells us that, according to Holtzmann, it is at present a "burning question" among critics "whether the relatively primitive narration and the root of the other synoptic texts is contained in Matthew or in Mark."* Yet while his own authority tells him that this is a burning question, he treats it as settled in favor of St. Mark, "beyond any rational doubt or dispute," and employs this assumption as sufficiently solid ground on which to rest his doubts of the genuineness of the Sermon on the Mount and the Lord's Prayer!

But let us pass to another point in Prof. Huxley's mode of argument. Let us grant, again, for the sake of argument, his *non sequitur* that the second Gospel is the nearest extant representative of the oldest tradition. "How comes it," he asks, "that it contains neither the Sermon on the Mount nor the Lord's Prayer?" Well, that is a very interesting inquiry, which has, in point of fact, often been considered by Christian divines; and various answers are conceivable, equally reasonable and sufficient. If it was St. Mark's object to record our Lord's acts rather than his teaching, what right has Prof. Huxley, from his purely human point of view, to find fault with him? If, from a Christian point of view, St. Mark was inspired by a divine guidance to present the most vivid, brief, and effective sketch possible of our Lord's action as a Saviour, and for that purpose to leave to another writer the description of our Lord as a teacher, the phenomenon is not less satisfactorily explained. St.

---

* Page 101.

Mark, according to that tradition of the Church which Prof. Huxley believes to be quite worthless, but which his authority Holtzmann does not, was in great measure the mouth-piece of St. Peter. Now, St. Peter is recorded in the Acts of the Apostles, in his address to Cornelius, as summing up our Lord's life in these words: "How God anointed Jesus of Nazareth with the Holy Ghost and with power, who went about doing good, and healing all who were oppressed of the devil; for God was with him"; and this is very much the point of view represented in St. Mark's Gospel. When, in fact, Prof. Huxley asks, in answer to Holtzmann, who is again unfavorable to his views, "What conceivable motive could Mark have for omitting it?" * the answers that arise are innumerable. Perhaps, as has been suggested, St. Mark was more concerned with acts than words; perhaps he wanted to be brief; perhaps he was writing for persons who wanted one kind of record and not another; and, above all, perhaps it was not so much a question of "omission" as of selection. It is really astonishing that this latter consideration never seems to cross the mind of Prof. Huxley and writers like him. The Gospels are among the briefest biographies in the world. I have sometimes thought that there is evidence of something superhuman about them in the mere fact that, while human biographers labor through volumes in order to give us some idea of their subject, every one of the Gospels, occupying no more than a chapter or two in length of an ordinary biography, nevertheless gives us an image of our Lord sufficiently vivid to have made him the living companion of all subsequent generations. But if "the

---

* Page 104.

gospel of Jesus Christ" was to be told within the compass of the sixteen chapters of St. Mark, some selection had to be made out of the mass of our Lord's words and deeds as recorded by the tradition of those "who from the beginning were eye-witnesses and ministers of the word." The very greatness and effectiveness of these four Gospels consist in this wonderful power of selection, like that by which a great artist depicts a character and a figure in half a dozen touches; and Prof. Huxley may, perhaps, to put the matter on its lowest level, find out a conceivable motive for St. Mark's omissions when he can produce such an effective narrative as St. Mark's. As St. John says at the end of his Gospel, "There are also many other things which Jesus did, the which, if they should be written every one, I suppose that even the world itself could not contain the books that should be written." So St. John, like St. Mark, had to make his selection, and selection involves omission.

But, after all, I venture to ask whether anything can be more preposterous than this supposition that because a certain tradition is the oldest authority, therefore every other authority is discredited? Boswell writes a life of Johnson; therefore every record of Johnson's acts or words which is not in Boswell is to be suspected. Carlyle writes a life of Sterling first, and Archdeacon Hare writes one afterward; therefore nothing in the archdeacon's life is to be trusted which was not also in Carlyle's. What seems to me so astonishing about Prof. Huxley's articles is not the wildness of their conclusions, but the rottenness of their ratiocination. To take another instance:

> Luke either knew the collection of loosely connected and aphoristic utterances which appear under the name of the "Sermon on

the Mount" in "Matthew," or he did not. If he did not, he must have been ignorant of the existence of such a document as our canonical "Matthew," a fact which does not make for the genuineness or the authority of that book. If he did, he has shown that he does not care for its authority on a matter of fact of no small importance; and that does not permit us to conceive that he believed the first Gospel to be the work of an authority to whom he ought to defer, let alone that of an apostolic eye-witness.

I pass by the description of the Sermon on the Mount as a "collection of loosely connected utterances," though it is a kind of begging of a very important question. But supposing St. Luke to have been ignorant of the existence of St. Matthew's Gospel, how does this reflect on the genuineness of that book unless we know, as no one does, that St. Matthew's Gospel was written before St. Luke's, and sufficiently long before it to have become known to him? Or, if he did know it, where is the disrespect to its authority in his having given for his own purposes an abridgment of that which St. Matthew gave more fully? Prof. Huxley might almost seem dominated by the mechanical theory of inspiration which he denounces in his antagonists. He writes as if there were something absolutely sacred, neither to be altered nor added to, in the mere words of some old authority of which he conceives himself to be in possession. Dr. Abbott, with admirable labor, has had printed for him, in clear type, the words or bits of words which are common to the first three Gospels, and he seems immediately to adopt the anathema of the book of Revelation, and to proclaim to every man, evangelists and apostles included, "if any man shall add unto these things, . . . and if any man shall take away from the words" of this "common tradition" of Dr. Abbott, he shall be forthwith scientifically excommunicated.

I venture to submit, as a mere matter of common sense, that if three persons used one document, it is the height of rashness to conclude that it contained nothing but what they all three quote; that it is not only possible but probable that, while certain parts were used by all, each may have used some parts as suitable to his own purpose which the others did not find suitable to theirs; and, lastly, that the fact of there having been one such document in existence is so far from being evidence that there were no others, that it even creates some presumption that there were. In short, I must beg leave to represent, not so much that Prof. Huxley's conclusions are wrong, but that there is absolutely no validity in the reasoning by which he endeavors to support them. It is not, in fact, reasoning at all, but mere presumption and guess-work, inconsistent, moreover, with all experience and common sense.

Of course, if Prof. Huxley's quibbles against the Sermon on the Mount go to pieces, so do his cavils at the authenticity of the Lord's Prayer; and, indeed, on these two points I venture to think that the case for which I was contending is carried by the mere fact that it seems necessary to Prof. Huxley's position to dispute them. If he can not maintain his ground without pushing his agnosticism to such a length as to deny the substantial genuineness of the Sermon on the Mount and the Lord's Prayer, I think he will be found to have allowed enough to satisfy reasonable men that his case must be a bad one. I shall not, therefore, waste more time on these points, as I must say something on his strange treatment of the third point in the evangelical records to which I referred, the story of the Passion. It is really difficult to take seriously what he says on this subject. He says:

I am not quite sure what Dr. Wace means by this—I am not aware that any one (with the exception of certain ancient heretics) has propounded doubts as to the reality of the crucifixion; and certainly I have no inclination to argue about the precise accuracy of every detail of that pathetic story of suffering and wrong. But if Dr. Wace means, as I suppose he does, that that which, according to the orthodox view, happened after the crucifixion, and which is, in a dogmatic sense, the most important part of the story, is founded on solid historical proofs, I must beg leave to express a diametrically opposite conviction.

Prof. Huxley is not quite sure what I mean by the story of the Passion, but supposes I mean the story of the resurrection! It is barely credible that he can have supposed anything of the kind; but by this gratuitous supposition he has again evaded the issue I proposed to him, and has shifted the argument to another topic, which, however important in itself, is entirely irrelevant to the particular point in question. If he really supposed that when I said the Passion I meant the resurrection, it is only another proof of his incapacity for strict argument, at least on these subjects. I not only used the expression "the story of the Passion," but I explicitly stated in my reply to him for what purpose I appealed to it. I said that "that story involves the most solemn attestation, again and again, of truths of which an agnostic coolly says he knows nothing"; and I mentioned particularly our Lord's final utterance, "Father, into thy hands I commend my spirit," as conveying our Lord's attestation in his death agony to his relation to God as his Father. That exclamation is recorded by St. Luke; but let me remind the reader of what is recorded by St. Mark, upon whom Prof. Huxley mainly relies. There we have the account of the agony in Gethsemane and of our Lord's prayer to his Father; we have the solemn challenge of the high priest, "Art thou the Christ, the son of the Blessed?" and our Lord's reply, "I am; and ye shall see the Son of man sitting on the right hand of power, and coming in the clouds of heaven," with his immediate condemnation, on the ground that in this statement he had spoken blasphemy. On the cross, moreover, St. Mark records his affecting appeal to his Father, "My God, my God, why hast thou forsaken me?" All this solemn evidence Prof. Huxley puts aside with the mere passing observation that he has "no inclination to argue about the precise accuracy of every detail of that pathetic story of suffering and wrong." But these prayers and declarations of our Lord are not mere details; they are of the very essence of the story of the Passion; and whether Prof. Huxley is inclined to argue about them or not, he will find that all serious people will be influenced by them to the end of time, unless they be shown to be unhistorical.

At all events, by refusing to consider their import, Prof. Huxley has again, in the most flagrant manner, evaded my challenge. I not only mentioned specifically "the story of the Passion," but I explained what I meant by it; and Prof. Huxley asks us to believe that he does not understand what I referred to; he refuses to face that story; and he raises an irrelevant issue about the resurrection. It is irrelevant, because the point specifically at issue between us is not the truth of the Christian creed, but the meaning of agnosticism, and the responsibilities which agnosticism involves. I say that whether agnosticism be justifiable or not, it involves a denial of the beliefs in which Jesus lived and died. It would equally involve a denial of them had he never risen; and if Prof. Huxley really thinks, therefore, that a denial of the resurrection affects the evidence afforded by the Passion, he must be incapable of distinguishing between two successive and entirely distinct occurrences.

But the manner in which Prof. Huxley has treated this irrelevant issue deserves perhaps a few words, for it is another characteristic specimen of his mode of argument. I note, by the way, that, after referring to "the facts of the case as stated by the oldest extant narrative of them"—he means the story in St. Mark, though this is not a part of that common tradition of the three Gospels on which he relies; for, as he observes, the accounts in St. Matthew and St. Luke present marked variations from it—he adds:

I do not see why any one should have a word to say against the inherent probability of that narrative; and, for my part, I am quite ready to accept it as an historical fact, that so much and no more is positively known of the end of Jesus of Nazareth.

We have, then, the important admission that Prof. Huxley has not a word to say against the historic credibility of the narrative in the fifteenth chapter of St. Mark, and accordingly he proceeds to quote its statements for the purpose of his argument. That argument, in brief, is that our Lord might very well have survived his crucifixion, have been removed still living to the tomb, have been taken out of it on the Friday or Saturday night by Joseph of Arimathea, and have recovered and found his way to Galilee. So much Prof. Huxley is prepared to believe, and he asks "on what grounds can a reasonable man be asked to believe any more?" But a prior question is on what grounds can a reasonable man be asked to believe as much as this? In the first place, if St. Mark's narrative is to be the basis of discussion, why does Prof. Huxley leave out of account the scourging, with the indication of weakness in our Lord's inability to bear his cross, and treat him as exposed to crucifixion in the condition simply of "temperate, strong men, such as the ordinary Galilean peasants were"? In the next place, I am informed by good medical authority that he is quite mistaken in saying that "no serious physical symptoms need at once arise from the wounds made by the nails in the hands and feet," and that, on the contrary, very grave symptoms would ordinarily arise in the course of no long time from such severe wounds, left to fester, with the nails in them, for six hours. In the third place, Prof. Huxley takes no account of the piercing of our Lord's side, and of the appearance of blood and water from the wound, which is solemnly attested by one witness. It is true that incident is not recorded by St. Mark; but Prof. Huxley must disprove the witness before he can leave it out of account. But, lastly, if Prof. Huxley's account of the matter be true, the first preaching of the church must have been founded on a deliberate fraud, of which some at least of our Lord's most intimate friends were guilty, or to which they were accessory; and I thought that supposition was practically out of account among reasonable men. Prof. Huxley argues as if he had only to deal with the further evidence of St. Paul. That, indeed, is evidence of a far more momentous nature than he recognizes; but it is by no means the most important. It is beyond question that the Christian society, from the earliest moment of its existence, believed in our Lord's resurrection. Baur frankly says that there is no doubt about the church having been founded on this belief, though he can not explain how the belief arose. If the resurrection be a fact, the belief is explained; but it is certainly not explained by the supposition of a fraud on the part of Joseph of Arimathea. As to Prof. Huxley's assertion that the accounts in the three Gospels are "hopelessly discrepant," it is easily made and as easily denied; but it is out of all reason that Prof. Huxley's bare assertion on such a point should outweigh the opinions of some of the most learned judges of evidence, who have thought no such thing. It would be absurd to attempt to discuss that momentous story as a side issue in a review. It is enough to have pointed out that Prof. Huxley discusses it without even taking into account the statements of the very narrative on which he relies. The manner in which he sets aside St. Paul is equally reckless:

> According to his own showing, Paul, in the vigor of his manhood, with every means of becoming acquainted, at first hand, with the evidence of eye-witnesses, not merely refused to credit them, but "persecuted the Church of God and made havoc of it." . . . Yet this strange man, because he has a vision one day, at once, and with equally headlong zeal, flies to the opposite pole of opinion.

"A vision!" The whole question is, what vision? How can Prof. Huxley be sure that no vision could be of such a nature as to justify a man in acting on it? If, as we are told, our Lord personally appeared to St. Paul, spoke to him, and gave him specific commands, was he to disbelieve his own eyes and ears, as well as his own conscience, and go up to Jerusalem to cross-examine Peter and John and James? If the vision was a real one he was at once under orders, and had to obey our Lord's injunctions. It is, to say the least, rash, if not presumptuous, for Prof. Huxley to declare that such a vision as St. Paul had would not have convinced him; and, at all events, the question is not disposed of by calling the manifestation "a vision." Two things are certain about St. Paul. One is that he was in the confidence of the Pharisees, and was their trusted agent in persecuting the Christians; and the other is that he was afterward in the confidence of the apostles, and knew all their side of the case. He holds, therefore, the unique position of having had equal access to all that would be alleged on both sides; and the result is that, being fully acquainted with all that the Pharisees could urge against the resurrection, he nevertheless gave up his whole life to attesting its truth, and threw in his lot, at the cost of martyrdom, with those whom he had formerly persecuted. Prof. Huxley reminds us that he did all this in the full vigor of manhood, and in spite of strong and even violent prejudices. This is not a witness to be put aside in Prof. Huxley's off-hand manner.

But the strangest part of Prof. Huxley's article remains to be noticed; and, so far as the main point at issue between us is concerned, I need hardly have noticed anything else. He proceeds to a long and intricate discussion, quite needless, as I think, for his main object, respecting the relations between the Nazarenes, Ebionites, Jewish and Gentile Christians, first in the time of Justin Martyr and then of St. Paul. Into this discussion, in the course of which he makes assumptions which, as Holtzmann will tell him, are as much questioned by the German criticism on which he relies as by English theologians, it is unnecessary for me to follow him. The object of it is to establish a conclusion, which is all with which I am concerned. That conclusion is that "if the primitive Nazarenes of whom the Acts speak were orthodox Jews, what sort of probability can there be that Jesus was anything else?"* But what more is necessary for the purpose of my argument? To say, indeed, that this *a priori*

---

* Page 124.

probability places us "in a position to form a safe judgment of the limits within which the teaching of Jesus of Nazareth must have been confined," is to beg a great question, for it assumes that our Lord could not have transcended those limits unless his disciples transcended them simultaneously with him. But if our Lord's beliefs were those of an orthodox Jew, we certainly know enough of them to be quite sure that they involved a denial of Prof. Huxley's agnosticism. An orthodox Jew certainly believed in God, and in his responsibility to God, and in a divine revelation and a divine law. It is, says Prof. Huxley, "extremely probable" that he appealed "to those noble conceptions of religion which constituted the pith and kernel of the teaching of the great prophets of his nation seven hundred years earlier." But, if so, his first principles involved the assertion of religious realities which an agnostic refuses to acknowledge. Prof. Huxley has, in fact, dragged his readers through this thorny question of Jewish and Gentile Christianity in order to establish, at the end of it, and, as it seems, quite unconsciously, an essential part of the very allegation which I originally made. I said that a person who "knows nothing" of God asserts the belief of Jesus of Nazareth to have been unfounded, repudiates his example, and denies his authority. Prof. Huxley, in order to answer this contention, offers to prove, with great elaboration, that Jesus was an orthodox Jew, and consequently that his belief did involve what an agnostic rejects. How much beyond these elementary truths Jesus taught is a further and a distinct question. What I was concerned to maintain is that a man can not be an agnostic with respect to even the elementary truths of religion without rejecting the example and authority of Jesus Christ; and Prof. Huxley, though he still endeavors to avoid facing the fact, has established it by a roundabout method of his own.

I suppose I must also reply to Prof. Huxley's further challenge respecting my belief in the story of the Gadarene swine, though the difficulty of which he makes so much seems to me too trivial to deserve serious notice. He says "there are two stories, one in 'Mark' and 'Luke,' and the other in 'Matthew.' In the former there is one possessed man, in the latter there are two," and he asks me which I believe? My answer is that I believe both, and that the supposition of there being any inconsistency between them can only arise on that mechanical view of inspiration from which Prof. Huxley seems unable to shake himself free. Certainly "the most unabashed of reconcilers can not well say that one man is the same as two, or two as one"; but no one need be abashed to say that the greater number includes the less, and that if two men met our Lord, one certainly did. If I go into the operating theatre of King's College Hospital, and see an eminent surgeon perform a new or rare operation on one or two patients, and if I tell a friend afterward that I saw the surgeon perform such and such an operation on a patient, will he feel in any perplexity if he meets another spectator half an hour afterward who says he saw the operation performed on two patients? All that I should have been thinking of was the nature of the operation, which is as well described by reference to one patient as to half a dozen; and similarly St. Mark and St. Luke may have thought that the only important point was the nature of the miracle itself, and not the number of possessed men who were the subjects of it. It is quite unnecessary, therefore, for me to consider all the elaborate dilemmas in which Prof. Huxley would entangle me respecting the relative authority of the first three Gospels. As two includes one, and as both witnesses are in my judgment equally to be trusted, I adopt the supposition which includes the statements of both. It is a pure assumption that inspiration requires verbal accuracy in the reporting of every detail, and an assumption quite inconsistent with our usual tests of truth. Just as no miracle has saved the texts of the Scriptures from corruption in secondary points, so no miracle has been wrought to exclude the ordinary variations of truthful reporters in the Gospel narratives. But a miracle, in my belief, has been wrought in inspiring four men to give, within the compass of their brief narratives, such a picture of the life and work and teaching, of the death and resurrection, of the Son of man as to illuminate all human existence for the future, and to enable men "to believe that Jesus is the Christ, and believing to have life through his name."

It is with different feelings from those which Prof. Huxley provokes that I turn for a while to Mrs. Humphrey Ward's article on "The New Reformation." Since he adopts that article as a sufficient confutation of mine, I feel obliged to notice it, though I am sorry to appear in any position of antagonism to its author. Apart from other considerations, I am under much obligation to Mrs. Ward for the valuable series of articles which she contributed to the "Dictionary of Christian Biography" under my editorship, upon the obscure but interesting history of the Goths in Spain. I trust that, in her account of the effect upon Robert Elsmere and Merriman of absorption in that barbarian scene, she is not describing her own experience and the source of her own aberrations. But I feel especially bound to treat her argument with consideration, and to waive any opposition which can be avoided. I am sorry that she, too, questions the possibility in this country of "a scientific, that is to say, an unprejudiced, an unbiased study of theology, under present conditions," and I should have hoped that she would have had too much confidence in her colleagues in the important work to which I refer than to cast this slur upon them. Their labors have, in fact, been received with sufficient appreciation by German scholars of all schools to render their vindication unnecessary; and if Prof. Huxley can extend his study of German theological literature much beyond Zeller's "Vorträge" of "a quarter of a century ago," or Ritschl's writings of "nearly forty years ago," he will not find himself countenanced by church historians in Germany in his contempt for the recent contributions of English scholars to early church history. However, it is the more easy for me to waive all differences of this nature with Mrs. Ward, because it is unnecessary for me to look beyond her article for its own refutation. Her main contention, or that at least for which Prof. Huxley appeals to her, seems to be that it is a mistake to suppose that the rationalistic movement of Germany has been defeated in the sphere of New Testament criticism, and she selects more particularly for her protest a recent statement in the "Quarterly Review" that this criticism, and particularly the movement led by Baur, is "an attack which has failed." The Quarterly Reviewer may be left to take care of himself; but I would only ask what is the evidence which Mrs. Ward adduces to the contrary? It may be summed up in two words—a prophecy and a romance. She does not adduce any evidence that the Tübingen school, which is the one we are chiefly concerned with, did not fail to establish its specific contentions; on the contrary, she says that "history protested," and she goes on to prophesy the success of other speculations which arose from that protest, concluding with an imaginary sketch, like that with which "Robert Elsmere" ends, of a "new Reformation preparing, struggling into utterance and being, all around us. . . . It is close upon us—it is prepared by all the forces of history and mind—its rise sooner or later is inevitable." This is prophesy, but it is not argument; and a little attention to Mrs. Ward's own statements will exhibit a very different picture. The Christian representative in her dialogue exclaims:

What is the whole history of German criticism but a series of brilliant failures, from Strauss downward? One theorist follows another—now Mark is uppermost as the Ur-Evangelist, now Matthew—now the Synoptics are sacrificed to St. John, now St. John to the Synoptics. Baur relegates one after another of the Epistles to the second century because his theory can not do with them in the first. Harnack tells you that Baur's theory is all wrong, and that Thessalonians and Philippians must go back again. Volkmar sweeps together Gospels and Epistles in a heap toward the middle of the second century as the earliest date for almost all of them; and Dr. Abbott, who, as we are told, has absorbed all the learning of the Germans, puts Mark before 70 A. D., Matthew just about 70 A. D., and Luke about 80 A. D.; Strauss's mythical theory is dead and buried by common consent; Baur's tendency theory is much the same; Renan will have none of the Tübingen school; Volkmar is already antiquated; and Pfleiderer's fancies are now in the order of the day.

A better statement could hardly be wanted of what is meant by an attack having failed, and now let the reader observe how Merriman in the dialogue meets it. Does he deny any of those allegations? Not one. "Very well," he says, "let us leave the matter there for the present. Suppose we go to the Old Testament"; and then he proceeds to dwell on the concessions made to the newest critical school of Germany by a few distinguished English divines at the last Church Congress. I must, indeed, dispute her representation of that rather one-sided debate as amounting to "a collapse of English orthodoxy," or as justifying her statement that "the Church of England practically gives its verdict" in favor, for instance, of the school which regards the Pentateuch or the Hexateuch as "the peculiar product of that Jewish religious movement which, beginning with Josiah, . . . yields its final fruits long after the exile." Not only has the Church of England given no such verdict, but German criticism has as yet given no such verdict. For example, in the introduction to the Old Testament by one of the first Hebrew scholars of Germany, Prof. Hermann Strack, contained in the valuable "Hand-book of the Theological Sciences," edited, with the assistance of several distinguished scholars, by Prof. Zöchler, I find, at page 215 of the third edition, published this year, the following brief summary of what, in Dr. Strack's opinion, is the result of the controversy so far:

> The future results of further labors in the field of Pentateuch criticism can not, of course, be predicted in particulars. But, in spite of the great assent which the view of Graf and Wellhausen at present enjoys, we are nevertheless convinced that it will not permanently lead to any essential alteration in the conception which has hitherto prevailed of the history of Israel, and in particular of the work of Moses. On the other hand, one result will certainly remain, that the Pentateuch was not composed by Moses himself, but was compiled by later editors from various original sources. . . . But the very variety of these sources may be applied in favor of the credibility of the Pentateuch.

In other words, it may be said that Dr. Strack regards it as established that "The Law of Moses" is a title of the same character as "The Psalms of David," the whole collection being denominated from its principal author. But he is convinced that the general conclusions of the prevalent school of Old Testament criticism, which involve an entire subversion of our present conceptions of Old Testament history, will not be maintained. In the face of this opinion, it does not seem presumptuous to express an apprehension that the younger school of Hebrew scholars in England, of whose concessions Mrs. Ward makes so much, have gone too far and too fast; and, at all events, it is clear from what Dr. Strack says —and I might quote also Delitzsch and Dillmann—that it is much too soon to assume that the school of whose conquests Mrs. Ward boasts is supreme. But, even supposing it were, what has this to do with the admitted and undoubted failures on the other side, in the field of New Testament criticism? If it be the fact, as Mrs. Ward does not deny, that not only Strauss's but Baur's theories and conclusions are now rejected; if it has been proved that Baur was entirely wrong in supposing the greater part of the New Testament books were late productions, written with a controversial purpose, what is the use of appealing to the alleged success of the German critics in another field? If Baur is confuted, he is confuted, and there is an end of his theories; though he may have been useful, as rash theorizers have often been, in stimulating investigation. In the same valuable hand-book of Dr. Zöchler's, already quoted, I find, under the "History of the Science of Introduction to the New Testament," the heading (page 15, vol. i, part 2), "Result of the controversy and end of the Tübingen school."

The Tübingen school (the writer concludes, p. 20) could not but fall as soon as its assumptions were recognized and given up. As Hilgenfeld confesses, "it went to an unjustifiable length, and inflicted too deep wounds on the Christian faith. . . . No enduring results in matters of substance have been produced by it."

Such is the judgment of an authoritative German hand-book on the writer to whom, in Merriman's opinion, "we owe all that we really *know* at the present moment about the New Testament," as though the Christian thought and life of eighteen hundred years had produced no knowledge on that subject!

In fact, Mrs. Ward's comparison seems to me to point in exactly the opposite direction:

> I say to myself (says her spokesman, p. 466) it has taken some thirty years for German critical science to conquer English opinion in the matter of the Old Testament. . . . How much longer will it take before we feel the victory of the same science . . . with regard to the history of Christian origins?

Remembering that the main movement of New Testament criticism in Germany dates not thirty, but more than fifty years back, and that thirty years ago Baur's school enjoyed the same applause in Germany as that of Wellhausen does now, does it not seem more in conformity with experience and with probability to anticipate that, as the Germans themselves, with longer experience, find they have been too hasty in following Baur, so with an equally long experience they may find they have been similarly too hasty in accepting Wellhausen? The fever of revolutionary criticism on the New Testament was at its height after thirty years, and the science has subsided into comparative health after twenty more. The fever of the revolutionary criticism of the Old Testament is now at its height, but the parallel suggests a similar return to a more sober and common-sense state of mind. The most famous name, in short, of German New Testament criticism is now associated with exploded theories;

and we are asked to shut our eyes to this undoubted fact because Mrs. Ward prophesies a different fate for the name now most famous in Old Testament criticism. I prefer the evidence of established fact to that of romantic prophecy.

But these observations suggest another consideration, which has a very important bearing on that general disparagement of English theology and theologians which Prof. Huxley expresses so offensively, and which Mrs. Ward encourages. She and Prof. Huxley talk as if German theology were all rationalistic and English theology alone conservative. Prof. Huxley invites his readers to study in Mrs. Ward's article

> the results of critical investigation as it is carried out among those theologians who are men of science and not mere counsel for creeds;

and he appeals to

> the works of scholars and theologians of the highest repute in the only two countries, Holland and Germany, in which, at the present time, professors of theology are to be found, whose tenure of their posts does not depend upon the results to which their inquiries lead them.

Well, passing over the insult to theologians in all other countries, what is the consequence of this freedom in Germany itself? Is it seen that all learned and distinguished theologians in that country are of the opinions of Prof. Huxley and Mrs. Ward? The quotations I have given will serve to illustrate the fact that the exact contrary is the case. If any one wants vigorous, learned, and satisfactory answers to Prof. Huxley and Mrs. Ward, Germany is the best place to which he can go for them. The professors and theologians of Germany who adhere substantially to the old Christian faith are at least as numerous, as distinguished, as learned, as laborious, as those who adhere to skeptical opinions. What is, by general consent, the most valuable and comprehensive work on Christian theology and church history which the last two generations of German divines have produced? Herzog's "Real-Encyclopädie für protestantische Theologie und Kirche," of which the second edition, in eighteen large volumes, was completed about a year ago. But it is edited and written in harmony with the general belief of Protestant Christians. Who have done the chief exegetical work of the last two generations? On the rationalistic side, though not exclusively so, is the "Kurzgefasstes exegetisches Handbuch," in which, however, at the present time, Dillmann represents an opposition to the view of Wellhausen respecting the Pentateuch; but on the other side we have Meyer on the New Testament—almost the standard work on the subject—Keil and Delitzsch on the Old Testament—and a great part of the New, Lange's immense "Bibelwerk," and the valuable "Kurzgefasster Kommentar" on the whole Scripture, including the Apocrypha, now in course of publication under the editorship of Profs. Strack and Zöchler. The Germans have more time for theoretical investigations than English theologians, who generally have a great deal of practical work to do; and German professors, in their numerous universities, in great measure live by them. But it was by German theologians that Baur was refuted; it is by German Hebraists like Strack that Wellhausen and Kuenen are now being best resisted. When Prof. Huxley and Mrs. Ward would leave an impression that, because German theological chairs are not shackled by articles like our own, therefore the best German thought and criticism is on the rationalistic side, they are conveying an entirely prejudiced representation of the facts. The effect of the German system is to make everything an open question; as though there were no such thing as a settled system of the spiritual universe, and no established facts in Christian history; and thus to enable any man of great ability with a skeptical turn to unsettle a generation and leave the edifice of belief to be built up again. But the edifice *is* built up again, and Germans take as large a part in rebuilding it as in undermining it. Because Prof. Huxley and Mrs. Ward can quote great German names on one side, let it not be forgotten that just as able German names can be quoted on the other side. Take, for instance, Harnack, to whom Mrs. Ward appeals, and whose "History of Dogmas" Prof. Huxley quotes. Harnack himself, in reviewing the history of his science, pays an honorable tribute to the late eminent divine, Thomasius, whose "History of Dogmas" has just been republished after his death, and who wrote in the devoutest spirit of the Lutheran communion. Of course, Harnack regards his point of view as narrow and unsatisfactory; but he adds that, "equally great are the valuable qualities of this work in particular, in regard of its exemplarily clear exposition, its eminent learning, and the author's living comprehension of religious problems." A man who studies the history of Christian theology in Harnack without reference to Thomasius will do no justice to his subject.

But, says Mrs. Ward, there is no real historical apprehension in the orthodox writers, whether of Germany or England, and the whole problem is one of "historical translation." Every statement, every apparent miracle, everything different from daily experience, must be translated into the language of that experience, or else we have not got real history. But this, it will be observed, under an ingenious disguise, is only the old method of assuming that nothing really miraculous can have happened, and that therefore everything which seems supernatural must be explained away into the natural. In other words, it is once more begging the whole question at issue. Mrs. Ward accuses orthodox writers of this fallacy; but it is really her own. Merriman is represented as saying that he learned from his Oxford teachers that

> it was imperatively right to endeavor to disentangle miracle from history, the marvelous from the real, in a document of the fourth, or third, or second century; . . . but the contents of the New Testament, however marvelous and however apparently akin to what surrounds them on either side, were to be treated from an entirely different point of view. In the one case there must be a desire on the part of the historian to discover the historical under the miraculous, . . . in the other case there must be a desire, a strong "affection," on the part of the theologian, toward proving the miraculous to be historical.

Mrs. Ward has entirely mistaken the point of view of Christian science. Certainly if any occurrence anywhere can be explained by natural causes, there is a strong presumption that it ought to be so explained; for, though a natural effect may be due in a given case to supernatural action, it is a fixed rule of philosophizing, according to Newton, that we should not assume unknown causes when known ones suffice. But the whole case of the Christian reasoner is that the records of the New Testament defy any attempt to explain them by natural causes. The German critics Hase, Strauss, Baur, Hausrath, Keim, all have made the attempt, and each, in the opinion of the others, and finally of Pfleiderer, has offered an insufficient solution of the problem. The case of the Christian is not that the evidence ought not to be explained naturally and translated into every-day experience, but that it can not be. But it is Mrs. Ward who assumes beforehand that simply because the "Life and Times of Jesus the Messiah," by that learned scholar and able writer, Dr. Edersheim, whose recent loss is so much to be deplored, does not "translate" all the Gospel narratives into natural occurrences, therefore it is essentially bad history. The story has been the same throughout. The whole German critical school, from the venerable Karl Hase—and, much as I differ from his conclusions, I can not mention without a tribute of respect and gratitude the name of that great scholar, the veteran of all these controversies, whose "Leben Jesu," published several years before Strauss was heard of, is still, perhaps, the most valuable book of reference on the subject—all, from that eminent man downward, have, by their own repeated confession, started from the assumption that the miraculous is impossible, and that the Gospels must, by some device or other, be so interpreted as to explain it away. "Affection" there is and ought to be in orthodox writers for venerable, profound, and consoling beliefs; but they start from no such invincible prejudice, and they are pledged by their principles to accept whatever interpretation may be really most consonant with the facts.

I have only one word to say, finally, in reply to Prof. Huxley. I am very glad to hear that he has always advocated the reading of the Bible and the diffusion of its study among the people; but I must say that he goes to work in a very strange way in order to promote this result. If he could succeed in persuading people that the Gospels are untrustworthy collections of legends, made by unknown authors, that St. Paul's epistles were the writings of "a strange man," who had no sound capacity for judging of evidence, or, with Mrs. Ward's friends, that the Pentateuch is a late forgery of Jewish scribes, I do not think the people at large would be likely to follow his well-meant exhortations. But I venture to remind him that the English Church has anticipated his anxiety in this matter. Three hundred years ago, by one of the greatest strokes of real government ever exhibited, the public reading of the whole Bible was imposed upon Englishmen; and by the public reading of the lessons on Sunday alone, the chief portions of the Bible, from first to last, have become stamped upon the minds of English-speaking people in a degree in which, as the Germans themselves acknowledge,* they are far behind us. He has too much reason for his lament over the melancholy spectacle presented by the intestine quarrels of churchmen over matters of mere ceremonial. But when he argues from this that the clergy of our day "can have but little sympathy with the old evangelical doctrine of the 'open Bible,'" he might have remembered that our own generation of English divines has, by the labor of years, endeavored at all events, whether successfully or not, to place the most correct version possible of the Holy Scriptures in the hands of the English people. I agree with him most cordially in seeing in the wide diffusion and the unprejudiced study of that sacred volume the best security for "true religion and sound learning." It is in the open Bible of England, in the general familiarity of all classes of Englishmen and English-women with it that the chief obstacle has been found to the spread of the

---

* See the preface to Riehm's "Handwörterbuch."

fantastic critical theories by which he is fascinated ; and, instead of Englishmen translating the Bible into the language of their natural experiences, it will in the future, as in the past, translate them and their experiences into a higher and a supernatural region.

VII.
AN EXPLANATION TO PROF. HUXLEY.

By W. C. MAGEE,
BISHOP OF PETERBOROUGH.

IN the February number of this review Prof. Huxley put into the mouth of Mr. Frederic Harrison the following sentence: " In his [the agnostic's] place, as a sort of navvy leveling the ground and cleansing it of such poor stuff as Christianity, he is a useful creature who deserves patting on the back—on condition that he does not venture beyond his last." The construction which I put upon these words—and of which I still think them quite capable—was that the professor meant to represent Mr. Harrison and himself as agreed upon the proper work of the agnostic, and as differing only as to whether he might or might not " venture beyond" that. On this supposition, my inference that he had called Christianity " sorry," or, as I ought to have said, " poor stuff" (the terms are, of of course, equivalent), would have been perfectly correct.

On re-reading the sentence in question, however, in connection with its context, I see that it may more correctly be regarded as altogether ironical; and this from the professor's implied denial in his last article of the correctness of my version, I conclude that he intended it to be. I accordingly at once withdraw my statement, and express my regret for having made it. May I plead, however, as some excuse for my mistake, that this picture of himself when engaged in his agnostic labors is so wonderfully accurate and life-like that I might almost be pardoned for taking for a portrait what was only meant for a caricature, or for supposing that he had expressed in so many words the contempt which displays itself in so many of his utterances respecting the Christian faith?

Nevertheless I gladly admit that the particular expression I had ascribed to him is not to be reckoned among the already too numerous illustrations of what I had described as his "readiness to say unpleasant," and —after reading his last article—I must add, offensive "things."

With this explanation and apology I take my leave of the professor and of our small personal dispute—small, indeed, beside the infinitely graver and greater issues raised in his reply to the unanswered arguments of Dr. Wace.

I do not care to distract the attention of the public from these to a fencing-match with foils between Prof. Huxley and myself. In sight of Gethsemane and Calvary such a fencing-match seems to me out of place.

VIII.

THE VALUE OF WITNESS TO THE MIRACULOUS.

By Prof. THOMAS H. HUXLEY.

CHARLES, or more properly, Karl, King of the Franks, consecrated Roman emperor in St. Peter's, on Christmas day, A. D. 800, and known to posterity as the Great (chiefly by his agglutinative Gallicized denomination of Charlemagne), was a man great in all ways, physically and mentally. Within a couple of centuries after his death Charlemagne became the center of innumerable legends; and the myth-making process does not seem to have been sensibly interfered with by the existence of sober and truthful histories of the emperor and of the times which immediately preceded and followed his reign, by a contemporary writer who occupied a high and confidential position in his court, and in that of his successor. This was one Eginhard, or Einhard, who appears to have been born about A. D. 770, and spent his youth at the court, being educated along with Charles's sons. There is excellent contemporary testimony not only to Eginhard's existence, but to his abilities, and to the place which he occupied in the circle of the intimate friends of the great ruler whose life he subsequently wrote. In fact, there is as good evidence of Eginhard's existence, of his official position, and of his being the author of the chief works attributed to him, as can reasonably be expected in the case of a man who lived more than a thousand years ago, and was neither a great king nor a great warrior. These works are—1. "The Life of the Emperor Karl." 2. " The Annals of the Franks." 3. "Letters." 4. " The History of the Translation of the Blessed Martyrs of Christ, SS. Marcellinus and Petrus."

It is to the last, as one of the most singular and interesting records of the period during which the Roman world passed into that of the middle ages, that I wish to direct attention.* It was written in the ninth century, somewhere, apparently, about the year 830, when Eginhard, ailing in health and weary of political life, had withdrawn to the monastery of Seligenstadt, of which he was the founder. A manuscript copy of the work, made in the tenth century, and once the property of the monastery of St. Bavon on the Scheldt, of which Eginhard was abbot, is still extant, and there is no reason to believe that, in this copy, the original has been in any way interpolated or otherwise tampered with. The main features of the strange story contained in the "Historia Translationis" are set forth in the following pages, in which, in regard to all matters of importance, I shall adhere as closely as possible to Eginhard's own words:

While I was still at court, busied with secular affairs, I often thought of the leisure which I hoped one day to enjoy in a solitary place, far away from the crowd, with which the liberality of Prince Louis, whom I then served, had provided me. This place is

---

* My citations are made from Teulet's "Einhardi omnia quæ extant opera," Paris, 1840–1843, which contains a biography of the author, a history of the text, with translations into French, and many valuable annotations.

situated in that part of Germany which lies between the Neckar and the Main,* and is nowadays called the Odenwald by those who live in and about it. And here having built, according to my capacity and resources, not only houses and permanent dwellings, but also a basilica fitted for the performance of divine service and of no mean style of construction, I began to think to what saint or martyr I could best dedicate it. A good deal of time had passed while my thoughts fluctuated about this matter, when it happened that a certain deacon of the Roman Church, named Deusdona, arrived at the court for the purpose of seeking the favor of the king in some affairs in which he was interested. He remained some time; and then having transacted his business, he was about to return to Rome, when one day, moved by courtesy to a stranger, we invited him to a modest refection; and while talking of many things at table, mention was made of the translation of the body of the blessed Sebastian,† and of the neglected tombs of the martyrs, of which there is such a prodigious number at Rome; and the conversation having turned toward the dedication of our new basilica, I began to inquire how it might be possible for me to obtain some of the true relics of the saints which rest at Rome. He at first hesitated, and declared that he did not know how that could be done. But observing that I was both anxious and curious about the subject, he promised to give me an answer some other day.

When I returned to the question, some time afterward, he immediately drew from his bosom a paper, which he begged me to read when I was alone, and to tell him what I was disposed to think of that which was therein stated. I took the paper, and, as he desired, read it alone and in secret. (Cap. i, 2, 3.)

I shall have occasion to return to Deacon Deusdona's conditions, and to what happened after Eginhard's acceptance of them. Suffice it, for the present, to say that Eginhard's notary, Ratleicus (Ratleig), was dispatched to Rome and succeeded in securing two bodies, supposed to

---

* At present included in the duchies of Hesse-Darmstadt and Baden.

† This took place in the year 826 A. D. The relics were brought from Rome and deposited in the Church of St. Medardus at Soissons.

be those of the holy martyrs Marcellinus and Petrus; and when he had got as far on his homeward journey as the Burgundian town of Solothurn or Soleure,* notary Ratleig dispatched to his master, at St. Bavon, a letter announcing the success of his mission.

As soon as by reading it I was assured of the arrival of the saints, I dispatched a confidential messenger to Maestricht, to gather together priests, other clerics, and also laymen, to go out to meet the coming saints as speedily as possible. And he and his companions, having lost no time, after a few days met those who had charge of the saints at Solothurn. Joined with them, and with a vast crowd of people who gathered from all parts, singing hymns, and amid great and universal rejoicings, they traveled quickly to the city of Argentoratum, which is now called Strasburg. Thence embarking on the Rhine they came to the place called Portus,† and landing on the east bank of the river, at the fifth station, thence they arrived at Michilinstadt, ‡ accompanied by an immense multitude, praising God. This place is in that forest of Germany which in modern times is called the Odenwald, and about six leagues from the Main. And here, having found a basilica recently built by me, but not yet consecrated, they carried the sacred remains into it and deposited them therein, as if it were to be their final resting-place. As soon as all this was reported to me, I traveled thither as quickly as I could. (Cap ii, 14.)

Three days after Eginhard's arrival began the series of wonderful events which he narrates, and for which we have his personal guarantee. The first thing that he notices is the dream of a servant of Ratleig the notary, who, being set to watch the holy relics in the church after vespers, went to sleep, and during his slumbers had a vision of two pigeons, one white and one gray and white,

---

* Now included in western Switzerland.

† Probably, according to Teulet, the present Sandhofer-fahrt, a little below the embouchure of the Neckar.

‡ The present Michilstadt, thirty miles northeast of Heidelberg.

which came and sat upon the bier over the relics; while, at the same time, a voice ordered the man to tell his master that the holy martyrs had chosen another resting-place and desired to be transported thither without delay.

Unfortunately, the saints seem to have forgotten to mention where they wished to go, and, with the most anxious desire to gratify their smallest wishes, Eginhard was naturally greatly perplexed what to do. While in this state of mind, he was one day contemplating his "great and wonderful treasure, more precious than all the gold in the world," when it struck him that the chest in which the relics were contained was quite unworthy of its contents; and after vespers he gave orders to one of the sacristans to take the measure of the chest in order that a more fitting shrine might be constructed. The man, having lighted a wax candle and raised the pall which covered the relics, in order to carry out his master's orders, was astonished and terrified to observe that the chest was covered with a blood-like exudation (*loculum mirum in modum humore sanguineo undique distillantem*), and at once sent a message to Eginhard.

> Then I and those priests who accompanied me beheld this stupendous miracle, worthy of all admiration. For just as when it is going to rain, pillars and slabs and marble images exude moisture, and, as it were, sweat, so the chest which contained the most sacred relics was found moist with the blood exuding on all sides. (Cap. ii, 16.)

Three days' fast was ordained in order that the meaning of the portent might be ascertained. All that happened, however, was that at the end of that time the "blood," which had been exuding in drops all the while, dried up. Eginhard is careful to say that the liquid " had a saline taste, something like that of tears, and was thin as water, though of the color of true blood," and he clearly thinks this satisfactory evidence that it was blood.

The same night another servant had a vision, in which still more imperative orders for the removal of the relics were given; and, from that time forth, "not a single night passed without one, two, or even three of our companions receiving revelations in dreams that the bodies of the saints were to be transferred from that place to another." At last a priest, Hildfrid, saw, in a dream, a venerable white-haired man in a priest's vestments, who bitterly reproached Eginhard for not obeying the repeated orders of the saints, and upon this the journey was commenced. Why Eginhard delayed obedience to these repeated visions so long does not appear. He does not say so in so many words, but the general tenor of the narrative leads one to suppose that Mulinheim (afterward Seligenstadt) is the "solitary place" in which he had built the church which awaited dedication. In that case all the people about him would know that he desired that the saints should go there. If a glimmering of secular sense led him to be a little suspicious about the real cause of the unanimity of the visionary beings who manifested themselves to his *entourage* in favor of moving on, he does not say so.

At the end of the first day's journey the precious relics were deposited in the church of St. Martin, in the village of Ostheim. Hither a paralytic nun (*sanctimonialis quædam paralytica*) of the name of Ruodlang was brought in a car by her friends and relatives from a monastery a league off. She spent the night watching and praying by the bier of the saints; "and health returning to all her members, on the morrow she went back to her place whence she came, on her feet, nobody supporting her, or in any way giving her assistance." (Cap. ii, 19).

On the second day the relics were carried to Upper Mulinheim, and finally, in accordance with the orders of the martyrs, deposited in the church of that place, which was therefore renamed Seligenstadt. Here, Daniel, a beggar boy of fifteen, and so bent that "he could not look at the sky without lying on his back," collapsed and fell down during the celebration of the mass. "Thus he lay a long time, as if asleep, and all his limbs straightening and his flesh strengthening (*recepta firmitate nervorum*), he arose before our eyes, quite well." (Cap. ii, 20.)

Some time afterward an old man entered the church on his hands and knees, being unable to use his limbs properly:

He, in the presence of all of us, by the power of God and the merits of the blessed martyrs, in the same hour in which he entered was so perfectly cured that he walked without so much as a stick. And he said that, though he had been deaf for five years, his deafness had ceased along with the palsy. (Cap. iii, 33.)

Eginhard was now obliged to return to the court at Aix-la-Chapelle, where his duties kept him through the winter; and he is careful to point out that the later miracles which he proceeds to speak of are known to him only at second hand. But, as he naturally observes, having seen such wonderful events with his own eyes, why should he doubt similar narrations when they are received from trustworthy sources?

Wonderful stories these are indeed, but as they are, for the most part, of the same general character as those already recounted, they may be passed over. There is, however, an account of a possessed maiden which is worth attention.

This is set forth in a memoir, the principal contents of which are the speeches of a demon who declared that he possessed the singular appellation of "Wiggo," and revealed himself in the presence of many witnesses, before the altar, close to the relics of the blessed martyrs. It is noteworthy that the revelations appear to have been made in the shape of replies to the questions of the exorcising priest, and there is no means of judging how far the answers are really only the questions to which the patient replied yes or no.

The possessed girl, about sixteen years of age, was brought by her parents to the basilica of the martyrs.

When she approached the tomb containing the sacred bodies, the priest, according to custom, read the formula of exorcism over her head. When he began to ask how and when the demon had entered her, she answered, not in the tongue of the barbarians, which alone the girl knew, but in the Roman tongue. And when the priest was astonished and asked how she came to know Latin, when her parents, who stood by, were wholly ignorant of it, "Thou hast never seen my parents," was the reply. To this the priest, "Whence art thou, then, if these are not thy parents?" And the demon, by the mouth of the girl, "I am a follower and disciple of Satan, and for a long time I was gatekeeper (janitor) in hell; but, for some years, along with eleven companions, I have ravaged the kingdom of the Franks." (Cap. v, 49.)

He then goes on to tell how they blasted the crops and scattered pestilence among beasts and men, because of the prevalent wickedness of the people.*

The enumeration of all these iniquities, in oratorical style, takes up a whole octavo page; and at the end it is stated, "All these things the demon spoke in Latin by the mouth of the girl."

---

* In the middle ages one of the most favorite accusations against witches was that they committed just these enormities.

And when the priest imperatively ordered him to come out, "I shall go," said he, "not in obedience to you, but on account of the power of the saints, who do not allow me to remain any longer." And, having said this, he threw the girl down on the floor and there compelled her to lie prostrate for a time, as though she slumbered. After a little while, however, he going away, the girl, by the power of Christ and the merits of the blessed martyrs, as it were awakening from sleep, rose up quite well, to the astonishment of all present; nor after the demon had gone out was she able to speak Latin: so that it was plain enough that it was not she who had spoken in that tongue, but the demon by her mouth. (Cap. v, 51.)

If the "Historia Translationis" contained nothing more than has been, at present, laid before the reader, disbelief in the miracles of which it gives so precise and full a record might well be regarded as hyper-skepticism. It might fairly be said: "Here you have a man, whose high character, acute intelligence, and large instruction are certified by eminent contemporaries; a man who stood high in the confidence of one of the greatest rulers of any age, and whose other works prove him to be an accurate and judicious narrator of ordinary events. This man tells you, in language which bears the stamp of sincerity, of things which happened within his own knowledge, or within that of persons in whose veracity he has entire confidence, while he appeals to his sovereign and the court as witnesses of others; what possible ground can there be for disbelieving him?"

Well, it is hard upon Eginhard to say so, but it is exactly the honesty and sincerity of the man which are his undoing as a witness to the miraculous. He himself makes it quite obvious that when his profound piety comes on the stage, his good sense and even his perception of right and wrong make their exit. Let us go back to the point at which we left him, secretly perusing the letter of Deacon Deusdona. As he tells us, its contents were—

that he (the deacon) had many relics of saints at home, and that he would give them to me if I would furnish him with the means of returning to Rome; he had observed that I had two mules, and, if I would let him have one of them and would dispatch with him a confidential servant to take charge of the relics, he would at once send them to me. This plausibly expressed proposition pleased me, and I made up my mind to test the value of the somewhat ambiguous promise at once;* so giving him the mule and money for his journey I ordered my notary Ratleig (who already desired to go to Rome to offer his devotions there) to go with him. Therefore, having left Aix-la-Chapelle (where the emperor and his court resided at the time) they came to Soissons. Here they spoke with Hildoin, abbot of the monastery of St. Medardus, because the said deacon had assured him that he had the means of placing in his possession the body of the blessed Tiburtius the martyr. Attracted by which promises he (Hildoin) sent with them a certain priest, Hunus by name, a sharp man (*hominem callidum*), whom he ordered to receive and bring back the body of the martyr in question. And so, resuming their journey, they proceeded to Rome as fast as they could. (Cap. i, 3.)

Unfortunately, a servant of the notary, one Reginbald, fell ill of a tertian fever, and impeded the progress of the party. However, this piece of adversity had its sweet uses; for, three days before they reached Rome, Reginbald had a vision. Somebody habited as a deacon appeared to him and asked why his master was in such a hurry to get to Rome; and when Reginbald explained their business, this visionary deacon, who seems to have taken the measure of his brother in the flesh with some accuracy, told him not by any means to expect that Dues-

---

* It is pretty clear that Eginhard had his doubts about the deacon, whose pledge he qualifies as *sponsiones incertæ*. But, to be sure, he wrote after events which fully justified skepticism.

dona would fulfill his promises. Moreover, taking the servant by the hand, he led him to the top of a high mountain, and, showing him Rome (where the man had never been), pointed out a church, adding: "Tell Ratleig the thing he wants is hidden there; let him get it as quickly as he can and go back to his master"; and, by way of a sign that the order was authoritative, the servant was promised that from that time forth his fever should disappear. And as the fever did vanish to return no more, the faith of Eginhard's people in Deacon Deusdona naturally vanished with it (*et fidem diaconi promissis non haberent*). Nevertheless, they put up at the deacon's house near St. Peter da Vincula. But time went on and no relics made their appearance, while the notary and the priest were put off with all sorts of excuses—the brother to whom the relics had been confided was gone to Beneventum and not expected back for some time, and so on —until Ratleig and Hunus began to despair, and were minded to return, *infecto negotio*.

But my notary, calling to mind his servant's dream, proposed to his companion that they should go to the cemetery which their host had talked about without him. So, having found and hired a guide, they went in the first place to the basilica of the blessed Tiburtius in the Via Labicana, about three thousand paces from the town, and cautiously and carefully inspected the tomb of that martyr, in order to discover whether it could be opened without any one being the wiser. Then they descended into the adjoining crypt, in which the bodies of the blessed martyrs of Christ, Marcellinus and Petrus, were buried; and, having made out the nature of their tomb, they went away thinking their host would not know what they had been about. But things fell out differently from what they had imagined. (Cap. i, 7.)

In fact, Deacon Duesdona, who doubtless kept an eye on his guests, knew all about their manœuvres and made haste to offer his services, in order that, "with the help of God" (*si Deus votis eorum favere dignaretur*), they should all work together. The deacon was evidently alarmed lest they should succeed without *his* help.

So, by way of preparation for the contemplated *vol avec effraction*, they fasted three days; and then, at night, without being seen, they betook themselves to the basilica of St. Tiburtius, and tried to break open the altar erected over his remains. But the marble proving too solid, they descended to the crypt, and "having invoked our Lord Jesus Christ and adored the holy martyrs," they proceeded to prise off the stone which covered the tomb, and thereby exposed the body of the most sacred martyr Marcellinus, " whose head rested on a marble tablet on which his name was inscribed." The body was taken up with the greatest veneration, wrapped in a rich covering, and given over to the keeping of the deacon and his brother Lunison, while the stone was replaced with such care that no sign of the theft remained.

As sacrilegious proceedings of this kind were punishable with death by the Roman law, it seems not unnatural that Deacon Deusdona should have become uneasy, and have urged Ratleig to be satisfied with what he had got and be off with his spoils. But the notary having thus cleverly captured the blessed Marcellinus, thought it a pity he should be parted from the blessed Petrus, side by side with whom he had rested for five hundred years and more in the same sepulchre (as Eginhard pathetically observes); and the pious man could neither eat, drink, nor sleep, until he had compassed his desire to reunite the saintly colleagues. This time, apparently in consequence of Duesdona's opposition to any further resurrectionist doings, he took counsel with a Greek monk, one Basil, and, accompanied by Hunus, but saying nothing to Deusdona, they committed another sacrilegious burglary, securing this time, not only the body of the blessed Petrus, but a quantity of dust, which they agreed the priest should take, and tell his employer that it was the remains of the blessed Tiburtius.

How Duesdona was "squared," and what he got for his not very valuable complicity in these transactions, does not appear. But at last the relics were sent off in charge of Lunison, the brother of Duesdona, and the priest Hunus, as far as Pavia, while Ratleig stopped behind for a week to see if the robbery was discovered, and, presumably, to act as a blind if any hue and cry were raised. But, as everything remained quiet, the notary betook himself to Pavia, where he found Lunison and Hunus awaiting his arrival. The notary's opinion of the character of his worthy colleagues, however, may be gathered from the fact that, having persuaded them to set out in advance along a road which he told them he was about to take, he immediately adopted another route, and, traveling by way of St. Maurice and the Lake of Geneva, eventually reached Soleure.

Eginhard tells all this story with the most *naïve* air of unconsciousness that there is anything remarkable about an abbot, and a high officer of state to boot, being an accessory both before and after the fact to a most gross and scandalous act of sacrilegious and burglarious robbery. And an amusing sequel to the story proves that, where relics were concerned, his friend Hildoin, another high ecclesiastical dignitary, was even less scrupulous than himself.

On going to the palace early one morning, after the

saints were safely bestowed at Seligenstadt, he found Hildoin waiting for an audience in the emperor's antechamber, and began to talk to him about the miracle of the bloody exudation. In the course of conversation, Eginhard happened to allude to the remarkable fineness of the garment of the blessed Marcellinus. Whereupon Abbot Hildoin replied (to Eginhard's stupefaction) that his observation was quite correct. Much astonished at this remark from a person who was supposed not to have seen the relics, Eginhard asked him how he knew that. Upon this, Hildoin saw that he had better make a clean breast of it, and he told the following story, which he had received from his priestly agent, Hunus: While Hunus and Lunison were at Pavia, waiting for Eginhard's notary, Hunus (according to his own account) had robbed the robbers. The relics were placed in a church, and a number of laymen and clerics, of whom Hunus was one, undertook to keep watch over them. One night, however, all the watchers, save the wide-awake Hunus, went to sleep; and then, according to the story which this "sharp" ecclesiastic foisted upon his patron—

it was borne in upon his mind that there must be some great reason why all the people, except himself, had suddenly become somnolent; and, determining to avail himself of the opportunity thus offered (*oblata occasione utendum*), he rose and, having lighted a candle, silently approached the chests. Then, having burned through the threads of the seals with the flame of the candle, he quickly opened the chests, which had no locks;* and, taking out portions of each of the bodies which were thus exposed, he closed the chests and connected the burned ends of the threads with the seals again, so that they appeared not to have been touched; and, no one having seen him, he returned to his place. (Cap. iii, 23.)

---

* The words are *scrinia sine clave*, which seem to mean "having no key." But the circumstances forbid the idea of breaking open.

Hildoin went on to tell Eginhard that Hunus at first declared to him that these purloined relics belonged to St. Tiburtius; but afterward confessed, as a great secret, how he had come by them, and he wound up his discourse thus:

> They have a place of honor beside St. Medardus, where they are worshiped with great veneration by all the people; but whether we may keep them or not is for your judgment. (Cap. iii, 23.)

Poor Eginhard was thrown into a state of great perturbation of mind by this revelation. An acquaintance of his had recently told him of a rumor that was spread about, that Hunus had contrived to abstract *all* the remains of SS. Marcellinus and Petrus while Eginhard's agents were in a drunken sleep; and that, while the real relics were in Abbot Hildoin's hands at St. Medardus, the shrine at Seligenstadt contained nothing but a little dust. Though greatly annoyed by this "execrable rumor, spread everywhere by the subtlety of the devil," Eginhard had doubtless comforted himself by his supposed knowledge of its falsity, and he only now discovered how considerable a foundation there was for the scandal. There was nothing for it but to insist upon the return of the stolen treasures. One would have thought that the holy man, who had admitted himself to be knowingly a receiver of stolen goods, would have made instant restitution and begged only for absolution. But Eginhard intimates that he had very great difficulty in getting his brother abbot to see that even restitution was necessary.

Hildoin's proceedings were not of such nature as to lead any one to place implicit trust in anything he might say; still less had his agent, priest Hunus, established much claim to confidence; and it is not surprising that

Eginhard should have lost no time in summoning his notary and Lunison to his presence, in order that he might hear what they had to say about the business. They, however, at once protested that priest Hunus's story was a parcel of lies, and that after the relics left Rome no one had any opportunity of meddling with them. Moreover, Lunison, throwing himself at Eginhard's feet, confessed with many tears what actually took place. It will be remembered that, after the body of St. Marcellinus was abstracted from its tomb, Ratleig deposited it in the house of Deusdona, in charge of the latter's brother, Lunison. But Hunus, being very much disappointed that he could not get hold of the body of St. Tiburtius, and afraid to go back to his abbot empty-handed, bribed Lunison with four pieces of gold and five of silver to give him access to the chest. This Lunison did, and Hunus helped himself to as much as would fill a gallon measure (*vas sextarii mensuram*) of the sacred remains. Eginhard's indignation at the "rapine" of this "nequissimus nebulo" is exquisitely droll. It would appear that the adage about the receiver being as bad as the thief was not current in the ninth century.

Let us now briefly sum up the history of the acquisition of the relics. Eginhard makes a contract with Deusdona for the delivery of certain relics which the latter says he possesses. Eginhard makes no inquiry how he came by them; otherwise, the transaction is innocent enough.

Deusdona turns out to be a swindler, and has no relics. Thereupon Eginhard's agent, after due fasting and prayer, breaks open the tombs and helps himself.

Eginhard discovers, by the self-betrayal of his brother

abbot, Hildoin, that portions of his relics have been stolen and conveyed to the latter. With much ado he succeeds in getting them back.

Hildoin's agent, Hunus, in delivering these stolen goods to him, at first declared they were the relics of St. Tiburtius, which Hildoin desired him to obtain; but afterward invented a story of their being the product of a theft, which the providential drowsiness of his companions enabled him to perpetrate from the relics which Hildoin well knew were the property of his friend.

Lunison, on the contrary, swears that all this story is false, and that he himself was bribed by Hunus to allow him to steal what he pleased from the property confided to his own and his brother's care by their guest Ratleig. And the honest notary himself seems to have no hesitation about lying and stealing to any extent, where the acquisition of relics is the object in view.

For a parallel to these transactions one must read a police report of the doings of a "long firm" or of a set of horse-coupers; yet Eginhard seems to be aware of nothing, but that he has been rather badly used by his friend Hildoin and the "nequissimus nebulo" Hunus.

It is not easy for a modern Protestant, still less for any one who has the least tincture of scientific culture, whether physical or historical, to picture to himself the state of mind of a man of the ninth century, however cultivated, enlightened, and sincere he may have been. His deepest convictions, his most cherished hopes, were bound up in the belief of the miraculous. Life was a constant battle between saints and demons for the possession of the souls of men. The most superstitious among our modern countrymen turn to supernatural agencies only when natural causes seem insufficient; to Eginhard and his friends the supernatural was the rule, and the sufficiency of natural causes was allowed only when there was nothing to suggest others.

Moreover, it must be recollected that the possession of miracle-working relics was greatly coveted, not only on high but on very low grounds. To a man like Eginhard, the mere satisfaction of the religious sentiment was obviously a powerful attraction. But, more than this, the possession of such a treasure was an immense practical advantage. If the saints were duly flattered and worshiped, there was no telling what benefits might result from their interposition on your behalf. For physical evils, access to the shrine was like the grant of the use of a universal pill and ointment manufactury; and pilgrimages thereto might suffice to cleanse the performers from any amount of sin. A letter to Lupus, subsequently abbot of Ferrara, written while Eginhard was smarting under the grief caused by the loss of his much-loved wife Imma, affords a striking insight into the current view of the relation between the glorified saints and their worshipers. The writer shows that he is anything but satisfied with the way in which he has been treated by the blessed martyrs whose remains he has taken such pains to "convey" to Seligenstadt, and to honor there as they would never have been honored in their Roman obscurity:

> It is an aggravation of my grief and a reopening of my wound, that our vows have been of no avail, and that the faith which we placed in the merits and intervention of the martyrs has been utterly disappointed.

We may admit, then, without impeachment of Eginhard's sincerity, or of his honor under all ordinary circumstances, that when piety, self-interest, the glory of the Church in general, and that of the church at Seligenstadt in particular, all pulled one way, even the work-a-day principles of morality were disregarded, and *a fortiori*, anything like proper investigation of the reality of the alleged miracles was thrown to the winds.

And if this was the condition of mind of such a man as Eginhard, what is it not legitimate to suppose may have been that of Deacon Deusdona, Lunison, Hunus, and company, thieves and cheats by their own confession; or of the probably hysterical nun; or of the professional beggars, for whose incapacity to walk and straighten themselves there is no guarantee but their own? Who is to make sure that the exorcist of the demon Wiggo was not just such another priest as Hunus; and is it not at least possible, when Eginhard's servants dreamed night after night in such a curiously coincident fashion, that a careful inquirer might have found they were very anxious to please their master?

Quite apart from deliberate and conscious fraud (which is a rarer thing than is often supposed), people whose mythopœic faculty is once stirred are capable of saying the thing that is not, and of acting as they should not, to an extent which is hardly imaginable by persons who are not so easily affected by the contagion of blind faith. There is no falsity so gross that honest men, and, still more, virtuous women, anxious to promote a good cause, will not lend themselves to it without any clear consciousness of the moral bearings of what they are doing.

The cases of miraculously effected cures of which Eginhard is ocular witness appear to belong to classes of disease in which malingering is possible or hysteria presumable. Without modern means of diagnosis, the names given to them are quite worthless. One "miracle," however, in which the patient was cured by the mere sight of the church in which the relics of the blessed martyrs lay, is an unmistakable case of dislocation of the lower jaw in a woman; and it is obvious that, as not unfrequently happens in such accidents to weakly subjects, the jaw slipped suddenly back into place, perhaps in consequence of a jolt, as the woman rode toward the church. (Cap. v, 53).*

There is also a good deal said about a very questionable blind man—one Albricus (Alberich?)—who, having been cured, not of his blindness, but of another disease under which he labored, took up his quarters at Seligenstadt, and came out as a prophet, inspired by the archangel Gabriel. Eginhard intimates that his prophecies were fulfilled; but, as he does not state exactly what they were or how they were accomplished, the statement must be accepted with much caution. It is obvious that he was not the man to hesitate to "case" a prophecy until it fitted, if the credit of the shrine of his favorite saints could be increased by such a procedure. There is no impeachment of his honor in the supposition. The logic of the matter is quite simple, if somewhat sophistical. The holiness of the church of the martyrs guarantees the reality of the appearance of the archangel Gabriel there, and what the archangel says must be true. Therefore, if anything seem to be wrong, that must be the mistake of the transmitter; and, in justice to the archangel, it must be suppressed or set right. This sort of "reconciliation" is not unknown in quite modern times, and among people

---

* Eginhard speaks with lofty contempt of the "*vana ac superstitiosa præsumptio*" of the poor woman's companions in trying to alleviate her sufferings with "herbs and frivolous incantations." Vain enough, no doubt, but the "mulierculæ" might have returned the epithet "superstitious" with interest.

who would be very much shocked to be compared with a "benighted papist" of the ninth century.

The readers of this review are, I imagine, very largely composed of people who would be shocked to be regarded as anything but enlightened Protestants. It is not unlikely that those of them who have accompanied me thus far may be disposed to say: "Well, this is all very amusing as a story; but what is the practical interest of it? We are not likely to believe in the miracles worked by the spolia of SS. Marcellinus and Petrus, or by those of any other saints in the Roman calendar."

The practical interest is this: If you do not believe in these miracles, recounted by a witness whose character and competency are firmly established, whose sincerity can not be doubted, and who appeals to his sovereign and other contemporaries as witnesses of the truth of what he says, in a document of which a MS. copy exists, probably dating within a century of the author's death, why do you profess to believe in stories of a like character which are found in documents, of the dates and of the authorship of which nothing is certainly determined, and no known copies of which come within two or three centuries of the events they record? If it be true that the four Gospels and the Acts were written by Matthew, Mark, Luke, and John, all that we know of these persons comes to nothing in comparison with our knowledge of Eginhard; and not only is there no proof that the traditional authors of these works wrote them, but very strong reasons to the contrary may be alleged. If, therefore, you refuse to believe that "Wiggo" was cast out of the possessed girl on Eginhard's authority, with what justice can you profess to believe that the legion of devils were cast out of the man among the tombs of the Gadarenes?

And if, on the other hand, you accept Eginhard's evidence, why do you laugh at the supposed efficacy of relics and the saint-worship of the modern Romanists? It can not be pretended, in the face of all evidence, that the Jews of the year 30, or thereabout, were less imbued with the belief in the supernatural than were the Franks of the year A. D. 800. The same influences were at work in each case, and it is only reasonable to suppose that the results were the same. If the evidence of Eginhard is insufficient to lead reasonable men to believe in the miracles he relates, *a fortiori* the evidence afforded by the Gospels and the Acts must be so.*

But it may be said that no serious critic denies the genuineness of the four great Pauline Epistles—Galatians, First and Second Corinthians, and Romans—and that, in three out of these four, Paul lays claim to the power of working miracles.† Must we suppose, therefore, that the Apostle to the Gentiles has stated that which is false? But to how much does this so-called claim amount? It may mean much or little. Paul nowhere tells us what he did in this direction, and, in his sore need to justify his assumption of apostleship against the sneers of his enemies, it is hardly likely that, if he had any very striking cases to bring forward, he would have neglected evidence so well calculated to put them to shame.

And, without the slightest impeachment of Paul's veracity, we must further remember that his strongly marked mental characteristics, displayed in unmistakable

---

* Of course, there is nothing new in this argument; but it does not grow weaker by age. And the case of Eginhard is far more instructive than that of Augustine, because the former has so very frankly, though incidentally, revealed to us not only his own mental and moral habits, but those of the people about him.

† See 1 Cor. xii, 10–28; 2 Cor. vi, 12; Rom. xv, 19.

fashion in these Epistles, are anything but those which would justify us in regarding him as a critical witness respecting matters of fact, or as a trustworthy interpreter of their significance. When a man testifies to a miracle, he not only states a fact, but he adds an interpretation of the fact. We may admit his evidence as to the former, and yet think his opinion as to the latter worthless. If Eginhard's calm and objective narrative of the historical events of his time is no guarantee for the soundness of his judgment where the supernatural is concerned, the fervid rhetoric of the Apostle of the Gentiles, his absolute confidence in the "inner light," and the extraordinary conceptions of the nature and requirements of logical proof which he betrays in page after page of his Epistles, afford still less security.

There is a comparative modern man who shared to the full Paul's trust in the "inner light," and who, though widely different from the fiery evangelist of Tarsus in various obvious particulars, yet, if I am not mistaken, shares his deepest characteristics. I speak of George Fox, who separated himself from the current Protestantism of England in the seventeenth century as Paul separated himself from the Judaism of the first century, at the bidding of the "inner light"—who went through persecutions as serious as those which Paul enumerates, who was beaten, stoned, cast out for dead, imprisoned nine times, sometimes for long periods, in perils on land and perils at sea. George Fox was an even more widely traveled missionary, and his success in founding congregations, and his energy in visiting them, not merely in Great Britain and Ireland and the West India Islands, but on the continent of Europe and that of North America, was no less remarkable. A few years after Fox began to preach there were reck-

THE VALUE OF WITNESS TO THE MIRACULOUS.

oned to be a thousand Friends in prison in the various jails of England; at his death, less than fifty years after the foundation of the sect, there were seventy thousand of them in the United Kingdom. The cheerfulness with which these people—women as well as men—underwent martyrdom in this country and in the New England States is one of the most remarkable facts in the history of religion.

No one who reads the voluminous autobiography of "Honest George" can doubt the man's utter truthfulness; and though, in his multitudinous letters, he but rarely rises far above the incoherent commonplaces of a street preacher, there can be no question of his power as a speaker, nor any doubt as to the dignity and attractiveness of his personality, or of his possession of a large amount of practical good sense and governing faculty.

But that George Fox had full faith in his own powers as a miracle-worker, the following passage of his autobiography (to which others might be added) demonstrates:

> Now after I was set at liberty from Nottingham gaol (where I had been kept prisoner a pretty long time) I traveled as before, in the work of the Lord. And coming to Mansfield Woodhouse, there was a distracted woman under a doctor's hand, with her hair let loose all about her ears; and he was about to let her blood, she being first bound, and many people being about her, holding her by violence; but he could get no blood from her. And I desired them to unbind her and let her alone; for they could not touch the spirit in her by which she was tormented. So they did unbind her, and I was moved to speak to her, and in the name of the Lord to bid her be quiet and still. And she was so. And the Lord's power settled her mind and she mended; and afterwards received the truth and continued in it to her death. And the Lord's name was honoured; to whom the glory of all his works belongs. Many great and wonderful things were wrought by the heavenly power in those days. For the Lord made bare his omnipotent arm and manifested his

power to the astonishment of many ; by the healing virtue whereof many have been delivered from great infirmities and the devils were made subject through his name : of which particular instances might be given beyond what this unbelieving age is able to receive or bear.*

It needs no long study of Fox's writings, however, to arrive at the conviction that the distinction between subjective and objective verities had not the same place in his mind as it has in that of ordinary mortals. When an ordinary person would say "I thought so and so," or "I made up my mind to do so and so," George Fox says "it was opened to me," or "at the command of God I did so and so." "Then at the command of God on the ninth day of the seventh month 1643 [Fox being just nineteen] I left my relations and brake off all familiarity or friendship with young or old." "About the beginning of the year 1647 I was moved of the Lord to go into Darbyshire." Fox hears voices and he sees visions, some of which he brings before the reader with apocalyptic power in simple and strong English, alike untutored and undefiled, of which, like John Bunyan, his contemporary, he was a master.

"And one morning, as I was sitting by the fire, a great cloud came over me, and a temptation beset me; and I sate still. And it was said, *All things come by Nature*. And the elements and stars came over me; so that I was in a manner quite clouded with it. . . . And, as I sate still under it, and let it alone, a living hope arose in me, and a true voice arose in me which said, *There is a living God who made all things*. And immediately the cloud and the temptation vanished away, and life rose

---

* "A Journal or Historical Account of the Life, Travels, Sufferings, and Christian Experiences, etc., of George Fox," ed. i, 1694, pp. 27, 28.

over it all, and my heart was glad and I praised the Living God" (p. 13).

If George Fox could speak as he proves in this and some other passages he could write, his astounding influence on the contemporaries of Milton and of Cromwell is no mystery. But this modern reproduction of the ancient prophet, with his "Thus saith the Lord," "This is the work of the Lord," steeped in supernaturalism and glorying in blind faith, is the mental antipodes of the philosopher, founded in naturalism and a fanatic for evidence, to whom these affirmations inevitably suggest the previous question: "How do you know that the Lord saith it?" "How do you know that the Lord doeth it?" and who is compelled to demand that rational ground for belief without which, to the man of science, assent is merely an immoral pretense.

And it is this rational ground of belief which the writers of the Gospels, no less than Paul, and Eginhard, and Fox, so little dream of offering that they would regard the demand for it as a kind of blasphemy.

IX.

AGNOSTICISM AND CHRISTIANITY.

By Prof. THOMAS H. HUXLEY.

Nemo ergo ex me scire quærat, quod me nescire scio, nisi forte ut nescire discat.*—Augustinus, *De Civ. Dei*, xii, 7.

Controversy, like most things in this world, has a good and a bad side. On the good side, it may be said that it stimulates the wits, tends to clear the mind, and often helps those engaged in it to get a better grasp of their subject than they had before; while, mankind being essentially fighting animals, a contest leads the public to interest themselves in questions to which, otherwise, they would give but a languid attention. On the bad side, controversy is rarely found to sweeten the temper, and generally tends to degenerate into an exchange of more or less effective sarcasms. Moreover, if it is long continued, the original and really important issues are apt to become obscured by disputes on the collateral and relatively insignificant questions which have cropped up in the course of the discussion. No doubt both of these aspects of controversy have manifested themselves in the course of the debate which has been in progress, for some

---

* Let no one therefore seek to know from me what I know I do not know, except in order to learn not to know.

months, in these pages. So far as I may have illustrated the second, I express repentance and desire absolution; and I shall endeavor to make amends for any foregone lapses by an endeavor to exhibit only the better phase in these concluding remarks.

The present discussion has arisen out of the use, which has become general in the last few years, of the terms "agnostic" and "agnosticism."

The people who call themselves "agnostics" have been charged with doing so because they have not the courage to declare themselves "infidels." It has been insinuated that they have adopted a new name in order to escape the unpleasantness which attaches to their proper denomination. To this wholly erroneous imputation I have replied by showing that the term "agnostic" did, as a matter of fact, arise in a manner which negatives it; and my statement has not been, and can not be, refuted. Moreover, speaking for myself, and without impugning the right of any other person to use the term in another sense, I further say that agnosticism is not properly described as a "negative" creed, nor indeed as a creed of any kind, except in so far as it expresses absolute faith in the validity of a principle which is as much ethical as intellectual. This principle may be stated in various ways, but they all amount to this: that it is wrong for a man to say that he is certain of the objective truth of any proposition unless he can produce evidence which logically justifies that certainty. This is what agnosticism asserts; and, in my opinion, it is all that is essential to agnosticism. That which agnostics deny and repudiate as immoral is the contrary doctrine, that there are propositions which men ought to believe, without logically satisfactory evidence; and that reprobation ought to attach to the profession of disbelief in such inadequately supported propositions. The justification of the agnostic principle lies in the success which follows upon its application, whether in the field of natural or in that of civil history; and in the fact that, so far as these topics are concerned, no sane man thinks of denying its validity.

Still speaking for myself, I add that, though agnosticism is not, and can not be, a creed, except in so far as its general principle is concerned; yet that the application of that principle results in the denial of, or the suspension of judgment concerning, a number of propositions respecting which our contemporary ecclesiastical "gnostics" profess entire certainty. And in so far as these ecclesiastical persons can be justified in the old-established custom (which many nowadays think more honored in the breach than the observance) of using opprobrious names to those who differ from them, I fully admit their right to call me and those who think with me "infidels"; all I have ventured to urge is that they must not expect us to speak of ourselves by that title.

The extent of the region of the uncertain, the number of the problems the investigation of which ends in a verdict of not proven, will vary according to the knowledge and the intellectual habits of the individual agnostic. I do not very much care to speak of anything as unknowable. What I am sure about is that there are many topics about which I know nothing, and which, so far as I can see, are out of reach of my faculties. But whether these things are knowable by any one else is exactly one of those matters which is beyond my knowledge, though I may have a tolerably strong opinion as to the probabilities of the case. Relatively to myself, I am quite sure that the region of uncertainty—the nebulous country in which words play the part of realities—is far more extensive than I could wish. Materialism and idealism; theism and atheism; the doctrine of the soul and its mortality or immortality—appear in the history of philosophy like the shades of Scandinavian heroes, eternally slaying one another and eternally coming to life again in a metaphysical "Nifelheim." It is getting on for twenty-five centuries, at least, since mankind began seriously to give their minds to these topics. Generation after generation, philosophy has been doomed to roll the stone up hill; and, just as all the world swore it was at the top, down it has rolled to the bottom again. All this is written in innumerable books; and he who will toil through them will discover that the stone is just where it was when the work began. Hume saw this; Kant saw it; since their time, more and more eyes have been cleansed of the films which prevented them from seeing it; until now the weight and number of those who refuse to be the prey of verbal mystification has begun to tell in practical life.

It was inevitable that a conflict should arise between agnosticism and theology; or rather I ought to say between agnosticism and ecclesiasticism. For theology, the science, is one thing; and ecclesiasticism, the championship of a foregone conclusion * as to the truth of a particular form of theology, is another. With scientific theology, agnosticism has no quarrel. On the contrary, the agnostic, knowing too well the influence of prejudice and idiosyncrasy, even on those who desire most earnestly to be impartial, can wish for nothing more urgently than that the scientific theologian should not only be at per-

---

* "Let us maintain, before we have proved. This seeming paradox is the secret of happiness." (Dr. Newman, "Tract 85," p. 85.)

fect liberty to thrash out the matter in his own fashion, but that he should, if he can, find flaws in the agnostic position, and, even if demonstration is not to be had, that he should put, in their full force, the grounds of the conclusions he thinks probable. The scientific theologian admits the agnostic principle, however widely his results may differ from those reached by the majority of agnostics.

But, as between agnosticism and ecclesiasticism, or, as our neighbors across the Channel call it, clericalism, there can be neither peace nor truce. The cleric asserts that it is morally wrong not to believe certain propositions, whatever the results of a strict scientific investigation of the evidence of these propositions. He tells us that " religious error is, in itself, of an immoral nature." * He declares that he has prejudged certain conclusions, and looks upon those who show cause for arrest of judgment as emissaries of Satan. It necessarily follows that, for him, the attainment of faith, not the ascertainment of truth, is the highest aim of mental life. And, on careful analysis of the nature of this faith, it will too often be found to be not the mystic process of unity with the divine, understood by the religious enthusiast—but that which the candid simplicity of a Sunday scholar once defined it to be. " Faith," said this unconscious plagiarist of Tertullian, " is the power of saying you believe things which are incredible."

Now I, and many other agnostics, believe that faith, in this sense, is an abomination; and though we do not indulge in the luxury of self-righteousness so far as to call those who are not of our way of thinking hard names, we do feel that the disagreement between ourselves and

---

* Dr. Newman, " Essay on Development," p. 357.

those who hold this doctrine is even more moral than intellectual. It is desirable there should be an end of any mistakes on this topic. If our clerical opponents were clearly aware of the real state of the case, there would be an end of the curious delusion, which often appears between the lines of their writings, that those whom they are so fond of calling "infidels" are people who not only ought to be, but in their hearts are, ashamed of themselves. It would be discourteous to do more than hint the antipodal opposition of this pleasant dream of theirs to facts.

The clerics and their lay allies commonly tell us that, if we refuse to admit that there is good ground for expressing definite convictions about certain topics, the bonds of human society will dissolve and mankind lapse into savagery. There are several answers to this assertion. One is, that the bonds of human society were formed without the aid of their theology, and in the opinion of not a few competent judges have been weakened rather than strengthened by a good deal of it. Greek science, Greek art, the ethics of old Israel, the social organization of old Rome, contrived to come into being without the help of any one who believed in a single distinctive article of the simplest of the Christian creeds. The science, the art, the jurisprudence, the chief political and social theories of the modern world have grown out of those of Greece and Rome—not by favor of, but in the teeth of, the fundamental teachings of early Christianity, to which science, art, and any serious occupation with the things of this world were alike despicable.

Again, all that is best in the ethics of the modern world, in so far as it has not grown out of Greek thought or barbarian manhood, is the direct development of the ethics of old Israel. There is no code of legislation, ancient or modern, at once so just and so merciful, so tender to the weak and poor, as the Jewish law; and if the Gospels are to be trusted, Jesus of Nazareth himself declared that he taught nothing but that which lay implicitly, or explicitly, in the religious and ethical system of his people.

And the scribe said unto him, Of a truth, Teacher, thou hast well said that he is one; and there is none other but he: and to love him with all the heart, and with all the understanding, and with all the strength, and to love his neighbor as himself, is much more than all whole burnt-offerings and sacrifices. (Mark xii, 32, 33.)

Here is the briefest of summaries of the teaching of the prophets of Israel of the eighth century; does the Teacher, whose doctrine is thus set forth in his presence, repudiate the exposition? Nay, we are told, on the contrary, that Jesus saw that he "answered discreetly," and replied, "Thou art not far from the kingdom of God."

So that I think that even if the creeds, from the so-called "Apostles'" to the so-called "Athanasian," were swept into oblivion; and even if the human race should arrive at the conclusion that whether a bishop washes a cup or leaves it unwashed, is not a matter of the least consequence, it will get on very well. The causes which have led to the development of morality in mankind, which have guided or impelled us all the way from the savage to the civilized state, will not cease to operate because a number of ecclesiastical hypotheses turn out to be baseless. And, even if the absurd notion that morality is more the child of speculation than of practical necessity and inherited instinct, had any foundation; if all the world is going to thieve, murder, and otherwise misconduct itself as soon as it discovers that certain portions of ancient history are mythical, what is the relevance of such arguments to any one who holds by the agnostic principle?

Surely the attempt to cast out Beelzebub by the aid of Beelzebub is a hopeful procedure as compared to that of preserving morality by the aid of immorality. For I suppose it is admitted that an agnostic may be perfectly sincere, may be competent, and may have studied the question at issue with as much care as his clerical opponents. But, if the agnostic really believes what he says, the "dreadful consequence" argufier (consistently I admit with his own principles) virtually asks him to abstain from telling the truth, or to say what he believes to be untrue, because of the supposed injurious consequences to morality. "Beloved brethren, that we may be spotlessly moral, before all things let us lie," is the sum total of many an exhortation addressed to the "infidel." Now, as I have already pointed out, we can not oblige our exhorters. We leave the practical application of the convenient doctrines of "reserve" and "non-natural interpretation" to those who invented them.

I trust that I have now made amends for my ambiguity, or want of fullness, in any previous exposition of that which I hold to be the essence of the agnostic doctrine. Henceforward, I might hope to hear no more of the assertion that we are necessarily materialists, idealists, atheists, theists, or any other *ists*, if experience had led me to think that the proved falsity of a statement was any guarantee against its repetition. And those who appreciate the nature of our position will see, at once, that when ecclesiasticism declares that we ought to believe this, that, and the other, and are very wicked if we don't, it is impossible for us to give any answer but this: We have not the slightest objection to believe anything you like, if you will give us good grounds for belief; but, if you can not, we must respectfully refuse, even if that refusal should wreck morality and insure our own damnation several times over. We are quite content to leave that to the decision of the future. The course of the past has impressed us with the firm conviction that no good ever comes of falsehood, and we feel warranted in refusing even to experiment in that direction.

In the course of the present discussion it has been asserted that the "Sermon on the Mount" and the "Lord's Prayer" furnish a summary and condensed view of the essentials of the teaching of Jesus of Nazareth, set forth by himself. Now this supposed *Summa* of Nazarene theology distinctly affirms the existence of a spiritual world, of a heaven, and of a hell of fire; it teaches the fatherhood of God and the malignity of the devil; it declares the superintending providence of the former and our need of deliverance from the machinations of the latter; it affirms the fact of demoniac possession and the power of casting out devils by the faithful. And, from these premises, the conclusion is drawn that those agnostics who deny that there is any evidence of such a character as to justify certainty, respecting the existence and the nature of the spiritual world, contradict the express declarations of Jesus. I have replied to this argumentation by showing that there is strong reason to doubt the historical accuracy of the attribution to Jesus of either the "Sermon on the Mount" or the "Lord's Prayer"; and, therefore, that the conclusion in question is not warranted, at any rate on the grounds set forth.

But, whether the Gospels contain trustworthy statements about this and other alleged historical facts or not, it is quite certain that from them, taken together with the other books of the New Testament, we may collect a pretty complete exposition of that theory of the spiritual world which was held by both Nazarenes and Christians; and which was undoubtedly supposed by them to be fully sanctioned by Jesus, though it is just as clear that they did not imagine it contained any revelation by him of something heretofore unknown. If the pneumatological doctrine which pervades the whole New Testament is nowhere systematically stated, it is everywhere assumed. The writers of the Gospels and of the Acts take it for granted, as a matter of common knowledge; and it is easy to gather from these sources a series of propositions, which only need arrangement to form a complete system.

In this system, man is considered to be a duality formed of a spiritual element, the soul; and a corporeal * element, the body. And this duality is repeated in the universe, which consists of a corporeal world embraced and interpenetrated by a spiritual world. The former consists of the earth, as its principal and central constituent, with the subsidiary sun, planets, and stars. Above the earth is the air, and below it the watery abyss. Whether the heaven, which is conceived to be above the air, and the hell in, or below, the subterranean deeps, are to be taken as corporeal or incorporeal is not clear.

However this may be, the heaven and the air, the earth and the abyss, are peopled by innumerable beings analogous in nature to the spiritual element in man, and

---

* It is by no means to be assumed that "spiritual" and "corporeal" are exact equivalents of "immaterial" and "material" in the minds of ancient speculators on these topics.

these spirits are of two kinds, good and bad. The chief of the good spirits, infinitely superior to all the others, and their Creator as well as the Creator of the corporeal world and of the bad spirits, is God. His residence is heaven, where he is surrounded by the ordered hosts of good spirits; his angels, or messengers, and the executors of his will throughout the universe.

On the other hand, the chief of the bad spirits is Satan—*the* devil *par excellence*. He and his company of demons are free to roam through all parts of the universe, except heaven. These bad spirits are far superior to man in power and subtlety, and their whole energies are devoted to bringing physical and moral evils upon him, and to thwarting, so far as their power goes, the benevolent intentions of the Supreme Being. In fact, the souls and bodies of men form both the theatre and the prize of an incessant warfare between the good and the evil spirits—the powers of light and the powers of darkness. By leading Eve astray, Satan brought sin and death upon mankind. As the gods of the heathen, the demons are the founders and maintainers of idolatry; as the "powers of the air," they afflict mankind with pestilence and famine; as "unclean spirits," they cause disease of mind and body.

The significance of the appearance of Jesus, as the Messiah or Christ, is the reversal of the satanic work, by putting an end to both sin and death. He announces that the kingdom of God is at hand, when the "prince of this world" shall be finally "cast out" (John xii, 31) from the cosmos, as Jesus, during his earthly career, cast him out from individuals. Then will Satan and all his deviltry, along with the wicked whom they have seduced to their destruction, be hurled into the abyss of unquenchable fire—there to endure continual torture, without a hope of winning pardon from the merciful God, their Father; or of moving the glorified Messiah to one more act of pitiful intercession; or even of interrupting, by a momentary sympathy with their wretchedness, the harmonious psalmody of their brother angels and men, eternally lapped in bliss unspeakable.

The straitest Protestant, who refuses to admit the existence of any source of divine truth, except the Bible, will not deny that every point of the pneumatological theory here set forth has ample scriptural warranty: the Gospels, the Acts, the Epistles, and the Apocalypse assert the existence of the devil and his demons and hell, as plainly as they do that of God and his angels and heaven. It is plain that the Messianic and the satanic conceptions of the writers of these books are the obverse and the reverse of the same intellectual coinage. If we turn from Scripture to the traditions of the fathers and the confessions of the churches, it will appear that in this one particular, at any rate, time has brought about no important deviation from primitive belief. From Justin onward, it may often be a fair question whether God, or the devil, occupies a larger share of the attention of the fathers. It is the devil who instigates the Roman authorities to persecute; the gods and goddesses of paganism are devils, and idolatry itself is an invention of Satan; if a saint falls away from grace, it is by the seduction of the demon; if a heresy arises, the devil has suggested it; and some of the fathers[*] go so far as to challenge the pagans to a sort of exorcising match, by way of testing the truth of Chris-

---

[*] Tertullian ("Apolog. adv. Gentes," cap. xxiii) thus challenges the Roman authorities: let them bring a possessed person into the presence of a Christian before their tribunal; and, if the demon does not confess himself

tianity. Mediæval Christianity is at one with patristic, on this head. The masses, the clergy, the theologians, and the philosophers alike, live and move and have their being in a world full of demons, in which sorcery and possession are every-day occurrences. Nor did the Reformation make any difference. Whatever else Luther assailed, he left the traditional demonology untouched; nor could any one have entertained a more hearty and uncompromising belief in the devil, than he and, at a later period, the Calvinistic fanatics of New England did. Finally, in these last years of the nineteenth century, the demonological hypotheses of the first century are, explicitly or implicitly, held and occasionally acted upon, by the immense majority of Christians of all confessions.

Only here and there has the progress of scientific thought, outside the ecclesiastical world, so far affected Christians that they and their teachers fight shy of the demonology of their creed. They are fain to conceal their real disbelief in one half of Christian doctrine by judicious silence about it; or by flight to those refuges for the logically destitute, accommodation or allegory. But the faithful who fly to allegory in order to escape absurdity resemble nothing so much as the sheep in the fable who—to save their lives—jumped into the pit. The allegory pit is too commodious, is ready to swallow up so much more than one wants to put into it. If the story of the temptation is an allegory; if the early recognition of Jesus as the Son of God by the demons is an allegory; if the plain declaration of the writer of the first Epistle of John (iii, 8), "To this end was the Son of God manifested that he might destroy the works of the devil,"

---

to be such, on the order of the Christian, let the Christian be executed out of hand.

is allegorical, then the Pauline version of the fall may be allegorical, and still more the words of consecration of the Eucharist, or the promise of the second coming; in fact, there is not a dogma of ecclesiastical Christianity the scriptural basis of which may not be whittled away by a similar process.

As to accommodation, let any honest man who can read the New Testament ask himself whether Jesus and his immediate friends and disciples can be dishonored more grossly than by the supposition that they said and did that which is attributed to them; while, in reality, they disbelieved in Satan and his demons, in possession and in exorcism? *

An eminent theologian has justly observed that we have no right to look at the propositions of the Christian faith with one eye open and the other shut. ("Tract 85," p. 29.) It really is not permissible to see with one eye, that Jesus is affirmed to declare the personality and the fatherhood of God, his loving providence, and his accessibility to prayer, and to shut the other to the no less definite teaching ascribed to Jesus in regard to the personality and the misanthropy of the devil, his malignant watchfulness, and his subjection to exorcistic formulæ and rites. Jesus is made to say that the devil "was a murderer from the beginning" (John viii, 44) by the same authority as that upon which we depend for his asserted declaration that "God is a spirit" (John iv, 24).

To those who admit the authority of the famous Vincentian dictum that the doctrine which has been held "always, everywhere, and by all" is to be received as

---

* See the expression of orthodox opinion upon the "accommodation" subterfuge, already cited, p. 20.

authoritative, the demonology must possess a higher sanction than any other Christian dogma, except, perhaps, those of the resurrection and of the Messiahship of Jesus; for it would be difficult to name any other points of doctrine on which the Nazarene does not differ from the Christian, and the different historical stages and contemporary subdivisions of Christianity from one another. And, if the demonology is accepted, there can be no reason for rejecting all those miracles in which demons play a part. The Gadarene story fits into the general scheme of Christianity, and the evidence for "Legion" and their doings is just as good as any other in the New Testament for the doctrine which the story illustrates.

It was with the purpose of bringing this great fact into prominence, of getting people to open both their eyes when they look at ecclesiasticism, that I devoted so much space to that miraculous story which happens to be one of the best types of its class. And I could not wish for a better justification of the course I have adopted than the fact that my heroically consistent adversary has declared his implicit belief in the Gadarene story and (by necessary consequence) in the Christian demonology as a whole. It must be obvious, by this time, that, if the account of the spiritual world given in the New Testament, professedly on the authority of Jesus, is true, then the demonological half of that account must be just as true as the other half. And, therefore, those who question the demonology, or try to explain it away, deny the truth of what Jesus said, and are, in ecclesiastical terminology, "infidels" just as much as those who deny the spirituality of God. This is as plain as anything can well be, and the dilemma for my opponent was either to assert that the Gadarene pig-bedevilment actually occurred, or to write himself down an "infidel." As was to be expected, he chose the former alternative; and I may express my great satisfaction at finding that there is one spot of common ground on which both he and I stand. So far as I can judge, we are agreed to state one of the broad issues between the consequences of agnostic principles (as I draw them), and the consequences of ecclesiastical dogmatism (as he accepts it), as follows:

Ecclesiasticism says: The demonology of the Gospels is an essential part of that account of that spiritual world, the truth of which it declares to be certified by Jesus.

Agnosticism (*me judice*) says: There is no good evidence of the existence of a demonic spiritual world, and much reason for doubting it.

Hereupon the ecclesiastic may observe: Your doubt means that you disbelieve Jesus; therefore you are an "infidel" instead of an "agnostic." To which the agnostic may reply: No; for two reasons: first, because your evidence that Jesus said what you say he said is worth very little; and, secondly, because a man may be an agnostic in the sense of admitting he has no positive knowledge; and yet consider that he has more or less probable ground for accepting any given hypothesis about the spiritual world. Just as a man may frankly declare that he has no means of knowing whether the planets generally are inhabited or not, and yet may think one of the two possible hypotheses more likely than the other, so he may admit that he has no means of knowing anything about the spiritual world, and yet may think one or other of the current views on the subject, to some extent, probable.

The second answer is so obviously valid that it needs no discussion. I draw attention to it simply in justice to those agnostics, who may attach greater value than I do to any sort of pneumatological speculations, and not because I wish to escape the responsibility of declaring that, whether Jesus sanctioned the demonological part of Christianity or not, I unhesitatingly reject it. The first answer, on the other hand, opens up the whole question of the claim of the biblical and other sources, from which hypotheses concerning the spiritual world are derived, to be regarded as unimpeachable historical evidence as to matters of fact.

Now, in respect of the trustworthiness of the Gospel narratives, I was anxious to get rid of the common assumption that the determination of the authorship and of the dates of these works is a matter of fundamental importance. That assumption is based upon the notion that what contemporary witnesses say must be true, or, at least, has always a *prima facie* claim to be so regarded; so that if the writers of any of the Gospels were contemporaries of the events (and still more if they were in the position of eye-witnesses) the miracles they narrate must be historically true, and, consequently, the demonology which they involve must be accepted. But the story of the "Translation of the Blessed Martyrs Marcellinus and Petrus," and the other considerations (to which endless additions might have been made from the fathers and the mediæval writers) set forth in this review for March last, yield, in my judgment, satisfactory proof that, where the miraculous is concerned, neither considerable intellectual ability, nor undoubted honesty, nor knowledge of the world, nor proved faithfulness as civil historians, nor profound piety, on the part of eye-witnesses and contemporaries, affords any guarantee of the objective truth of their statements, when we know that a firm belief in the miraculous was ingrained in their minds, and was the pre-supposition of their observations and reasonings.

Therefore, although it be, as I believe, demonstrable that we have no real knowledge of the authorship, or of the date of composition of the Gospels, as they have come down to us, and that nothing better than more or less probable guesses can be arrived at on that subject, I have not cared to expend any space on the question. It will be admitted, I suppose, that the authors of the works attributed to Matthew, Mark, Luke, and John, whoever they may be, are personages whose capacity and judgment in the narration of ordinary events are not quite so well certified as those of Eginhard; and we have seen what the value of Eginhard's evidence is when the miraculous is in question.

I have been careful to explain that the arguments which I have used in the course of this discussion are not new; that they are historical, and have nothing to do with what is commonly called science; and that they are all, to the best of my belief, to be found in the works of theologians of repute.

The position which I have taken up, that the evidence in favor of such miracles as those recorded by Eginhard, and consequently of mediæval demonology, is quite as good as that in favor of such miracles as the Gadarene, and consequently of Nazarene demonology, is none of my discovery. Its strength was, wittingly or unwittingly, suggested a century and a half ago by a theological scholar of eminence; and it has been, if not exactly occupied, yet so fortified with bastions and redoubts by a living ecclesiastical Vauban, that, in my judgment, it has been rendered impregnable. In the early part of the last century, the ecclesiastical mind in this country was much exercised by the question, not exactly of miracles, the occurrence of which in biblical times was axiomatic, but by the problem, When did miracles cease? Anglican divines were quite sure that no miracles had happened in their day, nor for some time past; they were equally sure that they happened sixteen or seventeen centuries earlier. And it was a vital question for them to determine at what point of time, between this *terminus a quo* and that *terminus ad quem*, miracles came to an end.

The Anglicans and the Romanists agreed in the assumption that the possession of the gift of miracle-working was *prima facie* evidence of the soundness of the faith of the miracle-workers. The supposition that miraculous powers might be wielded by heretics (though it might be supported by high authority) led to consequences too frightful to be entertained by people who were busied in building their dogmatic house on the sands of early church history. If, as the Romanists maintained, an unbroken series of genuine miracles adorned the records of their Church, throughout the whole of its existence, no Anglican could lightly venture to accuse them of doctrinal corruption. Hence, the Anglicans, who indulged in such accusations, were bound to prove the modern, the mediæval Roman, and the later patristic miracles false; and to shut off the wonder-working power from the Church at the exact point of time when Anglican doctrine ceased and Roman doctrine began. With a little adjustment— a squeeze here and a pull there—the Christianity of the first three or four centuries might be made to fit, or seem to fit, pretty well into the Anglican scheme. So the miracles, from Justin, say, to Jerome, might be recognized; while, in later times, the Church having become "corrupt"—that is to say, having pursued one and the same line of development further than was pleasing to Anglicans—its alleged miracles must needs be shams and impostures.

Under these circumstances, it may be imagined that the establishment of a scientific frontier, between the earlier realm of supposed fact and the later of asserted delusion, had its difficulties; and torrents of theological special pleading about the subject flowed from clerical pens; until that learned and acute Anglican divine, Conyers Middleton, in his "Free Inquiry," tore the sophistical web they had laboriously woven to pieces, and demonstrated that the miracles of the patristic age, early and late, must stand or fall together, inasmuch as the evidence for the later is just as good as the evidence for the earlier wonders. If the one set are certified by contemporaneous witnesses of high repute, so are the other; and, in point of probability, there is not a pin to choose between the two. That is the solid and irrefragable result of Middleton's contribution to the subject. But the Free Inquirer's freedom had its limits; and he draws a sharp line of demarkation between the patristic and the New Testament miracles—on the professed ground that the accounts of the latter, being inspired, are out of the reach of criticism.

A century later, the question was taken up by another divine, Middleton's equal in learning and acuteness, and far his superior in subtlety and dialectic skill; who, though an Anglican, scorned the name of Protestant; and, while yet a Churchman, made it his business to parade, with infinite skill, the utter hollowness of the arguments of those of his brother Churchmen who dreamed that they could be both Anglicans and Protestants. The argument of the "Essay on the Miracles recorded in the Ecclesiastical History of the Early Ages,"* by the present Roman cardinal, but then Anglican doctor, John Henry Newman, is compendiously stated by himself in the following passage:

> If the miracles of church history can not be defended by the arguments of Leslie, Lyttleton, Paley, or Douglas, how many of the Scripture miracles satisfy their conditions? (p. cvii).

And, although the answer is not given in so many words, little doubt is left on the mind of the reader that in the mind of the writer it is: None. In fact, this conclusion is one which can not be resisted, if the argument in favor of the Scripture miracles is based upon that which laymen, whether lawyers, or men of science, or historians, or ordinary men of affairs call evidence. But there is something really impressive in the magnificent contempt with which, at times, Dr. Newman sweeps aside alike those who offer and those who demand such evidence.

> Some infidel authors advise us to accept no miracles which would not have a verdict in their favor in a court of justice; that is, they employ against Scripture a weapon which Protestants would confine to attacks upon the Church, as if moral and religious questions required legal proofs, and evidence were the test of truth † (p. cvii).

"As if evidence were the test of truth"!—although the truth in question is the occurrence or non-occurrence of

---

* I quote the first edition (1843). A second edition appeared in 1870. Tract 85 of the "Tracts for the Times" should be read with this "Essay." If I were called upon to compile a primer of "infidelity," I think I should save myself trouble by making a selection from these works, and from the "Essay on Development" by the same author.

† Yet, when it suits his purpose, as in the introduction to the "Essay

certain phenomena at a certain time and in a certain place. This sudden revelation of the great gulf fixed between the ecclesiastical and the scientific mind is enough to take away the breath of any one unfamiliar with the clerical organon. As if, one may retort, the assumption that miracles may, or have, served a moral or a religious end in any way alters the fact that they profess to be historical events, things that actually happened; and, as such, must needs be exactly those subjects about which evidence is appropriate and legal proofs (which are such merely because they afford adequate evidence) may be justly demanded. The Gadarene miracle either happened, or it did not. Whether the Gadarene "question" is moral or religious, or not, has nothing to do with the fact that it is a purely historical question whether the demons said what they are declared to have said, and the devil-possessed pigs did or did not rush over the cliffs of the Lake of Gennesareth on a certain day of a certain year, after A. D. 26 and before A. D. 36; for, vague and uncertain as New Testament chronology is, I suppose it may be assumed that the event in question, if it happened at all, took place during the procuratorship of Pilate. If that is not a matter about which evidence ought to be required, and not only legal but strict scientific proof demanded by sane men who are asked to believe the story —what is? Is a reasonable being to be seriously asked to credit statements which, to put the case gently, are not exactly probable, and on the acceptance or rejection of which his whole view of life may depend, without asking for as much "legal" proof as would send an alleged pick-

---

on Development," Dr. Newman can demand strict evidence in religious questions as sharply as any "infidel author"; and he can even profess to yield to its force ("Essays on Miracles," 1870, note, p. 391).

pocket to jail, or as would suffice to prove the validity of a disputed will?

"Infidel authors" (if, as I am assured, I may answer for them) will decline to waste time on mere darkenings of counsel of this sort; but to those Anglicans who accept his premises, Dr. Newman is a truly formidable antagonist. What, indeed, are they to reply when he puts the very pertinent question:

"whether persons who, not merely question, but prejudge the ecclesiastical miracles on the ground of their want of resemblance, whatever that be, to those contained in Scripture—as if the Almighty could not do in the Christian church what he had not already done at the time of its foundation, or under the Mosaic covenant—whether such reasoners are not siding with the skeptic,"

and

"whether it is not a happy inconsistency by which they continue to believe the Scriptures while they reject the Church"* (p. liii).

Again, I invite Anglican orthodoxy to consider this passage:

the narrative of the combats of St. Antony with evil spirits is a development rather than a contradiction of revelation, viz., of such texts as speak of Satan being cast out by prayer and fasting. To be shocked, then, at the miracles of ecclesiastical history, or to ridicule them for their strangeness, is no part of a scriptural philosophy (p. liii–liv).

Further on, Dr. Newman declares that it has been admitted

that a distinct line can be drawn in point of character and circumstance between the miracles of Scripture and of church history; but this is by no means the case (p. lv). . . . Specimens are not want-

---

* Compare "Tract 85," p. 110: "I am persuaded that were men but consistent who oppose the Church doctrines as being unscriptural, they would vindicate the Jews for rejecting the gospel."

ing in the history of the Church of miracles as awful in their character and as momentous in their effects as those which are recorded in Scripture. The fire interrupting the rebuilding of the Jewish Temple, and the death of Arius, are instances in ecclesiastical history of such solemn events. On the other hand, difficult instances in the Scripture history are such as these: the serpent in Eden, the ark, Jacob's vision for the multiplication of his cattle, the speaking of Balaam's ass, the axe swimming at Elisha's word, the miracle on the swine, and various instances of prayers or prophecies, in which, as in that of Noah's blessing and curse, words which seem the result of private feeling are expressly or virtually ascribed to a divine suggestion (p. lvi).

Who is to gainsay our ecclesiastical authority here? "Infidel authors" might be accused of a wish to ridicule the Scripture miracles by putting them on a level with the remarkable story about the fire which stopped the rebuilding of the Temple, or that about the death of Arius —but Dr. Newman is above suspicion. The pity is that his list of what he delicately terms "difficult" instances is so short. Why omit the manufacture of Eve out of Adam's rib, on the strict historical accuracy of which the chief argument of the defenders of an iniquitous portion of our present marriage law depends? Why leave out the account of the "Bene Elohim" and their gallantries, on which a large part of the worst practices of the mediæval inquisitors into witchcraft was based? Why forget the angel who wrestled with Jacob, and, as the account suggests, somewhat overstepped the bounds of fair play at the end of the struggle? Surely we must agree with Dr. Newman that, if all these camels have gone down, it savors of affectation to strain at such gnats as the sudden ailment of Arius in the midst of his deadly, if prayerful,[*]

---

[*] According to Dr. Newman, "This prayer [that of Bishop Alexander, who begged God to 'take Arius away'] is said to have been offered about

enemies; and the fiery explosion which stopped the Julian building operations. Though the *words* of the "Conclusion" of the "Essay on Miracles" may, perhaps, be quoted against me, I may express my satisfaction at finding myself in substantial accordance with a theologian above all suspicion of heterodoxy. With all my heart, I can declare my belief that there is just as good reason for believing in the miraculous slaying of the man who fell short of the Athanasian power of affirming contradictories, with respect to the nature of the Godhead, as there is for believing in the stories of the serpent and the ark told in Genesis, the speaking of Balaam's ass in Numbers, or the floating of the axe, at Elisha's order, in the second book of Kings.

It is one of the peculiarities of a really sound argument that it is susceptible of the fullest development; and that it sometimes leads to conclusions unexpected by those who employ it. To my mind it is impossible to refuse to follow Dr. Newman when he extends his reasoning from the miracles of the patristic and mediæval ages backward in time as far as miracles are recorded. But, if the rules of logic are valid, I feel compelled to extend the argument forward to the alleged Roman miracles of the present day, which Dr. Newman might not have admitted,

---

3 P. M. on the Saturday; that same evening Arius was in the great square of Constantine, when he was suddenly seized with indisposition" (p. clxx). The "infidel" Gibbon seems to have dared to suggest that "an option between poison and miracle" is presented by this case; and it must be admitted, that if the bishop had been within reach of a modern police magistrate, things might have gone hardly with him. Modern "infidels," possessed of a slight knowledge of chemistry, are not unlikely, with no less audacity, to suggest an "option between fire-damp and miracle" in seeking for the cause of the fiery outburst at Jerusalem.

but which Cardinal Newman may hardly reject. Beyond question, there is as good, or perhaps better, evidence for the miracles worked by our Lady of Lourdes, as there is for the floating of Elisha's axe or the speaking of Balaam's ass. But we must go still further; there is a modern system of thaumaturgy and demonology which is just as well certified as the ancient.* Veracious, excellent, sometimes learned and acute persons, even philosophers of no mean pretension, testify to the "levitation" of bodies much heavier than Elisha's axe; to the existence of "spirits" who, to the mere tactile sense, have been indistinguishable from flesh and blood, and occasionally have wrestled with all the vigor of Jacob's opponent; yet, further, to the speech, in the language of raps, of spiritual beings, whose discourses, in point of coherence and value, are far inferior to that of Balaam's humble but sagacious steed. I have not the smallest doubt that, if these were persecuting times, there is many a worthy "spiritualist"

---

* A writer in a spiritualist journal takes me roundly to task for venturing to doubt the historical and literal truth of the Gadarene story. The following passage in his letter is worth quotation: "Now to the materialistic and scientific mind, to the uninitiated in spiritual verities, certainly this story of the Gadarene or Gergesene swine presents insurmountable difficulties; it seems grotesque and nonsensical. To the experienced, trained, and cultivated Spiritualist this miracle is, as I am prepared to show, one of the most instructive, the most profoundly useful, and the most beneficent which Jesus ever wrought in the whole course of his pilgrimage of redemption on earth." Just so. And the first page of this same journal presents the following advertisement, among others of the same kidney:

"To WEALTHY SPIRITUALISTS.—A lady medium of tried power wishes to meet with an elderly gentleman who would be willing to give her a comfortable home and maintenance in exchange for her spiritualistic services, as her guides consider her health is too delicate for public sittings: London preferred.—Address 'Mary,' office of 'Light.'"

Are we going back to the days of the Judges, when wealthy Micah set up his private ephod, teraphim, and Levite?

who would cheerfully go to the stake in support of his pneumatological faith, and furnish evidence, after Paley's own heart, in proof of the truth of his doctrines. Not a few modern divines, doubtless struck by the impossibility of refusing the spiritualist evidence, if the ecclesiastical evidence is accepted, and deprived of any *a priori* objection by their implicit belief in Christian demonology, show themselves ready to take poor Sludge seriously, and to believe that he is possessed by other devils than those of need, greed, and vainglory.

Under these circumstances, it was to be expected, though it is none the less interesting to note the fact, that the arguments of the latest school of "spiritualists" present a wonderful family likeness to those which adorn the subtle disquisitions of the advocate of ecclesiastical miracles of forty years ago. It is unfortunate for the "spiritualists" that, over and over again, celebrated and trusted media, who really, in some respects, call to mind the Montanist * and gnostic seers of the second century, are either proved in courts of law to be fraudulent impostors; or, in sheer weariness, as it would seem, of the honest dupes who swear by them, spontaneously confess their long-continued iniquities, as the Fox women did the other day in New York.† But whenever a catastrophe of this

---

* Consider Tertullian's "sister" ("hodie apud nos"), who conversed with angels, saw and heard mysteries, knew men's thoughts, and prescribed medicine for their bodies ("De Anima," cap. 9). Tertullian tells us that this woman saw the soul as corporeal, and described its color and shape. The "infidel" will probably be unable to refrain from insulting the memory of the ecstatic saint by the remark that Tertullian's known views about the corporeality of the soul may have had something to do with the remarkable perceptive powers of the Montanist medium, in whose revelations of the spiritual world he took such profound interest.

† See the New York "World" for Sunday, October 21, 1888; and the "Report of the Seybert Commission," Philadelphia, 1887.

kind takes place, the believers are nowise dismayed by it. They freely admit that not only the media, but the spirits whom they summon, are sadly apt to lose sight of the elementary principles of right and wrong; and they triumphantly ask: How does the occurrence of occasional impostures disprove the genuine manifestations (that is to say, all those which have not yet been proved to be impostures or delusions)? And, in this, they unconsciously plagiarize from the churchman, who just as freely admits that many ecclesiastical miracles may have been forged; and asks, with the same calm contempt, not only of legal proofs, but of common-sense probability, Why does it follow that none are to be supposed genuine? I must say, however, that the spiritualists, so far as I know, do not venture to outrage right reason so boldly as the ecclesiastics. They do not sneer at "evidence"; nor repudiate the requirement of legal proofs. In fact, there can be no doubt that the spiritualists produce better evidence for their manifestations than can be shown either for the miraculous death of Arius, or for the invention of the cross.*

From the "levitation" of the axe at one end of a period of near three thousand years to the "levitation" of Sludge & Co. at the other end, there is a complete continuity of the miraculous with every gradation from the childish to the stupendous, from the gratification of a caprice to the illustration of sublime truth. There is no drawing a line in the series that might be set out of plaus-

---

* Dr. Newman's observation that the miraculous multiplication of the pieces of the true cross (with which "the whole world is filled," according to Cyril of Jerusalem; and of which some say there are enough extant to build a man-of-war) is no more wonderful than that of the loaves and fishes, is one that I do not see my way to contradict. See "Essay on Miracles," second edition, p. 163.

ibly attested cases of spiritual intervention. If one is true, all may be true; if one is false, all may be false.

This is, to my mind, the inevitable result of that method of reasoning which is applied to the confutation of Protestantism, with so much success, by one of the acutest and subtlest disputants who have ever championed ecclesiasticism—and one can not put his claims to acuteness and subtlety higher.

> ... the Christianity of history is not Protestantism. If ever there were a safe truth it is this. ... "To be deep in history is to cease to be a Protestant." *

I have not a shadow of doubt that these anti-Protestant epigrams are profoundly true. But I have as little that, in the same sense, the "Christianity of history is not" Romanism; and that to be deeper in history is to cease to be a Romanist. The reasons which compel my doubts about the compatibility of the Roman doctrine, or any other form of Catholicism, with history, arise out of exactly the same line of argument as that adopted by Dr. Newman in the famous essay which I have just cited. If, with one hand, Dr. Newman has destroyed Protestantism, he has annihilated Romanism with the other; and the total result of his ambidextral efforts is to shake Christianity to its foundations. Nor was any one better aware that this must be the inevitable result of his arguments—if the world should refuse to accept Roman doctrines and Roman miracles—than the writer of "Tract 85."

Dr. Newman made his choice and passed over to the Roman Church half a century ago. Some of those who

---

† "An Essay on the Development of Christian Doctrine," by J. H. Newman, D. D., pp. 7 and 8. (1878.)

were essentially in harmony with his views preceded, and many followed him. But many remained; and, as the quondam Puseyite and present Ritualistic party, they are continuing that work of sapping and mining the Protestantism of the Anglican Church which he and his friends so ably commenced. At the present time they have no little claim to be considered victorious all along the line. I am old enough to recollect the small beginnings of the Tractarian party; and I am amazed when I consider the present position of their heirs. Their little leaven has leavened, if not the whole, yet a very large, lump of the Anglican Church; which is now pretty much of a preparatory school for Papistry. So that it really behooves Englishmen (who, as I have been informed by high authority, are all, legally, members of the state Church, if they profess to belong to no other sect) to wake up to what that powerful organization is about, and whither it is tending. On this point, the writings of Dr. Newman, while he still remained within the Anglican fold, are a vast store of the best and the most authoritative information. His doctrines on ecclesiastical miracles and on development are the corner-stones of the Tractarian fabric. He believed that his arguments led either Romeward, or to what ecclesiastics call "infidelity," and I call agnosticism. I believe that he was quite right in this conviction; but while he chooses the one alternative, I choose the other; as he rejects Protestantism on the ground of its incompatibility with history, so, *a fortiori*, I conceive that Romanism ought to be rejected, and that an impartial consideration of the evidence must refuse the authority of Jesus to anything more than the Nazarenism of James and Peter and John. And let it not be supposed that this is a mere "infidel" perversion of the facts. No one has more openly and clearly admitted the possibility that they may be fairly interpreted in this way than Dr. Newman. If, he says, there are texts which seem to show that Jesus contemplated the evangelization of the heathen:

... Did not the apostles hear our Lord? and what was *their* impression from what they heard? Is it not certain that the apostles did not gather this truth from his teaching? ("Tract 85," p. 63.)

He said, "Preach the gospel to every creature." These words *need* have only meant "Bring all men to Christianity through Judaism." Make them Jews, that they may enjoy Christ's privileges which are lodged in Judaism; teach them those rites and ceremonies, circumcision and the like, which hitherto have been dead ordinances, and now are living; and so the apostles seem to have understood them (Ibid., p. 65).

So far as Nazarenism differentiated itself from contemporary orthodox Judaism, it seems to have tended toward a revival of the ethical and religious spirit of the prophetic age, accompanied by the belief in Jesus as the Messiah, and by various accretions which had grown round Judaism subsequently to the exile. To these belong the doctrines of the resurrection, of the last judgment of heaven and hell; of the hierarchy of good angels; of Satan and the hierarchy of evil spirits. And there is very strong ground for believing that all these doctrines, at least in the shapes in which they were held by the post-exilic Jews, were derived from Persian and Babylonian * sources, and are essentially of heathen origin.

---

* Dr. Newman faces this question with his customary ability. "Now, I own, I am not at all solicitous to deny that this doctrine of an apostate angel and his hosts was gained from Babylon: it might still be divine nevertheless. God who made the prophet's ass speak, and thereby instructed the prophet, might instruct his church by means of heathen Babylon"

How far Jesus positively sanctioned all these indrainings of circumjacent paganism into Judaism; how far any one has a right to say that the refusal to accept one or other of these doctrines as ascertained verities comes to the same thing as contradicting Jesus, it appears to me not easy to say. But it is hardly less difficult to conceive that he could have distinctly negatived any of them; and, more especially, that demonology which has been accepted by the Christian churches in every age and under all their mutual antagonisms. But, I repeat my conviction that, whether Jesus sanctioned the demonology of his time and nation or not, it is doomed. The future of Christianity as a dogmatic system and apart from the old Israelitish ethics which it has appropriated and developed, lies in the answer which mankind will eventually give to the question whether they are prepared to believe such stories as the Gadarene and the pneumatological hypotheses which go with it, or not. My belief is they will decline to do anything of the sort, whenever and wherever their minds have been disciplined by science. And that discipline must and will at once follow and lead the footsteps of advancing civilization.

The preceding pages were written before I became acquainted with the contents of the May number of this review, wherein I discover many things which are decidedly not to my advantage. It would appear that "evasion" is my chief resource, "incapacity for strict argument" and "rottenness of ratiocination" my main mental characteristics, and that it is "barely credible" that a statement which I profess to make of my own

---

("Tract 85," p. 83). There seems to be no end to the apologetic burden that Balaam's ass can carry.

knowledge is true. All which things I notice, merely to illustrate the great truth, forced on me by long experience, that it is only from those who enjoy the blessing of a firm hold of the Christian faith that such manifestations of meekness, patience, and charity are to be expected.

I had imagined that no one who had read my preceding papers could entertain a doubt as to my position in respect of the main issue as it has been stated and restated by my opponent:

> an agnosticism which knows nothing of the relation of man to God must not only refuse belief to our Lord's most undoubted teaching, but must deny the reality of the spiritual convictions in which he lived and died.*

That is said to be "the simple question which is at issue between us," and the three testimonies to that teaching and those convictions selected are the Sermon on the Mount, the Lord's Prayer, and the Story of the Passion.

My answer, reduced to its briefest form, has been: In the first place, the evidence is such that the exact nature of the teachings and the convictions of Jesus is extremely uncertain, so that what ecclesiastics are pleased to call a denial of them may be nothing of the kind. And, in the second place, if Jesus taught the demonological system involved in the Gadarene story—if a belief in that system formed a part of the spiritual convictions in which he lived and died—then I, for my part, unhesitatingly refuse belief in that teaching, and deny the reality of those spiritual convictions. And I go further and add, that exactly in so far as it can be proved that Jesus sanctioned the essentially pagan demonological theories

---

* Page 131.

current among the Jews of his age, exactly in so far, for me, will his authority in any matter touching the spiritual world be weakened.

With respect to the first half of my answer, I have pointed out that the Sermon on the Mount, as given in the first Gospel, is, in the opinion of the best critics, a "mosaic work" of materials derived from different sources, and I do not understand that this statement is challenged. The only other Gospel, the third, which contains something like it, makes not only the discourse, but the circumstances under which it was delivered, very different. Now, it is one thing to say that there was something real at the bottom of the two discourses—which is quite possible; and another to affirm that we have any right to say what that something was, or to fix upon any particular phrase and declare it to be a genuine utterance. Those who pursue theology as a science, and bring to the study an adequate knowledge of the ways of ancient historians, will find no difficulty in providing illustrations of my meaning. I may supply one which has come within range of my own limited vision.

In Josephus's "History of the Wars of the Jews" (chap. xix) that writer reports a speech which he says Herod made at the opening of a war with the Arabians. It is in the first person, and would naturally be supposed by the reader to be intended for a true version of what Herod said. In the "Antiquities," written some seventeen years later, the same writer gives another report, also in the first person, of Herod's speech on the same occasion. This second oration is twice as long as the first, and though the general tenor of the two speeches is pretty much the same, there is hardly any verbal identity, and a good deal of matter is introduced into the one which is absent from the other. Now Josephus prides himself on his accuracy; people whose fathers might have heard Herod's oration were his contemporaries; and yet his historical sense is so curiously undeveloped, that he can, quite innocently, perpetuate an obvious literary fabrication; for one of the two accounts must be incorrect. Now, if I am asked whether I believe that Herod made some particular statement on this occasion; whether, for example, he uttered the pious aphorism, "Where God is, there is both multitude and courage," which is given in the "Antiquities," but not in the "Wars," I am compelled to say I do not know. One of the two reports must be erroneous, possibly both are: at any rate, I cannot tell how much of either is true. And, if some fervent admirer of the Idumean should build up a theory of Herod's piety upon Josephus's evidence that he propounded the aphorism, is it a "mere evasion" to say, in reply, that the evidence that he did utter it is worthless?

It appears again that, adopting the tactics of Conachar when brought face to face with Hal o' the Wynd, I have been trying to get my simple-minded adversary to follow me on a wild-goose chase through the early history of Christianity, in the hope of escaping impending defeat on the main issue. But I may be permitted to point out that there is an alternative hypothesis which equally fits the facts; and that, after all, there may have been method in the madness of my supposed panic.

For suppose it to be established that Gentile Christianity was a totally different thing from the Nazarenism of Jesus and his immediate disciples; suppose it to be demonstrable that, as early as the sixth decade of our era at least, there were violent divergencies of opinion among the followers of Jesus; suppose it to be hardly doubtful that the Gospels and the Acts took their present shapes under the influence of these divergencies; suppose that their authors, and those through whose hands they passed, had notions of historical veracity not more eccentric than those which Josephus occasionally displays—surely the chances that the Gospels are altogether trustworthy records of the teachings of Jesus become very slender. And as the whole of the case of the other side is based on the supposition that they are accurate records (especially of speeches, about which ancient historians are so curiously loose), I really do venture to submit that this part of my argument bears very seriously on the main issue ; and, as ratiocination, is sound to the core.

Again, when I passed by the topic of the speeches of Jesus on the cross, it appears that I could have had no other motive than the dictates of my native evasiveness. An ecclesiastical dignitary may have respectable reasons for declining a fencing-match " in sight of Gethsemane and Calvary " ; but an ecclesiastical " infidel " ! Never. It is obviously impossible that, in the belief that " the greater includes the less," I, having declared the Gospel evidence in general, as to the sayings of Jesus, to be of questionable value, thought it needless to select, for illustration of my views, those particular instances which were likely to be most offensive to persons of another way of thinking. But any supposition that may have been entertained that the old familiar tones of the ecclesiastical war-drum will tempt me to engage in such needless discussion had better be renounced. I shall do nothing of the kind. Let it suffice that I ask my readers to turn to the twenty-third chapter of Luke (revised version), verse thirty-four, and he will find in the margin

> Some ancient authorities omit: And Jesus said, "Father, forgive them, for they know not what they do."

So that, even as late as the fourth century, there were ancient authorities, indeed some of the most ancient and weightiest, who either did not know of this utterance, so often quoted as characteristic of Jesus, or did not believe it had been uttered.

Many years ago, I received an anonymous letter, which abused me heartily for my want of moral courage in not speaking out. I thought that one of the oddest charges an anonymous letter-writer could bring. But I am not sure that the plentiful sowing of the pages of the article with which I am dealing with accusations of evasion, may not seem odder to those who consider that the main strength of the answers with which I have been favored (in this review and elsewhere) is devoted not to anything in the text of my first paper, but to a note which occurs at page 171.* In this I say:

> Dr. Wace tells us: "It may be asked how far we can rely on the accounts we possess of our Lord's teaching on these subjects." And he seems to think the question appropriately answered by the assertion that it "ought to be regarded as settled by M. Renan's practical surrender of the adverse case."

I requested Dr. Wace to point out the passages of M. Renan's works, in which, as he affirms, this "practical surrender" (not merely as to the age and authorship of the Gospels, be it observed, but as to their historical value) is made, and he has been so good as to do so. Now let us consider the parts of Dr. Wace's citation from Renan which are relevant to the issue:

---

* Page 17.

The author of this Gospel [Luke] is certainly the same as the author of the Acts of the Apostles. Now the author of the Acts seems to be a companion of St. Paul—a character which accords completely with St. Luke. I know that more than one objection may be opposed to this reasoning; but one thing, at all events, is beyond doubt, namely, that the author of the third Gospel and of the Acts is a man who belonged to the second apostolic generation; and this suffices for our purpose.

This is a curious " practical surrender of the adverse case." M. Renan thinks that there is no doubt that the author of the third Gospel is the author of the Acts—a conclusion in which I suppose critics generally agree. He goes on to remark that this person *seems* to be a companion of St. Paul, and adds that Luke was a companion of St. Paul. Then, somewhat needlessly, M. Renan points out that there is more than one objection to jumping, from such data as these, to the conclusion that " Luke " is the writer of the third Gospel. And, finally, M. Renan is content to reduce that which is " beyond doubt " to the fact that the author of the two books is a man of the second apostolic generation. Well, it seems to me that I could agree with all that M. Renan considers "beyond doubt " here, without surrendering anything, either "practically " or theoretically.

Dr. Wace (" Nineteenth Century," March, p. 363)* states that he derives the above citation from the preface of the fifteenth edition of the " Vie de Jésus." My copy of " Les Evangiles," dated 1877, contains a list of Renan's " Œuvres Complètes," at the head of which I find " Vie de Jésus," 15ᵉ édition. It is, therefore, a later work than the edition of the " Vie de Jésus " which Dr. Wace quotes. Now " Les Evangiles," as its name implies, treats fully of

---

* Page 77.

the questions respecting the date and authorship of the Gospels; and any one who desired, not merely to use M. Renan's expressions for controversial purposes, but to give a fair account of his views in their full significance, would, I think, refer to the later source.

If this course had been taken, Dr. Wace might have found some as decided expressions of opinion in favor of Luke's authorship of the third Gospel as he has discovered in "The Apostles." I mention this circumstance because I desire to point out that, taking even the strongest of Renan's statements, I am still at a loss to see how it justifies that large-sounding phrase "practical surrender of the adverse case." For, on p. 438 of "Les Evangiles," Renan speaks of the way in which Luke's "excellent intentions" have led him to torture history in the Acts; he declares Luke to be the founder of that "eternal fiction which is called ecclesiastical history"; and, on the preceding page, he talks of the "myth" of the Ascension—with its *mise en scène voulue*. At p. 435, I find "Luc, ou l'auteur quel qu'il soit du troisième Evangile" [Luke, or whoever may be the author of the third Gospel]; at p. 280, the accounts of the Passion, the death and the resurrection of Jesus are said to be "peu historiques" [little historical]; at p. 283, "La valeur historique du troisième Evangile est sûrement moindre que celles des deux premiers" [the historical value of the third Gospel is surely less than that of the first two].

A Pyrrhic sort of victory for orthodoxy this "surrender"! And, all the while, the scientific student of theology knows that the more reason there may be to believe that Luke was the companion of Paul, the more doubtful becomes his credibility, if he really wrote the Acts. For, in that case, he could not fail to have been acquainted with Paul's account of the Jerusalem conference, and he must have consciously misrepresented it. We may next turn to the essential part of Dr. Wace's citation ("Nineteenth Century," p. 365)* touching the first Gospel:

> St. Matthew evidently deserves peculiar confidence for the discourses. Here are "the oracles"—the very notes taken while the memory of the instruction of Jesus was living and definite.

M. Renan here expresses the very general opinion as to the existence of a collection of "logia," having a different origin from the text in which they are imbedded, in Matthew. "Notes" are somewhat suggestive of a shorthand writer, but the suggestion is unintentional, for M. Renan assumes that these "notes" were taken, not at the time of the delivery of the "logia," but subsequently, while (as he assumes) the memory of them was living and definite; so that, in this very citation, M. Renan leaves open the question of the general historical value of the first Gospel, while it is obvious that the accuracy of "notes," taken, not at the time of delivery, but from memory, is a matter about which more than one opinion may be fairly held. Moreover, Renan expressly calls attention to the difficulty of distinguishing the authentic "logia" from later additions of the same kind ("Les Evangiles," p. 201). The fact is, there is no contradiction here to that opinion about the first Gospel which is expressed in "Les Evangiles" (p. 175.)

> The text of the so-called Matthew supposes the pre-existence of that of Mark, and does little more than complete it. He completes it in two fashions—first, by the insertion of those long discourses which gave their chief value to the Hebrew Gospels; then by adding traditions of a more modern formation, results of successive devel-

---

* Page 80.

opments of the legend, and to which the Christian consciousness already attached infinite value.

M. Renan goes on to suggest that besides "Mark," "pseudo-Matthew" used an Aramaic version of the Gospel originally set forth in that dialect. Finally, as to the second Gospel ("Nineteenth Century," p. 365):*

> He [Mark] is full of minute observations, proceeding, beyond doubt, from an eye-witness. There is nothing to conflict with the supposition that this eye-witness . . . was the apostle Peter himself, as Papias has it.

Let us consider this citation also by the light of "Les Evangiles":

> This work, although composed after the death of Peter, was, in a sense, the work of Peter; it represents the way in which Peter was accustomed to relate the life of Jesus (p. 116).

M. Renan goes on to say that, as an historical document, the Gospel of Mark has a great superiority (p. 116), but Mark has a motive for omitting the discourses; and he attaches a "puerile importance" to miracles (p. 117). The Gospel of Mark is less a legend than a biography written with credulity (p. 118). It would be rash to say that Mark has not been interpolated and retouched (p. 120).

If any one thinks that I have not been warranted in drawing a sharp distinction between "scientific theologians" and "counsel for creeds"; or that my warning against the too ready acceptance of certain declarations as to the state of biblical criticism was needless; or that my anxiety as to the sense of the word "practical" was superfluous, let him compare the statement that M. Renan has

---

* Page 81.

made a "practical surrender of the adverse case" with the facts just set forth. For what is the adverse case? The question, as Dr. Wace puts it, is, "It may be asked how far can we rely on the accounts we possess of our Lord's teaching on these subjects." It will be obvious that M. Renan's statements amount to an adverse answer —to a "practical" denial that any great reliance can be placed on these accounts. He does not believe that Matthew, the apostle, wrote the first Gospel; he does not profess to know who is responsible for the collection of "logia," or how many of them are authentic; though he calls the second Gospel the most historical, he points out that it is written with credulity, and may have been interpolated and retouched; and as to the author "quel qu'il soit" of the third Gospel, who is to "rely on the accounts" of a writer who deserves the cavalier treatment which "Luke" meets with at M. Renan's hands?

I repeat what I have already more than once said, that the question of the age and the authorship of the Gospels has not, in my judgment, the importance which is so commonly assigned to it; for the simple reason that the reports, even of eye-witnesses, would not suffice to justify belief in a large and essential part of their contents; on the contrary, these reports would discredit the witnesses. The Gadarene miracle, for example, is so extremely improbable, that the fact of its being reported by three, even independent, authorities could not justify belief in it unless we had the clearest evidence as to their capacity as observers and as interpreters of their observations. But it is evident that the three authorities are not independent; that they have simply adopted a legend, of which there were two versions; and instead of their proving its truth, it suggests their superstitious credulity;

so that, if "Matthew," "Mark," and "Luke" are really responsible for the Gospels, it is not the better for the Gadarene story, but the worse for them.

A wonderful amount of controversial capital has been made out of my assertion in the note to which I have referred, as an *obiter dictum* of no consequence to my argument, that, if Renan's work* were non-extant, the main results of biblical criticism as set forth in the works of Strauss, Baur, Reuss, and Volkmar, for example, would not be sensibly affected. I thought I had explained it satisfactorily already, but it seems that my explanation has only exhibited still more of my native perversity, so I ask for one more chance.

In the course of the historical development of any branch of science, what is universally observed is this: that the men who make epochs and are the real architects of the fabric of exact knowledge are those who introduce fruitful ideas or methods. As a rule, the man who does this pushes his idea or his method too far; or, if he does not, his school is sure to do so, and those who follow have to reduce his work to its proper value, and assign it its place in the whole. Not unfrequently they, in their turn, overdo the critical process, and, in trying to eliminate errors, throw away truth.

Thus, as I said, Linnæus, Buffon, Cuvier, Lamarck, really "set forth the results" of a developing science, although they often heartily contradict one another. Notwithstanding this circumstance, modern classificatory method and nomenclature have largely grown out of the results of the work of Linnæus; the modern conception of biology, as a science, and of its relation to climatology,

---

* I trust it may not be supposed that I undervalue M. Renan's labors or intended to speak slightingly of them.

geography, and geology, are as largely rooted in the results of the labors of Buffon; comparative anatomy and paleontology owe a vast debt to Cuvier's results; while invertebrate zoölogy and the revival of the idea of evolution are intimately dependent on the results of the work of Lamarck. In other words, the main results of biology up to the early years of this century are to be found in, or spring out of, the works of these men.

So, if I mistake not, Strauss, if he did not originate the idea of taking the mythopœic faculty into account in the development of the Gospel narratives; and, though he may have exaggerated the influence of that faculty, obliged scientific theology hereafter to take that element into serious consideration; so Baur, in giving prominence to the cardinal fact of the divergence of the Nazarene and Pauline tendencies in the primitive Church; so Reuss, in setting a marvelous example of the cool and dispassionate application of the principles of scientific criticism over the whole field of Scripture; so Volkmar, in his clear and forcible statement of the Nazarene limitations of Jesus, contributed results of permanent value in scientific theology. I took these names as they occurred to me. Undoubtedly, I might have advantageously added to them; perhaps I might have made a better selection. But it really is absurd to try to make out that I did not know that these writers widely disagree; and I believe that no scientific theologian will deny that, in principle, what I have said is perfectly correct. Ecclesiastical advocates, of course, can not be expected to take this view of the matter. To them, these mere seekers after truth, in so far as their results are unfavorable to the creed the clerics have to support, are more or less "infidels," or favorers of "infidelity"; and the only thing they care to see, or probably can see, is the fact that, in a great many matters, the truth-seekers differ from one another, and therefore can easily be exhibited to the public, as if they did nothing else; as if any one who referred to them, as having each and all contributed his share to the results of theological science, was merely showing his ignorance; and, as if a charge of inconsistency could be based on the fact that he himself often disagrees with what they say. I have never lent a shadow of foundation to the assumption that I am a follower of either Strauss, or Baur, or Reuss, or Volkmar, or Renan; my debt to these eminent men—so far my superiors in theological knowledge—is, indeed, great; yet it is not for their opinions, but for those I have been able to form for myself, by their help.

In "Agnosticism: a Rejoinder" (p. 96) I have referred to the difficulties under which those professors of the science of theology, whose tenure of their posts depends on the results of their investigations, must labor; and, in a note, I add:

Imagine that all our chairs of astronomy had been founded in the fourteenth century, and that their incumbents were bound to sign Ptolemaic articles. In that case, with every respect for the efforts of persons thus hampered to attain and expound the truth, I think men of common sense would go elsewhere to learn astronomy.

I did not write this paragraph without a knowledge that its sense would be open to the kind of perversion which it has suffered; but, if that was clear, the necessity for the statement was still clearer. It is my deliberate opinion: I reiterate it; and I say that, in my judgment, it is extremely inexpedient that any subject which calls itself a science should be intrusted to teachers who are debarred from freely following out scientific methods to their legitimate conclusions, whatever those conclusions may be. If I may borrow a phrase paraded at the Church Congress, I think it "ought to be unpleasant" for any man of science to find himself in the position of such a teacher.

Human nature is not altered by seating it in a professorial chair, even of theology. I have very little doubt that if, in the year 1859, the tenure of my office had depended upon my adherence to the doctrines of Cuvier, the objections to those set forth in the "Origin of Species" would have had a halo of gravity about them that, being free to teach what I pleased, I failed to discover. And, in making that statement, it does not appear to me that I am confessing that I should have been debarred by "selfish interests" from making candid inquiry, or that I should have been biased by "sordid motives." I hope that even such a fragment of moral sense as may remain in an ecclesiastical "infidel" might have got me through the difficulty; but it would be unworthy to deny or disguise the fact that a very serious difficulty must have been created for me by the nature of my tenure. And let it be observed that the temptation, in my case, would have been far slighter than in that of a professor of theology; whatever biological doctrine I had repudiated, nobody I cared for would have thought the worse of me for so doing. No scientific journals would have howled me down, as the religious newspapers howled down my too honest friend, the late Bishop of Natal; nor would my colleagues in the Royal Society have turned their backs upon me, as his episcopal colleagues boycotted him.

I say these facts are obvious, and that it is wholesome

and needful that they should be stated. It is in the interests of theology, if it be a science, and it is in the interests of those teachers of theology who desire to be something better than counsel for creeds, that it should be taken to heart. The seeker after theological truth, and that only, will no more suppose that I have insulted him than the prisoner who works in fetters will try to pick a quarrel with me, if I suggest that he would get on better if the fetters were knocked off; unless, indeed, as it is said does happen in the course of long captivities, that the victim at length ceases to feel the weight of his chains or even takes to hugging them, as if they were honorable ornaments.*

---

* To-day's "Times" contains a report of a remarkable speech by Prince Bismarck, in which he tells the Reichstag that he has long given up investing in foreign stock, lest so doing should mislead his judgment in his transactions with foreign states. Does this declaration prove that the chancellor accuses himself of being "sordid" and "selfish," or does it not rather show that, even in dealing with himself, he remains the man of realities?

X.

"COWARDLY AGNOSTICISM."*

A WORD WITH PROFESSOR HUXLEY.

By W. H. MALLOCK.

I WELCOME the discussion which, in this review and elsewhere, has been lately revived in earnest as to the issue between positive science and theology. I especially welcome Prof. Huxley's recent contribution to it, to which presently I propose to refer in detail. In that contribution—an article with the title "Agnosticism," which appeared a month or two since in "The Nineteenth Century"—I shall point out things which will probably startle the public, the author himself included, in case he cares to attend to them.

Before going further, however, let me ask and answer this question. If Prof. Huxley should tell us that he does not believe in God, why should we think the statement, as coming from him, worthy of an attention which we certainly should not give it if made by a person less distinguished than himself? The answer to this question is as follows: We should think Prof. Huxley's statement

---

* "The Bishop of Peterborough departed so far from his customary courtesy and self-respect as to speak of 'cowardly agnosticism.'"—PROF. HUXLEY, p. 15.

worth considering for two reasons: Firstly, he speaks as a man pre-eminently well acquainted with certain classes of facts. Secondly, he speaks as a man eminent, if not pre-eminent, for the vigor and honesty with which he has faced these facts, and drawn certain conclusions from them. Accordingly, when he sums up for us the main conclusions of science, he speaks not in his own name, but in the name of the physical universe, as modern science has thus far apprehended it; and similarly, when from these conclusions he reasons about religion, the bulk of the arguments which he advances against theology are in no way peculiar to himself, or gain any of their strength from his reputation; they are virtually the arguments of the whole non-Christian world. He may possibly have, on some points, views peculiar to himself. He may also have certain peculiar ways of stating them. But it requires no great critical acuteness, it requires only ordinary fairness, to separate those of his utterances which represent facts generally accepted, and arguments generally influential, from those which represent only some peculiarity of his own. Now, all this is true not of Prof. Huxley only. With various qualifications, it is equally true of writers with whom Prof. Huxley is apparently in constant antagonism, and who also exhibit constant antagonism among themselves. I am at this moment thinking of two especially—Mr. Frederic Harrison and Mr. Herbert Spencer. Mr. Harrison, in his capacity of religious teacher, is constantly attacking both Mr. Spencer and Prof. Huxley. Prof. Huxley repays Mr. Harrison's blows with interest; and there are certain questions of a religious and practical character as to which he and Mr. Spencer would be hardly on better terms. But, underneath the several questions they quarrel about, there is a solid substructure of conclusions, methods, and arguments, as to which they all agree—agree in the most absolute way. What this agreement consists in, and what practical bearing, if taken by itself, it must have on our views of life, I shall now try to explain in a brief and unquestionable summary; and in that summary, what the reader will have before him is not the private opinion of these eminent men, but ascertained facts with regard to man and the universe; and the conclusions which, if we have nothing else to assist us, are necessarily drawn from those facts by the necessary operations of the mind. The mention of names, however, has this signal convenience—it will keep the reader convinced that I am not speaking at random, and will supply him with standards by which he can easily test the accuracy and the sufficiency of my assertions.

The case, then, of science, or modern thought, against theological religion or theism, and the Christian religion in particular, substantially is as follows:

In the first place, it is now an established fact that the physical universe, whether it ever had a beginning or no, is, at all events, of an antiquity beyond what the imagination can realize; and also that, whether or no it is limited, its extent is so vast as to be equally unimaginable. Science may not pronounce it absolutely to be either eternal or infinite, but science does say this, that so far as our faculties can carry us they reveal to us no hint of either limit, end, or beginning.

It is further established that the stuff out of which the universe is made is the same everywhere and follows the same laws—whether at Clapham Common or in the farthest system of stars—and that this has always been so to the remotest of the penetrable abysses of time. It is established yet further that the universe in its present condition has evolved itself out of simpler conditions, solely in virtue of the qualities which still inhere in its elements, and make to-day what it is, just as they have made all yesterdays.

Lastly, in this physical universe science has included man—not alone his body, but his life and his mind also. Every operation of thought, every fact of consciousness, it has shown to be associated in a constant and definite way with the presence and with certain conditions of certain particles of matter, which are shown, in their turn, to be in their last analysis absolutely similar to the matter of gases, plants, or minerals. The demonstration has every appearance of being morally complete. The interval between mud and mind, seemingly so impassable, has been traversed by a series of closely consecutive steps. Mind, which was once thought to have descended into matter, is shown forming itself, and slowly emerging out of it. From forms of life so low that naturalists can hardly decide whether it is right to class them as plants or animals, up to the life that is manifested in saints, heroes, or philosophers, there is no break to be detected in the long process of development. There is no step in the process where science finds any excuse for postulating or even suspecting the presence of any new factor.

And the same holds good of the lowest forms of life, and what Prof. Huxley calls "the common matter of the universe." It is true that experimentalists have been thus far unable to observe the generation of the former out of the latter, but this failure may be accounted for in many ways, and does nothing to weaken the overwhelming evidence of analogy that such generation really does take place or has taken place at some earlier period.

"Carbonic acid, water, and ammonia," says Prof. Huxley, "certainly possess no properties but those of ordinary matter. . . . But when they are brought together under certain conditions they give rise to protoplasm; and this protoplasm exhibits the phenomenon of life. I see no breach in this series of steps in molecular complication, and I am unable to understand why the language which is applicable to any one form of the series may not be used to any of the others." *

So much, then, for what modern science teaches us as to the universe and the evolution of man. We will presently consider the ways, sufficiently obvious as they are, in which this seems to conflict with the ideas of all theism and theology. But first for a moment let us turn to what it teaches us also with regard to the history and the special claims of Christianity. Approaching Christianity on the side of its alleged history, it establishes the three following points: It shows us first that this alleged history, with the substantial truth of which Christianity stands or falls, contains a number of statements which are demonstrably at variance with fact; secondly, that it contains others which, though very probably true, are entirely misinterpreted through the ignorance of the writers who recorded them; and, thirdly, that though the rest may not be demonstrably false, yet those among them most essential to the Christian doctrine are so monstrously improbable and so utterly unsupported by evidence that we have no more ground for believing in them than we have in the wolf of Romulus.

Such, briefly stated, are the main conclusions of science in so far as they bear on theology and the theologic

---

* " Lay Sermons, Addresses, and Reviews," pp. 114, 117.

conception of humanity. Let us now consider exactly what their bearing is. Prof. Huxley distinctly tells us that the knowledge we have reached as to the nature of things in general does not enable us to deduce from it any absolute denial either of the existence of a personal God or of an immortal soul in man, or even of the possibility and the actual occurence of miracles. On the contrary, he would believe to-morrow in the miraculous history of Christianity if only there were any evidence sufficiently cogent in its favor; and on the authority of Christianity he would believe in God and in man's immortality. Christianity, however, is the only religion in the world whose claims to a miraculous authority are worthy of serious consideration, and science, as we have seen, considers these claims to be unfounded. What follows is this—whether there be a God or no, and whether he has given us immortal souls or no, science declares bluntly that he has never informed us of either fact; and if there is anything to warrant any belief in either, it can be found only in the study of the natural universe. Accordingly, to the natural universe science goes, and we have just seen what it finds there. Part of what it finds bears specially on the theologic conception of God, and part bears specially on the theologic conception of man. With regard to God, to an intelligent creator and ruler, it finds him on every ground to be a baseless and a superfluous hypothesis. In former conditions of knowledge it admits that this was otherwise—that the hypothesis then was not only natural but necessary; for there were many seeming mysteries which could not be explained without it. But now the case has been altogether reversed. One after another these mysteries have been analyzed, not entirely, but to this extent at all events, that the hypothesis of an intelligent creator is not only nowhere necessary, but it generally introduces far more difficulties than it solves. Thus, though we can not demonstrate that a creator does not exist, we have no grounds whatever for supposing that he does. With regard to man, what science finds is analogous. According to theology, he is a being specially related to God, and his conduct and his destinies have an importance which dwarfs the sum of material things into insignificance. But science exhibits him in a very different light; it shows that in none of the qualities once thought peculiar to him does he differ essentially from other phenomena of the universe. It shows that just as there are no grounds for supposing the existence of a creator, so there are none for supposing the existence of an immortal human soul; while as for man's importance relative to the rest of the universe, it shows that, not only as an individual, but also as a race, he is less than a bubble of foam is when compared with the whole sea. The few thousand years over which history takes us are as nothing when compared with the ages for which the human race has existed. The whole existence of the human race is as nothing when compared with the existence of the earth; and the earth's history is but a second and the earth but a grain of dust in the vast duration and vast magnitude of the All. Nor is this true of the past only, it is true of the future also. As the individual dies, so also will the race die; nor would a million of additional years add anything to its comparative importance. Just as it emerged out of lifeless matter yesterday, so will it sink again into lifeless matter to-morrow. Or, to put the case more briefly still, it is merely one fugitive manifestation of the same matter and force which, always obedient to the same unchanging laws, manifest themselves equally in a dung-heap, in a pig, and in a planet—matter and force which, so far as our faculties can carry us, have existed and will exist everywhere and forever, and which nowhere, so far as our faculties avail to read them, show any sign, as a whole, of meaning, of design, or of intelligence.

It is possible that Prof. Huxley, or some other scientific authority, may be able to find fault with some of my sentences or my expressions, and to show that they are not professionally or professorially accurate. If they care for such trifling criticism they are welcome to the enjoyment of it; but I defy any one to show, putting expression aside and paying attention only to the general meaning of what I have stated, that the foregoing account of what science claims to have established is not substantially true, and is not admitted to be so by any contemporary thinker who opposes science to theism, from Mr. Frederic Harrison to Prof. Huxley himself.

And now let us pass on to something which in itself is merely a matter of words, but which will bring what I have said thus far into the circle of contemporary discussion. The men who are mainly responsible for having forced the above views on the world, who have unfolded to us the verities of nature and human history, and have felt constrained by these to abandon their old religious convictions—these men and their followers have by common consent agreed, in this country, to call themselves by the name of agnostics. Now there has been much quarreling of late among these agnostics as to what agnosticism—the thing which unites them—is. It must be obvious, however, to every impartial observer, that the differences between them are little more than verbal, and arise from bad writing rather than from different reasoning. Substantially the meaning of one and all of them is the same. Let us take, for instance, the two who are most ostentatiously opposed to each other, and have lately been exhibiting themselves, in this and other reviews, like two terriers each at the other's throat. I need hardly say that I mean Prof. Huxley and Mr. Harrison.

Some writers, Prof. Huxley says, Mr. Harrison among them, have been speaking of agnosticism as if it was a creed or a faith or a philosophy. Prof. Huxley proclaims himself to be "dazed" and "bewildered" by the statements. Agnosticism, he says, is not any one of these things. It is simply—I will give his definition in his own words—

a method, the essence of which lies in the vigorous application of a single principle. . . . Positively, the principle may be expressed: In matters of the intellect, follow your reason as far as it will take you, without regard to any other consideration. And negatively: In matters of the intellect, do not pretend that conclusions are certain which are not demonstrated or demonstrable. That I take to be the agnostic faith, which if a man keep whole and undefiled, he shall not be ashamed to look the universe in the face, whatever the future may have in store for him.

Now anything worse expressed than this for the purpose of the discussion he is engaged in, or, indeed, for the purpose of conveying his own general meaning, it is hardly possible to imagine. Agnosticism, as generally understood, may, from one point of view, be no doubt rightly described as "a method." But is it a method with no results, or with results that are of no interest? If so, there would be hardly a human being idiot enough to waste a thought upon it. The interest resides in its results, and its results solely, and specially in those results that effect our ideas about religion. Accordingly, when the word agnosticism is now used in discussion, the meaning uppermost in the minds of those who use it is not a method, but the results of a method, in their religious bearings; and the method is of interest only in so far as it leads to these. Agnosticism means, therefore, precisely what Prof. Huxley says it does not mean. It means a creed, it means a faith, it means a religious or irreligious philosophy. And this is the meaning attributed to it not only by the world at large, but in reality by Prof. Huxley also quite as much as by anybody. I will not lay too much stress on the fact that, in the passage just quoted, having first fiercely declared agnosticism to be nothing but a method, in the very next sentence he himself speaks of it as a "faith." I will pass on to a passage that is far more unambiguous. It is taken from the same essay. It is as follows:

" 'Agnosticism [says Mr. Harrison] is a stage in the evolution of religion, an entirely negative stage, the point reached by physicists, a purely mental conclusion, with no relation to things social at all.' I am [says Prof. Huxley] quite dazed by this declaration. Are there then any 'conclusions' that are not 'purely mental'? Is there no relation to things social in 'mental conclusions' which affect men's whole conception of life? . . . 'Agnosticism is a stage in the evolution of religion.' If . . . Mr. Harrison, like most people, means by 'religion' theology, then, in my judgment, agnosticism can be said to be a stage in its evolution only as death may be said to be the final stage in the evolution of life."

Let us consider what this means. It means precisely what every one else has all along been saying, that agnosticism is to all intents and purposes a doctrine, a creed, a faith, or a philosophy, the essence of which is the negation of theologic religion. Now the fundamental propositions of theologic religion are these: There is a personal

God, who watches over the lives of men ; and there is an immortal soul in man, distinct from the flux of matter. Agnosticism, then, expressed in the briefest terms, amounts to two articles—not of belief, but of disbelief. *I do not believe in any God, personal, intelligent, or with a purpose ; or, at least, with any purpose that has any concern with man. I do not believe in any immortal soul, or in any personality or consciousness surviving the dissolution of the body.*

Here I anticipate from many quarters a rebuke, which men of science are very fond of administering. I shall be told that agnostics never say " there is no God," and never say " there is no immortal soul." Prof. Huxley is often particularly vehement on this point, He would have us believe that a dogmatic atheist is, in his view, as foolish as a dogmatic theist ; and that an agnostic, true to the etymology of his name, is not a man who denies God, but who has no opinion about him. But this—even if true in some dim and remote sense—is for practical purposes a mere piece of solemn quibbling, and is utterly belied by the very men who use it whenever they raise their voices to speak to the world at large. The agnostics, if they shrink from saying that there is no God, at least tell us that there is nothing to suggest that there is one, and much to suggest that there is not. Surely, if they never spoke more strongly than this, for practical purposes this is an absolute denial. Prof. Huxley, for instance, is utterly unable to demonstrate that an evening edition of the " Times " is not printed in Sirius ; but if any action depended on our believing this to be true, he would certainly not hesitate to declare that it was a foolish and fantastic falsehood. Who would think the better of him—who would not think the worse—if in this matter he gravely declared himself to be an agnostic? And precisely the same may be said of him with regard to the existence of God. For all practical purposes he is not in doubt about it. He denies it. I need not, however, content myself with my own reasoning. I find Prof. Huxley himself indorsing every word that I have just uttered. He declares that such questions as are treated of in volumes of divinity "are essentially questions of lunar politics, . . . not worth the attention of men who have work to do in the world": and he cites Hume's advice with regard to such volumes as being "most wise"— "Commit them to the flames, for they can contain nothing but sophistry and illusion." * Quotations of a similar import might be indefinitely multiplied; but it will be enough to add to this the statements quoted already, that agnosticism is to theologic religion what death is to life; and that physiology does but deepen and complete the gloom of the gloomiest motto of paganism—"*Debemur morti.*" If then agnosticism is not an absolute and dogmatic denial of the fundamental propositions of theology, it differs from an absolute and dogmatic denial in a degree that is so trivial as to be, in the words of Prof. Huxley himself, "not worth the attention of men who have work to do in the world." For all practical purposes and according to the real opinion of Prof. Huxley and Mr. Harrison equally, agnosticism is not doubt, is not suspension of judgment; but it is a denial of what "most people mean by religion"—that is to say, the fundamental propositions of theology, so absolute that Prof. Huxley compares it to their death.

And now let us pass on to the next point in our argu-

---

* "Lay Sermons, Addresses, and Reviews," p. 125.

ment, which I will introduce by quoting Prof. Huxley again. This denial of the fundamental propositions of theology "affects," he says, "men's whole conception of life." Let us consider how. By the Christian world, life was thought to be important owing to its connection with some unseen universe, full of interests and issues which were too great for the mind to grasp at present, but in which, for good or evil, we should each of us one day share, taking our place among the awful things of eternity. But at the touch of the agnostic doctrine this unseen universe bursts like a bubble, melts like an empty dream; and all the meaning which it once imparted to life vanishes from its surface like mists from a field at morning. In every sense but one, which is exclusively physical, man is remorselessly cut adrift from the eternal; and whatever importance or interest anything has for any of us, must be derived altogether from the shifting pains or pleasures which go to make up our momentary span of life, or the life of our race, which in the illimitable history of the All is an incident just as momentary.

Now supposing the importance and interest which life has thus lost can not be replaced in any other way, will life really have suffered any practical change and degradation? To this question our agnostics with one consent say Yes. Prof. Huxley says that if theologic denial leads us to nothing but materialism, "the beauty of a life may be destroyed," and "its energies paralyzed";[*] and that no one, not historically blind, "is likely to underrate the importance of the Christian faith as a factor in human history, or to doubt that some substitute genuine enough and worthy enough to replace it will arise."[†] Mr. Spen-

---

[*] "Lay Sermons, Addresses, and Reviews," p. 127.   [†] Page 50.

cer says the same thing with even greater clearness: while, as for Mr. Harrison, it is needless to quote from him; for half of what he has written is an amplification of these statements.

It is admitted, then, that life, in some very practical sense, will be ruined if science, having destroyed theologic religion, can not put, or allow to be put, some other religion in place of it. But we must not content ourselves with this general language. Life will be ruined, we say. Let us consider to what extent and how. There is a good deal in life which obviously will not be touched at all— that is to say, a portion of which is called the moral code. Theft, murder, some forms of lying and dishonesty, and some forms of sexual license, are inconsistent with the welfare of any society; and society, in self-defense, would still condemn and prohibit them, even supposing it had no more religion than a tribe of gibbering monkeys. But the moral code thus retained would consist of prohibitions only, and of such prohibitions only as could be enforced by external sanctions. Since, then, this much would survive the loss of religion, let us consider what would be lost along with it. Mr. Spencer, in general terms, has told us plainly enough. What would be lost, he says, is, in the first place, "our ideas of goodness, rectitude, or duty," or, to use a single word, "morality." This is no contradiction of what has just been said, for morality is not obedience, enforced or even instinctive, to laws which have an external sanction, but an active coöperation with the spirit of such laws, under pressure of a sanction that resides in our own wills. But not only would morality be lost, or this desire to work actively for the social good; there would be lost also every higher conception of what the social good or of what our own good is; and men would, as Mr. Spencer says, "become chiefly absorbed in the immediate and the relative."* Prof. Huxley admits in effect precisely the same thing when he says that the tendency of systematic materialism is to "paralyze the energies of life," and "to destroy its beauty."

Let us try to put the matter a little more concisely. It is admitted by our agnostics that the most valuable element in our life is our sense of duty, coupled with obedience to its dictates; and this sense of duty derives both its existence and its power over us from religion, and from religion alone. How it derived them from the Christian religion is obvious. The Christian religion prescribed it to us as the voice of God to the soul, appealing as it were to all our most powerful passions—to our fear, to our hope, and to our love. Hope gave it a meaning to us, and love and fear gave it a sanction. The agnostics have got rid of God and the soul together, with the loves, and fears, and hopes by which the two were connected. The problem before them is to discover some other considerations—that is, some other religion—which shall invest duty with the solemn meaning and authority derivable no longer from these. Our agnostics, as we know, declare themselves fully able to solve it. Mr. Spencer and Mr. Harrison, though the solution of each is different, declare not only that some new religion is ready for us, but that it is a religion higher and more efficacious than the old; while Prof. Huxley, though less prophetic and sanguine, rebukes those "who are alarmed lest

---

* "Since the beginning, religion has had the all-essential office of preventing men from being chiefly absorbed in the relative or the immediate, and of awaking them to a consciousness of something beyond it."—"First Principles," p. 100.

man's moral nature be debased," and declares that a wise man like Hume would merely "smile at their perplexities."*

Let us now consider what this new religion is—or rather these new religions, for we are offered more than one. So far as form goes, indeed, we are offered several. They can, however, all of them be resolved into two, resting on two entirely different bases, though sometimes, if not usually, offered to our acceptance in combination. One of these, which is called by some of its literary adherents Positivism or the Religion of Humanity, is based on two propositions with regard to the human race. The first proposition is that it is constantly though slowly improving, and will one day reach a condition thoroughly satisfactory to itself. The second proposition is that this remote consummation can be made so interesting to the present and to all intervening generations that they will strain every nerve to bring it about and hasten it. Thus, though humanity is admitted to be absolutely a fleeting phenomenon in the universe, it is presented relatively as of the utmost moment to the individual; and duty is supplied with a constant meaning by hope, and with a constant motive by sympathy. The basis of the other religion is not only different from this, but opposed to it. Just as this demands that we turn away from the universe, and concentrate our attention upon humanity, so the other demands that we turn away from humanity and concentrate our attention on the universe. Mr. Herbert Spencer calls this the Religion of the Unknowable; and though many agnostics consider the name fantastic, they one and all of them, if they resign the religion of hu-

---

* "Lay Sermons," pp. 123, 124.

manity, consider and appeal to this as the only possible alternative.

Now I have already in this review, not many months since, endeavored to show how completely absurd and childish the first of these two religions, the Religion of Humanity, is. I do not propose, therefore, to discuss it further here, but will beg the reader to consider that for the purpose of the present argument it is brushed aside like rubbish, unworthy of a second examination. Perhaps this request will sound somewhat arbitrary and arrogant, but I have something to add which will show that it is neither. The particular views which I now aim at discussing are the views represented by Prof. Huxley; and Prof. Huxley rejects the Religion of Humanity as completely as I do, and with a great deal less ceremony, as the following passage will demonstrate:

> Out of the darkness of prehistoric ages man emerges with the marks of his lowly origin strong upon him. He is a brute, only more intelligent than the other brutes; a blind prey to impulses, which, as often as not, lead him to destruction; a victim to endless illusions which, as often as not, make his mental existence a terror and a burden, and fill his physical life with barren toil and battle. He attains a certain degree of physical comfort, and develops a more or less workable theory of life, in such favorable situations as the plains of Mesopotamia or Egypt, and, then, for thousands and thousands of years, struggles with varying fortunes, attended by infinite wickedness, bloodshed, and misery, to maintain himself at this point against the greed and the ambition of his fellow-men. He makes a point of killing or otherwise persecuting all those who try to get him to move on; and when he has moved on a step, foolishly confers post-mortem deification on his victims. He exactly repeats the process with all who want to move a step yet further. And the best men of the best epoch are simply those who make the fewest blunders and commit the fewest sins. . . . I know of no study so unutterably saddening as that of the evolution of humanity

as it is set forth in the annals of history ; . . . [and] when the positivists order men to worship humanity—that is to say, to adore the generalized conception of men, as they ever have been, and probably ever will be—I must reply that I could just as soon bow down and worship the generalized conception of a "wilderness of apes."*

Let us pause here for a moment and look about us, so as to see where we stand. Up to a certain point the agnostics have all gone together with absolute unanimity, and I conceive myself to have gone with them. They have all been unanimous in their rejection of theology, and in regarding man and the race of men as a fugitive manifestation of the all-enduring something, which always, everywhere, and in an equal degree, is behind all other phenomena of the universe. They are unanimous also in affirming that, in spite of its fugitive character, life can afford us certain considerations and interests, which will still make duty binding on us, will still give it a meaning. At this point, however, they divide into two bands. Some of them assert that the motive and the meaning of duty is to be found in the history of humanity, regarded as a single drama, with a prolonged and glorious conclusion, complete in itself, satisfying in itself, and imparting, by the sacrament of sympathy, its own meaning and grandeur to the individual life, which would else be petty and contemptible. This is what some assert, and this is what others deny. With those who assert it we have now parted company, and are standing alone with those others who deny it—Prof. Huxley among them, as one of their chief spokesmen.

And now addressing myself to Prof. Huxley in this character, let me explain what I shall try to prove to him.

---

* Pages 51, 52.

If he could believe in God and in the divine authority of Christ, he admits he could account for duty and vindicate a meaning for life ; but he refuses to believe, even though for some reasons he might wish to do so, because he holds that the beliefs in question have no evidence to support them. He complains that an English bishop has called this refusal "cowardly"—" has so far departed from his customary courtesy and self-respect as to speak of ' cowardly agnosticism.' " I agree with Prof. Huxley that, on the grounds advanced by the bishop, this epithet " cowardly " is entirely undeserved ; but I propose to show him that, if not deserved on them, it is deserved on others, entirely unsuspected by himself. I propose to show that his agnosticism is really cowardly, but cowardly not because it refuses to believe enough, but because, tried by its own standards, it refuses to deny enough. I propose to show that the same method and principle, which is fatal to our faith in the God and the future life of theology, is equally fatal to anything which can give existence a meaning, or which can—to have recourse to Prof. Huxley's own phrases—" prevent our ' energies ' from being ' paralyzed,' and ' life's beauty ' from being destroyed." I propose, in other words, to show that his agnosticism is cowardly, not because it does not dare to affirm the authority of Christ, but because it does not dare to deny the meaning and the reality of duty. I propose to show that the miserable rags of argument with which he attempts to cover the life which he professes to have stripped naked of superstition, are part and parcel of that very superstition itself—that, though they are not the chasuble and the embroidered robe of theology, they are its hair-shirt, and its hair-shirt in tatters—utterly useless for the purpose to which it is despairingly applied, and serving only to make the forlorn wearer ridiculous. I propose to show that in retaining this dishonored garment, agnosticism is playing the part of an intellectual Ananias and Sapphira ; and that in professing to give up all that it can not demonstrate, it is keeping back part, and the larger part of the price—not, however, from dishonesty, but from a dogged and obstinate cowardice, from a terror of facing the ruin which its own principles have made.

Some, no doubt, will think that this is a rash undertaking, or else that I am merely indulging in the luxury of a little rhetoric. I hope to convince the reader that the undertaking is not rash, and that I mean my expressions to be taken in a frigid and literal sense. Let me begin then by repeating one thing, which I have said before. When I say that agnosticism is fatal to our conception of duty, I do not mean that it is fatal to those broad rules and obligations which are obviously necessary to any civilized society, which are distinctly defensible on obvious utilitarian grounds, and which, speaking generally, can be enforced by external sanctions. These rules and obligations have existed from the earliest ages of social life, and are sure to exist as long as social life exists. But so far are they from giving life a meaning, that on Prof. Huxley's own showing they have barely made life tolerable. A general obedience to them for thousands and thousands of years has left " the evolution of man, as set forth in the annals of history," the " most unutterably saddening study" that Prof. Huxley knows. From the earliest ages to the present—Prof. Huxley admits this—the nature of man has been such that, despite their laws and their knowledge, most men have made themselves miserable by yielding to "greed" and to "ambition," and by practicing "infinite wickedness." They have proscribed their wisest when alive, and accorded them a "foolish" hero-worship when dead. Infinite wickedness, blindness, and idiotic emotion have, then, according to Prof. Huxley's deliberate estimate, marked and marred men from the earliest ages to the present; and he deliberately says also, that "as men ever have been, they probably ever will be."

To do our duty, then, evidently implies a struggle. The impulses usually uppermost in us have to be checked, or chastened, by others, and these other impulses have to be generated, by fixing our attention on considerations which lie somehow beneath the surface. If this were not so, men would always have done their duty; and their history would not have been "unutterably saddening," as Prof. Huxley says it has been. What sort of considerations, then, must those we require be? Before answering this question let us pause for a moment, and, with Prof. Huxley's help, let us make ourselves quite clear what duty is. I have already shown that it differs from a passive obedience to external laws, in being a voluntary and active obedience to a law that is internal; but its logical aim is analogous—that is to say, the good of the community, ourselves included. Prof. Huxley describes it thus—"to devote one's self to the service of humanity, including intellectual and moral self-culture under that name"; "to pity and help all men to the best of one's ability"; "to be strong and patient," "to be ethically pure and noble"; and to push our devotion to others "to the extremity of self-sacrifice." All these phrases are Prof. Huxley's own. They are plain enough in themselves; but, to make what he means yet plainer, he tells us that the best examples of the duty he has been describing are to be found among Christian martyrs and saints, such as Catherine of Sienna, and above all in the ideal Christ—"the noblest ideal of humanity," he calls it, "which mankind has yet worshiped." Finally, he says that "religion, properly understood, is simply the reverence and love for [this] ethical ideal, and the desire to realize that ideal in life which every man ought to feel." That man "ought" to feel this desire, and "ought" to act on it, "is," he says, "surely indisputable," and "agnosticism has no more to do with it than it has with music or painting."

Here, then, we come to something at last which Prof. Huxley, despite all his doubts, declares to be certain—to a conclusion which agnosticism itself, according to his view, admits to be "indisputable." Agnosticism, however, as he has told us already, lays it down as a "fundamental axiom" that no conclusions are indisputable but such as are "demonstrated or demonstrable." The conclusion, therefore, that we ought to do our duty, and that we ought to experience what Prof. Huxley calls "religion," is evidently a conclusion which, in his opinion, is demonstrated or demonstrable with the utmost clearness and cogency. Before, however, inquiring how far this is the case, we must state the conclusion in somewhat different terms, but still in terms which we have Prof. Huxley's explicit warrant for using. Duty is a thing which men in general, "as they always have been, and probably ever will be," have lamentably failed to do, and to do which is very difficult, going as it does against some of the strongest and most victorious instincts of our nature. Prof. Huxley's conclusion, then, must be expressed thus: "We ought to do something which most of us do not do, and which we can not do without a severe and painful struggle, often involving the extremity of self-sacrifice."

And now, such being the case, let us proceed to this crucial question—What is the meaning of the all-important word "*ought*"? It does not mean merely that on utilitarian grounds the conduct in question can be defended as tending to certain beneficent results. This conclusion would be indeed barren and useless. It would merely amount to saying that some people would be happier if other people would for their sake consent to be miserable; or that men would be happier as a race if their instincts and impulses were different from "what they always have been and probably ever will be." When we say that certain conduct ought to be followed, we do not mean that its ultimate results can be shown to be beneficial to other people, but that they can be exhibited as desirable to the people to whom the conduct is recommended—and not only as desirable, but as desirable in a pre-eminent degree—desirable beyond all other results that are immediately beneficial to themselves. Now the positivists, or any other believers in the destinies of humanity, absurd as their beliefs may be, still have in their beliefs a means by which, theoretically, duty could be thus recommended. According to them, our sympathy with others is so keen, and the future in store for our descendants is so satisfying, that we have only to think of this future and we shall burn with a desire to work for it. But Prof. Huxley, and those who agree with him, utterly reject both of these suppositions. They say, and very rightly, that our sympathies are limited; and that the blissful future, which it is supposed will appeal to them, is moonshine. The utmost, then, in the way of objective results, that any of us can accomplish by following the path of duty, is not only little in itself, but there is no reason for supposing that it will contribute to anything great. On the contrary, it will only contribute to something which, as a whole, is "unutterably saddening."

Let us suppose, then, an individual with two ways of life open to him—the way of ordinary self-indulgence, and the way of pain, effort, and self-sacrifice. The first seems to him obviously the most advantageous; but he has heard so much fine talk in favor of the second, that he thinks it at least worth considering. He goes, we will suppose, to Prof. Huxley, and asks to have it demonstrated that this way of pain is preferable. Now what answer to that could Prof. Huxley make—he, or any other agnostic who agrees with him? He has made several answers. I am going to take them one by one; and while doing to each of them, as I hope, complete justice, to show that they are not only absolutely and ridiculously impotent to prove what is demanded of them, but they do not even succeed in touching the question at issue.

One of the answers hardly needs considering, except to show to what straits the thinker must be put who uses it. A man, says Prof. Huxley, ought to choose the way of pain and duty, because it conduces in some small degree to the good of others; and to do good to others ought to be his predominant desire, or, in other words, his religion. But the very fact in human nature that makes the question at issue worth arguing, is the fact that men naturally do not desire the good of others, or, at least, desire it in a very lukewarm way; and every consideration which the positivist school advance to make the good of others attractive and interesting to ourselves Prof. Huxley dismisses with what we may call an uproarious contempt. If, then, we are not likely to be nerved to our duty by a belief that duty done tends to produce and hasten a change that shall really make the whole human lot beautiful, we are not likely to be nerved to it by the belief that its utmost possible result will be some partial and momentary benefit to a portion of a "wilderness of apes." The positivist says to the men of the present day: "Work hard at the foundation of things social; for on these foundations one day will arise a glorious edifice." Prof. Huxley tells them to work equally hard, only he adds that the foundation will never support anything better than pig-sties. His attempt, then, on social grounds, to make duty binding, and give force to the moral imperative, is merely a fragment of Mr. Harrison's system, divorced from anything that gave it a theoretical meaning. Prof. Huxley has shattered that system against the hard rock of reality, and this is one of the pieces which he has picked up out of the mire.

The social argument, then, we may therefore put aside, as good perhaps for showing what duty is, but utterly useless for creating any desire to do it. Indeed, to render Prof. Huxley justice, it is not the argument on which he mainly relies. The argument, or rather the arguments, on which he mainly relies have no direct connection with things social at all. They seek to create a religion, or to give a meaning to duty, by dwelling on man's connection, not with his fellow-men, but with the universe, and thus developing in the individual a certain ethical self-reverence, or rather, perhaps, preserving his existing self-reverence from destruction. How any human being who pretends to accurate thinking can conceive that these arguments would have the effect desired —that they would either tend in any way to develop self-reverence of any kind, or that this self-reverence, if developed, could connect itself with practical duty—passes my comprehension. Influential and eminent men, however, declare that such is their opinion; and for that reason the arguments are worth analyzing. Mr. Herbert Spencer is here in almost exact accord with Prof. Huxley; we will therefore begin by referring to his way of stating the matter.

"We are obliged," he says, "to regard every phenomenon as a manifestation of some power by which we are acted on; though omnipresence is unthinkable, yet, as experience discloses no bounds to the diffusion of phenomena, we are unable to think of limits to the presence of this power; while the criticisms of science teach us that this power is incomprehensible. And this consciousness of an incomprehensible power, called omnipresent from inability to assign its limits, is just that consciousness on which religion dwells." * Now Prof. Huxley, it will be remembered, gives an account of religion quite different. He says it is a desire to realize a certain ideal in life. His terminology therefore differs from that of Mr. Spencer; but of the present matter, as the following quotation will show, his view is substantially the same.

"Let us suppose," he says, "that knowledge is absolute, and not relative, and therefore that our conception of matter represents that which really is. Let us suppose further that we do know more of cause and effect than a certain succession; and I for my part do not see what escape there is from utter materialism and necessarianism." And this materialism, were it really what science forces on us, he admits would amply justify the darkest fears that are entertained of it. It would "drown man's

---

* "First Principles," p. 99.

soul," "impede his freedom," "paralyze his energies," "debase his moral nature," and "destroy the beauty of his life." * But, Prof. Huxley assures us, these dark fears are groundless. There is indeed only one avenue of escape from them; but that avenue truth open to us.

"For," he says, "after all, what do we know of this terrible 'matter,' except as a name for the unknown and hypothetical cause of states of our own consciousness? And what do we know of that 'spirit' over whose extinction by matter a great lamentation is arising, . . . except that it also is a name for an unknown and hypothetical cause or condition of states of consciousness? . . . And what is the dire necessity and iron law under which men groan? Truly, most gratuitously invented bugbears. I suppose if there be an 'iron' law it is that of gravitation; and if there be a physical necessity it is that a stone unsupported must fall to the ground. But what is all we really know and can know about the latter phenomena? Simply that in all human experience stones have fallen to the ground under these conditions; that we have not the smallest reason for believing that any stone so circumstanced will not fall to the ground; and that we have, on the contrary, every reason to believe that it will so fall. . . . But when, as commonly happens, we change *will* into *must*, we introduce an idea of necessity which . . . has no warranty that I can discover anywhere. . . . Force I know, and Law I know; but who is this Necessity, save an empty shadow of my own mind's throwing?"

Let us now compare the statements of these two writers. Each states that the reality of the universe is unknowable; that just as surely as matter is always one aspect of mind, so mind is equally one aspect of matter; and that if it is true to say that the thoughts of man are material, it is equally true to say that the earth from which man is taken is spiritual. Further, from these statements each writer deduces a similar moral. The only

---

* "Lay Sermons," pp. 122, 123, 127.

difference between them is, that Mr. Spencer puts it positively, and Prof. Huxley negatively. Mr. Spencer says that a consciousness of the unknowable nature of the universe fills the mind with religious emotion. Prof. Huxley says that the same consciousness will preserve from destruction the emotion that already exists in it. We will examine the positive and negative propositions in order, and see what bearing, if any, they have on practical life.

Mr. Spencer connects his religion with practical life thus: The mystery and the immensity of the All, and our own inseparable connection with it, deepen and solemnize our own conception of ourselves. They make us regard ourselves as "elements in that great evolution of which the beginning and the end are beyond our knowledge or conception"; and in especial they make us so regard our "own innermost convictions."

"It is not for nothing," says Mr. Spencer, "that a man has in him these sympathies with some principles, and repugnance to others. . . . He is a descendant of the past; he is a parent of the future; and his thoughts are as children born to him, which he may not carelessly let die. He, like every other man, may properly consider himself as one of the myriad agencies through whom works the Unknown Cause and when the Unknown Cause produces in him a certain belief, he is thereby authorized to profess and act with this belief." *

In all the annals of intellectual self-deception it would be hard to find anything to outdo or even to approach this. What a man does or thinks, what he professes or acts out, can have no effect whatever, conceivable to ourselves, beyond such effects as it produces within the limits of this planet; and hardly any effect, worth

---

* "First Principles," p. 123.

our consideration, beyond such as it produces on himself and a few of his fellow-men. Now, how can any of these effects be connected with the evolution of the universe in such a way as to enable a consciousness of the universe to inform us that one set of effects should be aimed at by us rather than another? The positivists say that our aim should be the progress of man; and that, as I have said, forms a standard of duty, though it may not supply a motive. But what has the universe to do with the progress of man? Does it know anything about it, or care anything about it? Judging from the language of Mr. Spencer and Prof. Huxley, one would certainly suppose that it did. Surely, in that case, here is anthropomorphism with a vengeance. "It is not for nothing," says Mr. Spencer, "that the Unknowable has implanted in a man certain impulses." What is this but the old theologic doctrine of design? Can anything be more inconsistent with the entire theory of the evolutionist? Mr. Spencer's argument means, if it means anything, that the Unknowable has implanted in us one set of sympathies in a sense in which it has not implanted others; else the impulse to deny one's belief, and not to act on it, which many people experience, would be authorized by the Unknowable as much as the impulse to profess it, and to act on it. And according to Mr. Spencer's entire theory, according to Prof. Huxley's entire theory, according to the entire theory of modern science, it is precisely this that is the case. If it is the fact that the Unknowable works through any of our actions, it works through all alike, bad, good, and indifferent, through our lies as well as through our truth-telling, through our injuries to our race as well as through our benefits to it. The attempt to connect the well-being of humanity with any general tendency observable in the universe, is in fact, on agnostic principles, as hopeless as an attempt to get, in a balloon, to Jupiter. It is utterly unfit for serious men to talk about; and its proper place, if anywhere, would be in one of Jules Verne's story-books. The destinies of mankind, so far as we have any means of knowing, have as little to do with the course of the Unknowable as a whole, as the destinies of an ant-hill in South Australia have to do with the question of home rule for Ireland.

Or even supposing the Unknowable to have any feeling in the matter, how do we know that its feeling would be in our favor, and that it would not be gratified by the calamities of humanity, rather than by its improvement? Or here is a question which is more important still. Supposing the Unknowable did desire our improvement, but we, as Prof. Huxley says of us, were obstinately bent against being improved, what could the Unknowable do to us for thus thwarting its wishes?

And this leads us to another aspect of the matter. If consciousness of the Unknowable does not directly influence action, it may yet be said that the contemplation of the universe as the wonderful garment of this unspeakable mystery, is calculated to put the mind into a serious and devout condition, which would make it susceptible to the solemn voice of duty. How any devotion so produced could have any connection with duty I confess I am at a loss to see. But I need not dwell on that point, for what I wish to show is this, that contemplation of the Unknowable, from the agnostic's point of view, is not calculated to produce any sense of devoutness at all. Devoutness is made up of three things, fear, love, and wonder; but were the agnostic's thoughts really controlled by his principles (which they are not) not one of these emotions could the Unknowable possibly excite in him. It need hardly be said that he has no excuse for loving it, for his own first principles forbid him to say that it is lovable, or that it possesses any character, least of all any anthropomorphic character. But perhaps it is calculated to excite fear or awe in him. This idea is more plausible than the other. The universe as compared with man is a revelation of forces that are infinite, and it may be said that surely these have something awful and impressive in them. There is, however, another side to the question. This universe represents not only infinite forces, but it represents also infinite impotence. So long as we conform ourselves to certain ordinary rules we may behave as we like for anything it can do to us. We may look at it with eyes of adoration, or make faces at it, and blaspheme it, but for all its power it can not move a finger to touch us. Why, then, should a man be in awe of this lubberly All, whose blindness and impotence are at least as remarkable as its power, and from which man is as absolutely safe as a mouse in a hole is from a lion? But there still remains the emotion of wonder to be considered. Is not the universe calculated to excite our wonder? From the agnostic point of view we must certainly say No. The further science reveals to us the constitution of things the feeling borne in on us more and more strongly is this, that it is not wonderful that things happen as they do, but that it would be wonderful if they happened otherwise: while as for the Unknown Cause that is behind what science reveals to us, we can not wonder at that, for we know nothing at all about it, and, if there is any wonder involved in the matter at all, it is nothing but wonder at our own ignorance.

So much, then, for our mere emotions toward the

Unknowable. There still remains, however, one way more in which it is alleged that our consciousness of it can be definitely connected with duty; and this is the way which our agnostic philosophers most commonly have in view, and to which they allude most frequently. I allude to the search after scientific truth and the proclamation of it, regardless of consequences. Whenever the agnostics are pressed as to the consequences of their principles, it is on this conception of duty that they invariably fall back. Mr. Herbert Spencer, on his own behalf, expresses the position thus:

> The highest truth he sees will the wise man fearlessly utter, knowing that, let what may come of it, he is thus playing his right part in the world, knowing that if he can effect the change [in belief] he aims at, well; if not, well also; though not *so* well.*

After what has been said already it will not be necessary to dwell long on this astonishing proposition. A short examination will suffice to show its emptiness. That a certain amount of truth in social intercourse is necessary for the continuance of society, and that a large number of scientific truths are useful in enabling us to add to our material comforts is, as Prof. Huxley would say "surely indisputable." And truth thus understood it is "surely indisputable" that we should cultivate. The reason is obvious. Such truth has certain social consequences, certain things that we all desire come of it; but the highest truth which Mr. Spencer speaks of stands, according to him, on a wholly different basis, and we are to cultivate it, not because of its consequences, but in defiance of them. And what are its consequences, so far as we can see? Prof. Huxley's answer is this: "I have

---

* "First Principles," p. 123.

had, and have, the firmest conviction that . . . the *verace via*, the straight road, has led nowhere else but into the dark depths of a wild and tangled forest." Now if this be the case, what possible justification can there be for following this *verace via?* In what sense is the man who follows it playing " his right part in the world "? And when Mr. Spencer says, with regard to his conduct, " it is well," with whom is it well, or in what sense is it well? We can use such language with any warrant or with any meaning only on the supposition that the universe, or the Unknowable as manifested through the universe, is concerned with human happiness in some special way, in which it is not concerned with human misery, and that thus our knowledge of it must somehow make men happier, even though it leads them into a wild and tangled forest. It is certain that our devotion to truth will not benefit the universe; the only question is, will knowledge of the universe, beyond a certain point, benefit us? But the supposition just mentioned is merely theism in disguise. It imputes to the Unknowable design, purpose, and affection. In every way it is contrary to the first principles of agnosticism. Could we admit it, then devotion to truth might have all the meaning that Mr. Spencer claims for it: but if this supposition is denied, as all agnostics deny it, this devotion to truth, seemingly so noble and so unassailable, sinks to a superstition more abject, more meaningless, and more ridiculous than that of any African savage, groveling and mumbling before his fetich.

We have now passed under review the main positive arguments by which our agnostics, while dismissing the existence of God as a question of lunar politics, endeavor to exhibit the reality of religion, and of duty, as a thing that is "surely indisputable." We will now pass on to their negative arguments. While by positive arguments they endeavor to prove that duty and religion are realities, by their negative arguments they endeavor to prove that duty and religion are not impossibilities. We have seen how absolutely worthless to their cause are the former; but if the former are worthless, the latter are positively fatal.

What they are the reader has already seen. I have taken the statement of them from Prof. Huxley, but Mr. Spencer uses language almost precisely similar. These arguments start with two admissions. Were all our actions linked one to another by mechanical necessity, it is admitted that responsibility and duty would be no longer conceivable. Our "energies," as Prof. Huxley admits, would be "paralyzed" by "utter necessarianism." Further, did our conception of matter represent a reality, were matter low and gross, as we are accustomed to think of it, then man, as the product of matter, would be low and gross also, and heroism and duty would be really successfully degraded, by being reduced to questions of carbon and ammonia. But from all of these difficulties Prof. Huxley professes to extricate us. Let us look back at the arguments by which he considers that he has done so.

We will begin with his method of liberating us from the "iron" law of necessity, and thus giving us back our freedom and moral character. He performs this feat, or rather, he thinks he has performed it, by drawing a distinction between what *will* happen and what *must* happen. On this distinction his entire position is based. Now in every argument used by any sensible man there is probably some meaning. Let us try fairly to see what is the meaning in this. I take it that the idea at the bottom of

Prof. Huxley's mind is as follows: Though all our scientific reasoning presupposes the uniformity of the universe, we are unable to assert of the reality behind the universe, that it might not manifest itself in ways by which all present science would be baffled. But what has an idea like this to do with any practical question? So far as man, and man's will, are concerned, we have to do only with the universe as we know it; and the only knowledge we have of it, worth calling knowledge, involves, as Prof. Huxley is constantly telling us, "the great act of faith," which leads us to take what has been as a certain index of what will be. Now, with regard to this universe, Prof. Huxley tells us that the progress of science has always meant, and "means now more than ever," "the extension of the province of . . . causation, and . . . the banishment of spontaneity."* And this applies, as he expressly says, to human thought and action as much as to the flowering of a plant. Just as there can be no voluntary action without volition, so there can be no volition without some preceding cause. Accordingly, if a man's condition at any given moment were completely known, his actions could be predicted with as much or with as little certainty as the fall of a stone could be predicted if released from the hand that held it. Now Prof. Huxley tells us that, with regard to certainty, we are justified in saying that the stone will fall; and we should, therefore, be justified in saying similarly of the man, that he will act in such and such a manner. Whether theoretically we are absolutely certain is no matter. We are absolutely certain for all practical purposes, and the question of human freedom is nothing if not practical. What then

---

* "Lay Sermons," p. 123.

is gained—is anything gained—is the case in any way altered—by telling ourselves that, though there is certainty in the case, there is no necessity? Suppose I held a loaded pistol to Prof. Huxley's ear, and offered to pull the trigger, should I reconcile him to the operation by telling him that, though it certainly would kill him, there was not the least necessity that it should do so? And with regard to volition and action, as the result of preceding causes, is not the case precisely similar? Let Prof. Huxley turn to all the past actions of humanity. Can he point to any smallest movement of any single human being, which has not been the product of causes, which in their turn have been the product of other causes? Or can he point to any causes which, under given conditions, could have produced any effects other than those they have produced, unless he uses the word *could* in the foolish and fantastic sense which would enable him to say that unsupported stones could possibly fly upward? For all practical purposes the distinction between *must* and *will* is neither more nor less than a feeble and childish sophism. Theoretically no doubt it will bear this meaning—that the Unknowable might have so made man, that at any given moment he could be a different being: but it does nothing to break the force of what all science teaches us—that man, formed as he is, can not act otherwise than as he does. The universe may have no necessity at the back of *it;* but its presence and its past alike are a necessity at the back of *us;* and it is not necessity, but it is doubt of necessity, that is really "the shadow of our own mind's throwing."

And now let us face Prof. Huxley's other argument, which is to save life from degradation by taking away the reproach from matter. If it is true, he tells us, to say that everything, mind included, is matter, it is equally true to say that everything, matter included, is mind; and thus, he argues, the dignity we all attribute to mind, at once is seen to diffuse itself throughout the entire universe. Mr. Herbert Spencer puts the same view thus:

> Such an attitude of mind [contempt for matter and dread of materialism] is significant not so much of a reverence for the Unknown Cause, as of an irreverence for those familiar forms in which the Unknown Cause is manifested to us.* . . . But whoever remembers that the forms of existence of which the uncultivated speak with so much scorn . . . are found to be the more marvelous the more they are investigated, and are also to be found to be in their natures absolutely incomprehensible . . . will see that the course proposed [a reduction of all things to terms of matter] does not imply a degradation of the so-called higher, but an elevation of the so-called lower.

The answer to this argument, so far as it touches any ethical or religious question, is at once obvious and conclusive. The one duty of ethics and of religion is to draw a distinction between two states of emotion and two courses of action—to elevate the one and to degrade the other. But the argument we are now considering, though undoubtedly true in itself, has no bearing on this distinction whatever. It is invoked to show that religion and duty remain spiritual in spite of all materialism; but it ends, with unfortunate impartiality, in showing the same thing of vice and of cynical worldliness. If the life of Christ is elevated by being seen in this light, so also is the life of Casanova; and it is as impossible in this way to make the one higher than the other as it is to make one man higher than another by taking them both up in a balloon.

---

* "First Principles," p. 556.

I have now gone through the whole case for duty and for religion, as stated by the agnostic school, and have shown that, as thus stated, there is no case at all. I have shown their arguments to be so shallow, so irrelevant, and so contradictory, that they never could have imposed themselves on the men who condescend to use them, if these men, upon utterly alien grounds, had not pledged themselves to the conclusion which they invoke the arguments to support. Something else, however, still remains to be done. Having seen how agnosticism fails to give a basis to either religion or duty, I will point out to the reader how it actively and mercilessly destroys them. Religion and duty, as has been constantly made evident in the course of the foregoing discussion, are, in the opinion of the agnostics, inseparably connected. Duty is a course of conduct which is more than conformity to human law; religion consists of the emotional reasons for pursuing that conduct. Now these reasons, on the showing of the agnostics themselves, are reasons that do not lie on the surface of the mind. They have to be sought out in moods of devoutness and abstraction, and the more we dwell on them, the stronger they are supposed to become. They lie above and beyond the ordinary things of life; but after communing with them, it is supposed that we shall descend to these things with our purposes sharpened and intensified. It is easy to see, however, if we divest ourselves of all prejudice, and really conceive ourselves to be convinced of nothing which is not demonstrable by the methods of agnostic science, that the more we dwell on the agnostic doctrine of the universe, the less and not the more shall duty seem to be binding on us.

I have said that agnosticism can supply us with no religion. Perhaps I was wrong in saying so, but if we will but invert the supposed tendency of religion, it can and it will supply us with a religion indeed. It will supply us with a religion which, if we describe it in theological language, we may with literal accuracy describe as the religion of the devil—of the devil, the spirit which denies. Instead of telling us of duty, that it has a meaning which does not lie on the surface, such meaning as may lie on the surface it will utterly take away. It will indeed tell us that the soul which sins shall die; but it will tell us in the same breath that the soul which does not sin shall die the same death. Instead of telling us that we are responsible for our actions, it will tell us that if anything is responsible for them it is the blind and unfathomable universe; and if we are asked to repent of any shameful sins we have committed, it will tell us we might as well be repentant about the structure of the solar system. These meditations, these communings with scientific truth, will be the exact inverse of the religious meditations of the Christian. Every man, no doubt, has two voices—the voice of self-indulgence or indifference, and the voice of effort and duty; but whereas the religion of the Christian enabled him to silence the one, the religion of the agnostic will forever silence the other. I say forever, but I probably ought to correct myself. Could the voice be silenced forever, then there might be peace in the sense in which Roman conquerors gave the name of peace to solitude. But it is more likely that the voice will still continue, together with the longing expressed by it, only to feel the pains of being again and again silenced, or sent back to the soul saying bitterly, I am a lie.

Such, then, is really the result of agnosticism on life, and the result is so obvious to any one who knows how to reason, that it could be hidden from nobody, except by one thing, and that is the cowardice characteristic of all our contemporary agnostics. They dare not face what they have done. They dare not look fixedly at the body of the life which they have pierced.

And now comes the final question to which all that I have thus far urged has been leading. What does theologic religion answer to the principles and to the doctrines of agnosticism? In contemporary discussion the answer is constantly obscured, but it is of the utmost importance that it should be given clearly. It says this: If we start from and are faithful to the agnostic's fundamental principles, that nothing is to be regarded as certain which is not either demonstrated or demonstrable, then the denial of God is the only possible creed for us. To the methods of science, nothing in this universe gives any hint of either a God or a purpose. Duty; and holiness, aspiration and love of truth, are "merely shadows of our own mind's throwing," but shadows which, instead of making the reality brighter, only serve to make it more ghastly and hideous. Humanity is a bubble; the human being is a puppet cursed with the intermittent illusion that he is something more, and roused from this illusion with a pang every time it flatters him. Now, from this condition of things is there no escape? Theologic religion answers, There is one, and one only, and this is the repudiation of the principle on which all agnosticism rests.

Let us see what this repudiation amounts to, and we shall then realize what, in the present day, is the intellectual basis which theologic religion claims. Theologic religion does not say that within limits the agnostic principle is not perfectly valid and has not led to the discovery of a vast body of truth. But what it does say is this: That the truths which are thus discovered are not the only truths which are certainly and surely discoverable. The fundamental principle of agnosticism is that nothing is certainly true but such truths as are demonstrated or demonstrable. The fundamental principle of theologic religion is that there are other truths of which we can be equally or even more certain, and that these are the only truths that give life a meaning and redeem us from the body of death. Agnosticism says nothing is certain which can not be proved by science. Theologic religion says, nothing which is important can be. Agnosticism draws a line round its own province of knowledge, and beyond that it declares is the unknown void which thought can not enter, and in which belief can not support itself. Where Agnosticism pauses, there religion begins. On what seems to science to be unsustaining air, it lays its foundations—it builds up its fabric of certainties. Science regards them as dreams, as an "unsubstantial pageant"; and yet even to science religion can give some account of them. Prof. Huxley says, as we have seen, that "from the nature of ratiocination," it is obvious that it must start "from axioms which can not be demonstrated by ratiocination"; and that in science it must start with "one great act of faith"—faith in the uniformity of nature. Religion replies to science: "And I, too, start with a faith in one thing. I start with a faith which you, too, profess to hold—faith in the meaning of duty and the infinite importance of life; and out of that faith my whole fabric of certainties, one after the other, is reared by the hands of reason. Do you ask for proof? Do you ask for verification? I can give you one only, which you may take or leave, as you choose. Deny the certainties which I declare to be certain—deny the existence of God, deny man's freedom and immortality, and by no other conceivable hypothesis can you vindicate for man's life any possible meaning, or save it from the degradation at which you profess to feel so aghast." "Is there no other way," I can conceive science asking, "no other way by which the dignity of life may be vindicated except this—the abandonment of my one fundamental principle? Must I put my lips, in shame and humiliation, to the cup of faith I have so contemptuously cast away from me? May not this cup pass from me? Is there salvation in no other?" And to this question, without passion or preference, the voice of reason and logic pitilessly answers "No."

Here is the dilemma which men, sooner or later, will see before them, in all its crudeness and nakedness, cleared from the rags with which the cowardice of contemporary agnosticism has obscured it; and they will then have to choose one alternative or the other. What their choice will be I do not venture to prophesy; but I will venture to call them happy if their choice prove to be this: To admit frankly that their present canon of certainity, true so far as it goes, is only the pettiest part of truth, and that the deepest certainties are those which, if tried by this canon, are illusions. To make this choice a struggle would be required with pride, and with what has long passed for enlightenment; and yet, when it is realized what depends on the struggle, there are some at least who will think that it must end successfully. The only way by which, in the face of science, we can ever logically arrive at a faith in life, is by the commission of what many at present will describe as an intellectual suicide. I do not for a moment admit that such an expression is justifiable, but, if I may use it provisionally, and because it points to the temper at present prevalent, I shall be simply pronouncing the judgment of frigid reason in saying that it is only through the grave and gate of death that the spirit of man can pass to its resurrection.

XI.

THE NEW REFORMATION.

A DIALOGUE.

By MRS. HUMPHRY WARD.

In a sitting-room belonging to a corner house in one of the streets running from the Strand toward the Embankment, a young man sat reading on a recent winter afternoon. Behind him was an old-fashioned semicircular window, through which the broad gray line of the river, the shipping on its stream, and the dark masses of building on the opposite shore could be as plainly seen as the fading light permitted. But a foggy evening was stealing rapidly on, and presently the young man dropped his book, and betook himself to his pipe, supplemented by a dreamy study of the fire. A sound was heard in the little hall down-stairs; the reader started up, went to the door, and listened; but all was quiet again, and he returned to his chair. As he moved he showed a figure, tall, and possessed of a certain slouching, broad-shouldered power. The hair was noticeably black, and curled closely over the head. The features were strongly cut, dashed in, a little by accident, as it seemed, so that only the mouth had fallen finely into drawing. But through the defects of the face, as through the student's stoop of the powerful frame, there breathed an attractive and vigorous individuality. You saw a man all alive, marked already by the intensity with which he had plied his trade, and curiously combining in his outward aspect the suggestions of a patient tenacity with those of a quick and irritable susceptibility.

"I must wait for him, I suppose," he said to himself, as he resumed his seat. "I wish it were over. Come here, Tony, and support me."

The Aberdeen terrier on the rug got up slowly, sleepily blinked at his master, and climbed into the chair beside him, where he had hardly established himself, after a long process of leisurely fidgeting, when the hall-door bell rang in good earnest, and Tony, hastily driven down, was left to meditate on the caprices of power.

His master threw open the door.

"Well, how are you, my dear old fellow?" said the new-comer. "I thought I never should get here. The lunch at Lambeth was interminable, and one saw so many people there whom one knew a little, and was glad to talk to, that even after lunch it was impossible to cut it short. But how are you? How glad I am to see you!"

And the speaker advanced into the room, still holding the other's hand affectionately. He was a slightly-built man, in a clerical coat, with a long, narrow face and piercing eyes. The whole aspect was singularly refined; all the lines were thin and prematurely worn; but the expression was sparkling and full of charm, and the strong priestly element in dress and manner clearly implied no lack of pliancy of mind, of sensitiveness and elasticity of feeling.

"Sit down there," said the owner of the rooms, putting the new-comer into the chair he himself had just vacated. "Tony—you impudence!—out of that! Really, that dog and I have been living so long by ourselves that *his* manners, at any rate, are past praying for—and I should be sorry to answer for my own."

"Well, and where have you been all this time, Merriman?" said the man in the chair, looking up at his companion with an expression in which a very strong and evident pleasure seemed to be crossed by something else. "Two years, isn't it, since we parted at Oxford, and since I went off to my first curacy? And not a line from you since—not one—not even an address on a postcard, till I heard from you that you would be in town to-day. Do you call that decent behavior, sir, to an old friend?"

"It is explainable, I think," said the other awkwardly and paused. "But, however— So you, Ronalds, are still at Mickledown, and it is your vicar Raynham who has been consecrated to-day to this new South African see?"

"Yes," said Ronalds, with a sigh. "Yes, it is a heavy loss to us all. If ever there was a true and effective Churchman, it is Raynham. It is hard to spare a man like that from the work here. However, he is absolutely guileless and self-sacrificing, and I like to believe that he knows best. But yourself, Merriman; you seem to forget that it is *you* who are the riddle and the mystery! It is nearly two years ago, isn't it, since you wrote to tell me you had postponed your ordination for the purpose of spending some time in Germany, and going through further theological training? But as to your whereabout in Germany I have been quite in the dark. Explain, old fellow."

And the speaker put up his hand and touched his companion's arm. Look and action were equally winning, and expressed the native inborn lovableness of the man.

Merriman named a small but famous German university.

"I have been eighteen months there," he added, briefly, his quick eye taking note of the shade which had fallen across his companion's expression. "I have had a splendid time."

"And have come back—what for?"

"To eat dinners and go to the Bar."

Ronalds started.

"So the old dream is given up?" he said, slowly. "How we used to cherish it together! When did you make up your mind to relinquish the Church?"

"Some eight or nine months ago."

The speaker paused a moment, then went on:

"That is why I did not write to you, Ronalds. At first I was too undecided, too overwhelmed by new ideas; and then, afterward, I knew you would be distressed, so I let it alone till we should meet."

Ronalds lay back in his chair, sheltering his eyes from the blaze of the fire with one hand. He did not speak for a minute or two; then he said, in a somewhat constrained voice:

"Is G—— one of their—what shall I call it?—liberal—advanced—universities?"

"Not particularly. The mass of students in the theological faculty there are on the road to being Lutheran pastors of a highly orthodox kind, and find plenty of professors to suit them. I was attracted by the reputation of a group of men, whose books are widely read, indeed, but whose lecture-rooms are very scantily filled. It seemed to me that in their teaching I should find that *historical* temper which I was above all in search of. You remember"—and the speaker threw back his head with a smile which pleasantly illumined the massive, irregular features—"how you used to laugh at me for a Teutophile—how that history prize of mine on Teutonic Arianism plunged me into quagmires of German you used to make merry over, and wherein, according to you, I had dropped forever all chances of a decent English style! Well, it was nothing but that experience of German methods, working together with all the religious ideas of which my mind and yours had been full for so long, that made me put off orders and go abroad. I think," he added slowly, "I was athirst to see what Germans, like those whose work on the fifth and sixth centuries had struck me with admiration, could make of the first and second centuries. I was full of problems and questionings. The historical work which I had begun so casually seemed to have roused a host of new forces and powers. I was unhappy. The old and the new wouldn't blend—wouldn't fuse. I was especially worried with that problem of *historical translation*, if I may call it so, which had risen up before me like a ghost out of all those interminable German books about the Goths, in which I had buried myself. My ghost walked. It touched matters I tried in vain to keep sacred from it. Finally, it drove me out of England."

A new flame of fire had wakened in the black, half-shut eyes. With such a growth of animation might Richard Rothe have described the tumults of heart and mind which drove him from Germany southward into the land of art, from Würtemberg to Rome, from the narrow thought-world of Lutheran Pietism into the wide horizons of a humaner faith.

"Historical *translation!*" said the other, looking up. "What do you mean by that?"

"Simply the transmutation of past witness into the language of the present. That was the point, the problem, which seized me from the beginning. Here, for instance, in my work among the Goths, I had before me a mass of original material—chronicles, ecclesiastical biographies, acts of councils, lives of saints, papal letters, religious polemics, and so forth. And I had also before me two different kinds of modern treatment of it, an older and a newer; the older represented by books written— what shall we say?—broadly speaking, before 1840; the newer by a series of works produced, of course, in the light of Niebuhr and Ranke, and differing altogether in tone from the earlier series. What *was* this difference in tone? Of course, we all know—in spite of Gibbon—that history has been reborn since the Revolution. Yes; but why? how? Put the development into words. Well, it seemed to me like nothing in the world so much as the difference between good and bad translation. The older books had had certain statements and products of the past to render into the language of the present. And they had rendered them inadequately with that vagueness and generality and convention which belong to bad translation. And the result was either merely flat and perfunctory, something totally without the breath of life and reality, or else the ideas and speech of the past were hidden away under what was in truth a disguise—often a magnificent disguise—woven out of the ideas and speech of the present. But the books since Niebuhr, since Ranke, since Mommsen! *There* you found a difference. At last you found out that these men and women, these kings and bishops and saints, these chroniclers and officials, were flesh and blood; that they had ideas, passions, politics; that they lived, as we do, under governing prepossessions; that they had theories of life and the universe; and till you understood these and could throw yourself back into them, you had no chance of understanding the men or their doings. The past woke up, lived and moved, and what it said came to you with a new accent, the accent of truth. And all this was brought about by nothing in the world fundamentally but *improved translation*, by the use of that same faculty, half-scientific, half-imaginative, which, in the rendering of a foreign language, enables a man to get into the very heart and mind of his author, to speak with his tones and feel with his feeling."

The speaker paused a moment as though to rein himself up. Ronalds looked at him, smiling at the strenuous attitude—hands on sides, head thrown back—which seemed to recall many by-gone moments to the spectator.

"If you mean by all this," he said, "that the modern historian throws less of himself into his work, shows more real detachment of mind than his predecessors, I can bring half a dozen instances against you. When is Carlyle anybody but Carlyle, fitting the whole of history to the clothes- and force-philosophy?"

"Oh, the subjective element, of course, is inevitable to some degree or other. But, in truth, paradox as it may sound, it is just this heightened individuality in the modern historian which makes him in many ways a better interpreter of the past. He is more sympathetic, more eager, more curious, more *romantic*, if you will; and, at the same time, the scientific temper, which is the twin sister of the romantic—and both the peculiar children of to-day—is always there to guide his eagerness, to instruct his curiosity, to discipline his sympathy. He understands the past better, because he carries more of the present into it than those who went before, because the culture of *this* present provides him with sharper and more ingenious tools wherewith to reconstruct the building of the past, and because, by virtue of a trained and developed imagination, he is able nowadays to live in the life, physical and moral, of the by-gone streets and temples, the long dead men and women, brought to light again by his knowledge and his skill, to a degree and in a manner unknown to any century but ours."

"Well said!" exclaimed Ronalds, smiling again. "Modern history has earned its pæan—far be it from me to grudge it."

"Ah! I run on," said the other, penitently, the arms falling and the attitude relaxing. "But to return to myself, if you really want the explanation—"

And he looked inquiringly at his friend.

"I want it," said Ronalds in a low voice. "But I dread it."

Merriman paused a moment, his keen black eyes resting on his friend. Then he said gently:

"I will say no more if it would be painful to you. And yet I should like to explain myself. You influenced me a great deal at Oxford. I doubt if I should ever have thought of taking orders but for you. Constantly in Germany my mind turned to you with a sense of responsibility. I could not write, but I always looked forward to talking it out."

"Go on, go on," said Ronalds, looking up at him. "I wish to understand—if I can."

"Well, then, you remember that, during the time I was hunting up Goths, I had to break off divinity lectures. But the day after the prize was sent in I remember gathering together the old books again, and I took up specially Edersheim's 'Jesus the Messiah,' which

Haigh of Trinity had lent me some weeks before. I read it for hours, and at the end I laid it down with an inward judgment, the strength of which I shall never forget. 'Learning up to a certain point, feeling up to a certain point, but all through bad history—*bad translation!*' Six months before, I should have been incapable of any such verdict. But my Germans, with their vile type and their abominable style, had taught me a good deal in between. If Edersheim's ways of using documents and conceiving history were right, then theirs were all wrong. But I knew them, on the contrary, to be abundantly right —at any rate, within their own sphere. *Must* the Christian documents be treated differently—*could* they be treated differently, in principle—from the documents of the declining empire, or of any other historical period? That evening was a kind of crisis. I was never at peace afterward. I remember turning to books on Inspiration and on the Canon, and resuming attendance on old S———'s lectures on Apologetics, which had been interrupted for me by reading for the Essay. Many times I recollect going to see X——— at Christchurch. He saw I was in difficulties, and talked to me a great deal and very kindly about the impossibility of mere *reason* supplying a solution for any of the prevalent doubts as to Christianity. One must *wish* to believe, or belief was impossible. He quoted Mansel's words to me: 'Affection is part of insight; it is wanted for gaining due acquaintance with the facts of the case.' All this fitted in very well with the Neo-Kantian ideas I believed myself to have adopted during my reading for Greats; and when he sent me to Mozley, and Newman's 'Grammar of Assent,' I followed his advice gladly enough. But the only result was that I found my whole conception of truth fissured and broken up. It came to this, that there were *two* truths—not only a truth of matter and a truth of spirit, but two truths of history, two truths of literary criticism, to which answered corresponding moods of mind on the part of the Christian. It was imperatively right to endeavor to disentagle miracle from history, the marvelous from the real, in a document of the fourth, or third, or second century; to see delusions in the Montanist visions, the growth of myth in Apocryphal gospels, or the Acts of Pilate, a natural credulity in Justin's demonology, careless reporting in the ascription by Papias to Jesus of a gross millenarian prophecy, and so on. But the contents of the New Testament, however marvelous, and however apparently akin to what surrounds them on either side, were to be treated from a totally different point of view. In the one case there must be a desire on the part of the historian to discover the historical under the miraculous, or he would be failing in his duty as a sane and competent observer; in the other case there must be a desire, a strong 'affection,' on the part of the theologian, toward proving the miraculous to be historical, or he would be failing in his duty as a Christian. Yet in both cases— the reflection was inevitable—the evidence was historical and literary, and the witnesses were human!—At this point I came across the first volume of Baur's 'Church History.' Now, Baur's main theories, you will remember, had been described to us in one or two of S——'s lectures. He had been held up to us as the head and front of the German system-making; the extravagance of his Simon Magus theory, the arbitrariness of his perpetual antitheses between 'Petrinismus' and 'Paulinismus,' 'Particularismus' and 'Universalismus,' had been brought out with a good deal of the dry old Oxford humor, and, naturally, not many of us had kept any thought of Baur in our minds. But now I began to read one of his chief books, and I can only describe what I felt in the words lately attributed by his biographer to Prof. Green: 'He thought the "Church History" the most *illuminating* book he had ever read.' Clearly it was overstrained and arbitrary in parts; the theory was forced, and the arrangement too symmetrical for historical or literary reality. But it seemed to me you might say the same of Niebuhr and Wolff. Yet they had been, and were still, the pioneers and masters of an age. Why not Baur in his line? At any rate, it was clear to me that his book was *history;* it fell into line with all other first-rate work in the historical department, whereas, whatever else they might be, Farrar's and Edersheim's were *not* history. That was my first acquaintance with German theology, except some translations of Weiss and Dorner. I had shrunk from it till then, and X—— had warned me from it. But after reading Baur's 'Church History' and the 'Paul,' I suddenly made up my mind to go abroad, and to give a year at least to the German critical school. Well, so far, Ronalds, do you blame me?"

And the speaker broke off abruptly, his almost excessive calm of manner wavering a little, his eye seeking his friend's.

Ronalds had sat till now shrunken together in the big arm-chair, which, standing out against the uncurtained window, through which came a winter twilight, seemed lost again among the confused lines of the houses on the opposite bank of the river, or of the barges going slowly up stream. He roused himself at this, and bent forward.

"Blame?" the word had an odd ring; "that depends. How much did it *cost* you, all this, Merriman?"

"What do you mean?"

"What I say. It gives me a shiver as I listen to you. I foresee the end—a dismal end, all through—and I keep wondering whether you had ever anything to lose, whether you were ever *inside?* If you were, could this process you describe have gone on with so little check, so little reaction?"

The firelight showed a flush on the fine ascetic cheek. He had roused himself to speak strongly, but the effort excited him.

Merriman left his post by the fire and began to pace up and down.

"I had meant only to describe to you," he said, at last, " an episode of intellectual history. The rest is between me—and God. It can not really be put into words. But, as you know, I was brought up strictly and religiously. You and I shared the same thoughts, the same influences, the same religious services at Oxford. These months I have been describing to you were months of great misery on the side of feeling and practice. I remember coming back one morning from an early service, and thinking with a kind of despair what would happen to me if I were ever forced to give up the Sacrament. Yet the process went on all the same. I believe it is very much a matter of temperament. I could not master the passionate desire to think the matter through, to harmonize knowledge and faith, to get to the bottom. You might have done it, I think." And he stood still, looking at his friend with a smile which had no satire in it.

"Of course, every Christian knows that there are doubts and difficulties in the path of the faith, and that he may succumb to them if he pleases," said Ronalds, after a pause; "but if he is true he keeps close to his Lord, and gives the answer of faith. He asks himself which solves most problems — Christianity or agnosticism. He looks round on the state of the world, on the history of his own life, and on the work of Christ in both. Is he going to give up the witness of the faith, of the 'holy men of old,' of the saints of the present, of his own inmost life, because men of science, in a world which is all inexplicable, tell him that miracle is impossible, or because a generation or two of German professors—who seem to him to spend most of their time, Penelope-like, in unraveling their own webs—persist, in the face of a living and divine reality, which attests itself to him every day of his life, in telling him that the Church is a mere human contrivance based upon a delusion and a lie? Above all, he will not venture himself deliberately, in a state of immaturity and disarmament, into the enemy's camp; for 'he is not his own,' and what he bears in his bosom, the treasure of the faith, is but confided to him to be guarded with his life."

The musical vibrating voice sank with the closing words. Merriman returned to his old position by the fire, and was silent a minute.

"But even you," he said presently with a smile, "can not deny reason some place in your scheme."

"Naturally," said the other, his tone of emotion changing for one of sarcasm. "To the freethinker of to-day we Christians are all sentimentalists—strong in emotion, weak in brains. A religion which boasts in England a Newton, a Hooker, a Butler, and a Newman among its sons, is conceived of as having nothing rational to say for itself. The charge is absurd on the face of it.

We say, indeed, that finally—in the last resort—a certain disposition of soul is required for the due apprehension of Christian truth; that the process of apprehension contains an act of faith which can not be evaded, and that the rationalist who will accept nothing but what his reason can indorse, is merely refusing the divine condition on which God's gift is offered to him. But that a religion which is not justified and ordered by reason is a religion full of danger—is not a religion, indeed, but a mysticism—we know as well as you do, and the English Church needs no one to teach her an elementary lesson. English theology wants no apologist, and the man who has not already gone over to the restlessness of unbelief need not leave his own church in quest of guides. Will you find more learning in all Germany than you can get in Westcott and Lightfoot? A better historian than Bishop Stubbs? A more omniscient knowledge of the history of criticism and the canon than Dr. Salmon will give you, if you take the trouble to read his books? In all that you have been saying I see—forgive me—a ludicrous want of perspective and proportion. Why this craze for German books and German professors? Are there no thinkers in the world but German ones? And what is the whole history of German criticism but a history of brilliant failures, from Strauss downward? One theorist follows another—now Mark is uppermost as the *Ur-Evangelist*, now Matthew—now the Synoptics are sacrificed to St. John, now St. John to the Synoptics. Baur relegates one after another of the Epistles to the second century because his theory can not do with them in the first. Harnack tells you that Baur's theory is all wrong, and that Thessalonians and Philippians must go back again. Volkmar sweeps together Gospels and Epistles in a heap toward the middle of the second century as the earliest date for almost all of them; and Dr. Abbot, who, as we are told, has absorbed all the learning of all the Germans, puts Mark before 70 A. D.; Matthew, just before 70 A. D.; and Luke, about 80 A. D.! Strauss's mythical theory is dead and buried by common consent; Baur's tendency theory is much the same; Renan will have none of the Tübingen school; Volkmar is already antiquated; and Pfleiderer's fancies are now in the order of the day. Meanwhile, we who believe in a risen Lord, look quietly on, while the 'higher criticism' swallows its own offspring. When you have settled your own case, we say to your friends and teachers, then ask us to listen to you. Meanwhile we are practical men: the poor and wretched are at our gates, and sin, sorrow, death, stand aside for no one!"

Merriman had been watching his companion during this outburst with a curious expression, half combative, half indulgent. When Ronalds stopped, he took a long breath.

"I don't know whether you have read many of the books?" he asked, shortly.

"No, I don't read German; and I am a busy parish clergyman with little time to spare for superfluities. But, as you remind me, S——'s lectures taught one a good deal, and I follow the matter in the press and the magazines, or in conversation, as I come across it."

Merriman smiled.

"I suppose your answer would be the answer of four fifths of English clergymen, if the question were put to them. Well, then, I am to take it for granted, Ronalds, that to you the whole of German New Testament *Wissenschaft*, or, at any rate, what calls itself 'the German critical school,' is practically indifferent. You regard it in the words of a recent 'Quarterly' article, as 'an attack' which has 'failed.' Very well, let us leave the matter there for the present. Suppose we go to the Old Testament. Were you at the Manchester Church Congress last year, and, if so, what was your impression?"

Ronalds leaned forward, looked steadily into the fire, and did not answer for a moment or two. An expression of pain and perplexity gradually rose in the delicate face, in strong contrast with the inspiration, the confidence of his previous manner.

"You mean as to the Historical Criticism debate?"

Merriman nodded.

"It was extraordinarily interesting—very painful in some ways. I doubt the wisdom of it. It raised more questions than it solved. Since then I have had it much in my mind; but my life gives me no time to work at the subjects in detail."

"Did it, or did it not, prove to your mind, as it did to mine, that there is a vital change going on, not only in the lay, but in the clerical conceptions of the Old Testament? Did your memory, like mine, travel back to Pusey, to the condemnation of Colenso by all the Bishops and five-sixths of Convocation, to the writers in the 'Speaker's Commentary' who refuted him?"

"There is a change, certainly," said Ronalds, slowly; "but"—and he raised his head with a light gesture, as of one shaking off a weight—"my faith is not bound up with the religious books of the Jews—'God spake through the prophets,' through Israel's training, through the Psalms—leave me that faith, which, indeed, in its broad essential elements, you have never yet been able to touch; give me the Gospels and St. Paul, and I at least am content."

"'My faith is not bound up with the religious books of the Jews,'" repeated Merriman. "I noticed almost a similar sentence in an article by the Bishop of Carlisle rather more than a year ago. What it means is that you and he have adopted, so far as the Old Testament is concerned, the standpoint of 'Essays and Reviews.' He is a Bishop, you a High Churchman. Yet thirty years ago the Bishops and the High Churchmen prosecuted 'Essays and Reviews' in two Ecclesiastical Courts; and Jowett's essay, in which the thoughts you have just expressed were practically embodied, cost him at Oxford his salary as professor. But to return to the Church Congress. The distinctive note of its most distinctive debate, as it seems to me, was the glorification of 'criticism,' especially, no doubt, in relation to the Old Testament. Turn to the passages. I have the report here"—and he drew the volume toward him and turned up some marked pages. "First, 'I hold to be established beyond all controversy that the Pentateuch in its present form was not written by Moses.' That comes from the Dean of Peterborough. The same speaker says, further, 'Of the composite character of the Hexateuch there can be no question. "The proofs have been often set forth," says Dr. Robertson Smith, "and never answered." To say that they have any connection with rationalistic principles is simply to say that scholarship and rationalism are identical, for on this point Hebraists of all schools are agreed.'—But if the Hexateuch be composite, a redaction of different documents from unknown hands, by an unknown editor, what becomes of its scriptural authority—what especially becomes of the doctrine of the Fall?—Poor Pusey! with his 'amazement' that any mind could be shaken by such arguments as those contained in the first book of Colenso; or poor Wilberforce, with his contempt for the 'old and often-refuted cavils' brought forward by the assailants of the Pentateuch!

"But there is another passage a little further on in the Congress debate, which would have touched Pusey still more nearly. 'The certainties already attained by criticism,' cries Prof. Cheyne triumphantly, 'are neither few nor unimportant. Think of the Pentateuch, Isaiah, Daniel, and Ecclesiastes!' *'Think of Daniel!'* One can still hear Pusey thundering away: 'Others who wrote in defense of the faith engaged in large subjects. I took for my province one more confined but definite issue. I selected the Book of Daniel. What I have proposed to myself in this course of lectures is to meet a boastful criticism upon its own grounds, and to show its failure where it claims to be most triumphant.' 'I have answered the objections raised,' he declares; but he can not 'affect to believe that they have any special plausibility.' What loftiness of tone all through! what a sternness of moral indignation toward the miserable skeptics, whose theories as to Daniel and the rest have been let loose, through 'Essays and Reviews,' 'on the young and uninstructed'! Well, five-and-twenty years go by, and the Church of England practically gives its verdict as between Pusey and the German or English infidels whom he trampled on, and, in spite of that tone of Apostolic certainty, judgment goes finally, even within the Church, not for the Anglican leader, but for the 'infidels'! The Book of Daniel, despite a hesitating protest here and there, like that of Dr. Stanley Leathes, or some bewildered country clergyman writing to the 'Guardian,' comes quietly and irrevocably down to 165 B.C., and the Hexateuch, dissolved more or less into its original sources, announces itself as the peculiar product of that Jewish religious movement which, beginning under Josiah, strengthens with the Exile, and yields its final fruits long after the Exile! . . .

"But this whole debate is remarkable to a degree—*as the debate of a Church Congress.* It is penetrated and preoccupied with the claims of 'criticism.' Its subject is whether 'critical *results*' (especially in connection with the Old Testament) are to be taught from the pulpits of the Church of England, and these results, as described by almost all the speakers, involve a complete reconstruction of an English Churchman's ideas on the subject of the early history, laws, and religion of the Jews—matters which he has always regarded, and which, indeed, he logically must regard, as intimately bound up with his Christian faith. Now all this, especially as one looks back twenty-five years, to the Synodical condemnation of Colenso, and of 'Essays and Reviews,' strikes one as a sufficiently remarkable phenomenon. The question is, *What forces have brought it about?* Well, there can be very little debate as to that. No doubt science and Prof. Huxley have had their way with the Mosaic cosmogony, and the methods and spirit of science provide an atmosphere which insensibly affects all our modes of thought. But we are passing out of the scientific phase of Old Testament criticism. That has, so to speak, done its work. It is the *literary and historical* phase which is now uppermost. And in the matter of the literary history of the Old Testament the present collapse of English orthodoxy is due to one cause, as far as I can see, and one cause only—*the invasion of English by German thought.* Instead of marching side by side with Germany and Holland during the last thirty years, as we might have done, had our theological faculties been other than what they are, we have been attacked and conquered by them; we have been skirmishing or protesting, feeding ourselves with the 'Record' and the 'Church Times,' reading the 'Speaker's Commentary,' or the productions of the Christian Evidence Society, till the process of penetration from without has slowly completed itself, and we find ourselves suddenly face to face with such a fact as this Church Congress debate, and the rise and marked success of a younger school of critics—Cheyne, Driver, Robertson Smith—whom the Germans may fairly regard as the captives of their bow and spear.

"For look at the names of scholars quoted in this very debate—all of them German, with the great exception of Kuenen! And look back over the history of the Pentateuchal controversy itself! It begins in Holland with Spinoza, or in France with the oratorian Richard Simon, two hundred years ago. Simon starts the literary criticism of the Mosaic books, from the Catholic side. Jean le Clerc, a Dutch Protestant theologian in Amsterdam, about 1685, starts the historical method, inquires as to the time and circumstances of composition, and so on—first conceives it, in fact, as an historical problem. Seventy years later comes the Montpellier physician, Jean Astruc. He first notices the key to the whole enigma, the distinctive use made of the words 'Elohim' and 'Jahveh.' This leads him to the supposition of different strata in the Pentateuch, and from him descend in direct line Kuenen and Wellhausen.—It is instructive, by-the-way, to notice that all the time Astruc will have nothing to say to arguments against the Mosaic authorship of the

Pentateuch. 'That,' he says, scornfully, 'was the disease of the last century'—an 'attack,' in fact, which had 'failed'!—Well, then Astruc's 'Conjectures' pass into Germany, and meet there at first with very much the same reception from German orthodoxy that English orthodoxy gave Colenso. Till Eichhorn's 'Einleitung' appears. From that point the patient, industrious mind of Germany throws itself seriously on the problem, and a whole new and vast development begins. Thenceforward not a name of any importance that is not German, except that of Kuenen, who is altogether German in method and science, down to our own day, when at last among ourselves a school of English scholars trained in the German results, and enthusiastically eager to diffuse them, has risen to take away our reproach, and has hardly begun to work before the effects on English popular religion are everywhere conspicuous.

"Well, I don't know what you feel, Ronalds, but all these things to me, at any rate, are immensely significant. I say to myself, it has taken some thirty years for German critical science to conquer English opinion in the matter of the Old Testament. But, except in the regions of an either illiterate or mystical prejudice, that conquest is now complete. How much longer will it take before we feel the victory of the same science, carried on by the same methods and with the sams ends, in a field of knowledge infinitely more precious and vital to English popular religion than the field of the Old Testament—before Germany imposes upon us not only her conceptions with regard to the history and literature of the Jews, but also those which she has been elaborating for half a century with regard to that history which is the natural heir and successor of the Jewish—the history of Christian origins?"

"In your opinion, no doubt, a very few years indeed," returned Ronalds, recovering that attractive cheerfulness of look which was characteristic of him. "As for me, I see no necessary connection between the two subjects. The period covered by the New Testament is much narrower, the material of a different quality, the evidence infinitely more accessible, the possibility of mistakes on the part of the Church infinitely less. And whatever may be said of our Old Testament scholarship, not even the most self-satisfied German can speak disrespectfully of us in the matter of the New. As I said before, with men like Lightfoot, Westcott, Hort, and Salmon as the leaders and champions of our faith on the intellectual side, we have very little, as it seems to me, to fear from any skeptical foreign *Wissenschaft*. Besides, what can be more unfair, Merriman, than to speak as if the whole of this *Wissenschaft* were on one side? Neander, Weiss, Dorner, Tischendorf, Luthardt; these are names as famous in the world as any of the so-called 'critical' names, and they are the names, not of assailants, but of defenders of our faith. And as to the assault on the Christian documents, we can appeal not only to Christian writers, but to a skeptic like Renan, in whose opinion the assault has been repulsed and discredited. No! here at least we are stronger, not weaker, than we were thirty years ago. Every weapon that a hostile science could suggest has been brought to bear against the tower of our faith, and it stands more victoriously than ever, foursquare to all the winds that blow."

"And meanwhile every diocesan conference rings with the wail over 'infidel opinions,'" said Merriman quietly. "It grows notoriously more and more difficult to get educated men to take any interest in the services or doctrines of the Church, though they will join eagerly in its philanthropy; literature and the periodical press are becoming either more indifferent or more hostile to the accepted Christianity year by year; the upper strata of the working class, upon whom the future of that class depends, either stand coldly aloof from all the Christian sects, or throw themselves into secularism; and Archdeacon Farrar, preaching on the prosecution of the Bishop of Lincoln, passionately appeals to all sections of Christians to close their ranks, not against each other, but against the 'skepticism rampant' among the cultivated class, and the religious indifference of the democracy.— But let me take your points in order. No doubt there is a large and flourishing school of orthodox theology in Germany. So, seventy years ago, there was a large and flourishing school in Germany of defenders of the Mosaic authorship and date of the Pentateuch. One can run over the names—Fritzsche, Scheibel, Jahn, Dahler, Rosenmüller, Herz, Hug, Sack, Pustkuchen, Kanne, Meyer, Stäudlin—who now remembers one of them? Of all their books, says a French Protestant, sketching the controversy, *il n'est resté que le souvenir d'un héroïque et impuissant effort.* It is not *their* work, but that of their opponents, which has lived and penetrated, has transformed opinion and is molding the future. They represented the exceptional, the traditional, the miraculous, and they have had to give way to the school representing the normal, the historical, the rational. And yet not one of them but did not believe that he had crushed De Wette and all his works! Is not all probability, all analogy, all the past, so to speak, on our side when we prophesy a like fate for those schools of the present which, in the field of Christian origins, represent the exceptional, the traditional, the miraculous? For what we have been witnessing so far is the triumph of a principle, of *an order of ideas*, and this principle, this order, belongs to us, not to you, and is as applicable to Christian history as it is to Jewish.

"Then as to our own theology. Let me be disrespectful to no one. But I should like to ask you what possibility is there in this country of a scientific, that is to say, an unprejudiced, an unbiased study of theology, under present conditions? All our theological faculties are subordinate to the Church; the professors are clergymen, the examiners in the theological schools must be in priest's orders. They are, in fact, in that position to which the reactionary orthodoxy of Germany tried—unsuccessfully—to reduce the German universities after '48. Read the protest of the theological faculty of Göttingen against an attempt of the sort. It is given, if I remember right, in Hausrath's 'Life of Strauss,' and you will realize the opinion of learned Germany as to the effect of such a relation between the Church and the universities as obtains here, on the progress of knowledge. The results of our English system are precisely what you might expect—great industry and great success in textual criticism in all the branches of what the Germans call the *niedere Kritik*, complete sterility, as far as the higher criticism—that is to say, the effort to reconceive Christianity in the light of the accumulations of modern knowledge—is concerned.* When Pattison made his proposals

---

* It is clear that Merriman has here overlooked certain names he might have mentioned—those of Dr. Hatch and Dr. Sanday, for instance—and outside the Church of England and the theological faculties, those of R. W. Macan, the author of one of the most comprehensive and scholarly monographs that exist in English; of the veteran Dr. Davidson; of Mr. R. F.

as to the reorganization of studies at Oxford, he did not trouble himself to include therein any proposals as to the theological faculty. Until the whole conditions under which that faculty exists could be altered, he knew that to meddle with it would be useless. All that could be expected from it was a certain amount of exegetical work and a more or less respectable crop of apologetic, and that it produced. But he did not leave the subject without drawing up a comparison between the opportunities of the theological student at Oxford and those of the same student at any German university—a comparison which set one thinking. His complaints of the quality and range of English theological research have been often repeated; they were echoed at last year's Church Congress by Prof. Cheyne—but, in fact, the matter is notorious. You have only to glance from the English field to the German, from our own cramped conditions and meager product to the German abundance and variety, to appreciate Pattison's remark in the 'Westminster,' in 1857. I forget the exact words—'it is a misnomer to speak of *German* theology. It is more properly the theology of the age'—the only scientific treatment of the materials which exists. Like other great movements, it rises in this country or that, but it ends by penetrating into all. For my own part, I believe that we in England, with regard to this German study of Chris-

---

Horton, whose illogical and interesting book on "The Inspiration of Scripture" breathes change and transition in every page; of Dr. Drummond, whose admirable "Philo" is full of the best spirit of modern learning. But three or four swallows do not make a summer, and Merriman's mind is evidently possessed with the thought of that atmosphere, that vast surrounding literature which in Germany supports and generates the individual effort.

tianity, are now at the beginning of an epoch of *popularization*. The books which record it have been studied in England, Scotland, and America with increasing eagerness during the last fifteen years by a small class; in the next fifteen years we shall probably see their contents reproduced in English form and penetrating public opinion in a new and surprising way. A minimum of readers among us read German, and translations only affect a small and mostly professional stratum of opinion. But when we get our own English lives of Christ and histories of the primitive Church, written on German principles in the tone and speech familiar to the English world, then will come the struggle. With regard to the Old Testament, this is precisely what has happened — the struggle has come—and already we see much of the result.

"Finally, as to Renan," Merriman lay back in his chair, and a smile broadened over the whole face—" I am always puzzled by the readiness with which the Englishman uses Renan as a stick to beat the Germans. Forgive me, Ronalds—but doesn't it sometimes occur to you that the Germans may have something to say about Renan? Isn't their whole contention about him that he is a great artist, a brilliant historian, but an uncertain critic? Amiel, who, though a Genevese, was brought up at Berlin, exactly expresses German opinion when he lays stress on the contradiction in Renan 'between the literary taste of the artist, which is delicate, individual, and true, and the opinions of the critic, which are borrowed, old-fashioned, and wavering.' In the course of time this judgment becomes patent to Renan, and the result appears in certain uncivil passages about young German professors in the preface to 'Les Evangiles,' and elsewhere. What matter? The face of Knowledge remains the same. Renan is still, as Taine long ago remarked, the main expounder of German theological *Wissenschaft* for the world in general; in spite of his own great learning the 'Origines du Christianisme' could not have been written without the thirty years of German labor lying behind it. And, as a principle—whether it is a great Frenchman determined to combine the artist with the *savant*, or an Englishman struggling to fuse Anglicanism with learning, as soon as it comes to serious differences between them and the German critical schools, I can only say that the impartial historical spectator will be all for the chances of the Germans, simply from his knowledge of the general lie of the field! Oh, these Germans!" and the speaker shook his head with an expression half humorous, half protesting. "Yes, we arraign them, and justly, for their type and their style, their manners or no-manners, their dullness and their length. And all the time what Taine said long ago in his study of Carlyle, remains as true as ever. Let me turn to the passage, I have pondered it often," and he drew a little note-book to him, which was lying beside his hand.

Thus, at the end of the last century there rose into being the philosophic genius of Germany, which, after engendering a new metaphysic, a new theology, a new poetry, a new literature, a new philology, a new exegesis, a new learning, is now descending into all the sciences, and there carrying on its evolution. No spirit more original, more universal, more fruitful in consequences of all sorts, more capable of transforming everything and remaking everything, has shown itself in the world for three hundred years. It is of the same significance, the same rank as that of the Renaissance and that of the Classical Period. Like those earlier forces, it draws to itself all the best endeavor of contemporary intelligence, it appears as they did in every civilized country, it represents as they did " un des moments de l'histoire du monde."

The enthusiast dropped the book, with a smile at his own warmth. Ronalds smiled too, but more sadly, and the two friends sat silent awhile. Merriman filled a new pipe, his keen look showing the rise within him of thoughts as quick and numerous as the spirals of blue smoke which presently came and went between him and his friend.

After a minute or two, he said, bending forward:

"But all that, Ronalds, was by-the-way. Let me go back to myself and this change of view I am trying to explain to you. You have given me your opinion, which I suppose is a very common one among English Churchmen, that the whole movement of German critical theology is an 'attack' which has 'failed,' that the orthodox position is really stronger than before it began, and so on. Well, let me put side by side with that conviction of yours, my own, which has been gained during eighteen months' intense effort, spent all of it on German soil, in the struggle to understand something of the past history and the present situation of German critical theology. Take it from 1835, fifty-four years. Practically, the movement which matters to us begins with the shock and scandal of Strauss's 'Leben Jesu,' which appeared in that year. Strauss, who, like Renan, was an artist and a writer, derived, as we all know, his philosophical impulse from Hegel, his critical impulse from Schleiermacher. Philosophically he appealed from Hegel the orthodox conservative to Hegel the thinker. 'You taught us,' he says in effect to his great teacher, 'that there are two elements in all religion, the passing and the eternal, the relative and the absolute, the *Vorstellung* and the *Begriff*. The particular system of dogmas put forward by any religion is the *Vorstellung* or presentation, the *Begriff* or idea is the underlying spiritual reality common to it and presumably other systems besides. Why in Christianity have you gone so far toward identifying the two? Why this exception? For what reasons have you allowed to the *Vorstellung* in Christianity a value which belongs only to the *Begriff*? Your reasons must rest upon the Christian evidence. But the evidence can not bear the weight. Examine it carefully, and you will see that the particular statements which it makes are really only *Vorstellung* as in other religions, the imaginative mythical elements which hide from us the Idea or *Begriff*. The idea which is expressed in Christian theology is the idea of God in man. The incarnation, death, and resurrection of Jesus are shadows of the eternal generation, the endless self-repetition of the Divine life. The single facts are mere sensuous symbols. "To the idea in the fact, to the race in the individual, our age wishes to be led.'" Naturally to achieve this end the Gospels as history had to be swept away. And they were remorselessly swept away. Something indeed remained. There was a Jewish teacher, Jesus of Nazareth, in whom contemporary truth saw first the Messiah, then the Son of God, then the Logos. But his life and character were comparatively unimportant—so it stood, at least, in the earliest and latest 'Leben Jesu'; what was important was the idealizing mythopœic faculty which from the Jesus of the Galilean Lake evolved the Christ of Bethlehem, of the miracles, of the resurrection, of theology. Thus the whole method was speculative and *a priori*. There was in it a minimum of history, a minimum indeed of literary criticism. Strauss criticised the *contents* of the Christian literature without understanding the literary and historical conditions which had produced it. Of the real life and culture of the men who wrote it, of the real historical conditions surrounding the person of Jesus, he had almost as little notion as the dogmatic historians who undertook to answer him.

"Luckily, however, not only orthodoxy, but the spirit of history, took alarm, and from the revolt of history against hypothesis began the Tübingen school. Baur, that veteran of knowledge, was struck, in the first place, with the fact which Strauss's book revealed, that a scientific knowledge of Christian sources was as yet wanting to theology; in the next, he was imbued with the conception that the Gospels had been till then placed in a false perspective both by Strauss and New Testament criticism generally—that not they, but the Pauline Epistles, represent the earliest and directest testimony we have to Christian belief. From this standpoint he began a complete re-examination of early Christian literature, conceiving it as a chapter in the history of thought. How did the circle of disciples surrounding Jesus of Nazareth broaden into the Catholic Church? Can the steps of that development be traced in the books of the New Testament? If so, how are the separate books to be classed and interpreted with relation to the general movement? We all know the famous answer, how the Catholic Church of the second century is but the product of a great compromise come to under the pressure of heresy by the two primitive opposing parties, the Petrine and the Pauline, which for about a hundred years had divided Christian literature between them, so that all its products, Gospels, Epistles, and Apocalypse, are, in a sense, pamphlets, controversial documents written in the interests of one or the other body of opinion. Well, here at last was history—as compared either with Strauss's philosophizing, or with the idyllic but unintelligible picture presented by the Early Church as it was drawn, say, by Neander. But it was not yet *pure history*. It was marred by a too great love of system-making, of arbitrary antithesis and formulæ, learned, of course, from Hegel, which took far too little account of the variety, the *nuances*, the complexity and many-sidedness which belonged to the early Christian life, as to all life, but especially the rich and fermenting life of a nascent religion. The clew was found, but in spite of the genius of Baur —and to my mind we owe to him all that we really *know* at the present moment about the New Testament—it had been too arbitrarily and confidently followed up.

"Again history protested, and again critical theology fell patiently to work.

"It was conscious of two wants—a deeper and more comprehensive understanding of the personality and work of Jesus, which Baur, who had thrown a flood of light on Paul, had notoriously left unattempted; and in the second place, it was striving toward a more lifelike and convincing picture of the early Christian society. From a study of Christian ideas, it passed to a closer study of the conditions under which they arose, of that whole culture, social and intellectual, Jewish or Hellenic, of which they were presumably the product. Collateral knowledge poured in on all sides—of the history of religions, of Roman institutions, of the developments and ramifications of Hellenic and Hellenistic thought. The workers following Baur fell into different groups; Hilgenfeld on the right, softening and moderating Baur's more negative conclusions; Volkmar on the left, developing them extravagantly, yet evolving in the process an amount of learning, ingenuity, and suggestiveness which will leave its mark when his specific conclusions as to the dates of the New Testament books are no longer remembered. Meanwhile two oppositions to the Tübingen school had shown themselves—the dogmatic and the scientific. Of the first not much need be said. Its most honored name is that of Bernhard Weiss, but the great majority of its books, written to meet the orthodox needs of the moment, are already forgotten. On the other hand, the scientific opposition represented by Reuss, Rothe, Ewald, and Ritschl did admirable work. It brought Baur's ideas to the test in every possible way, and it supplied fresh ideas, fresh solutions of its own. Reuss's cautious and exhaustive method led the student to think out the whole problem for himself anew; Rothe drew out the debt of Christianity to Greek and Latin institutions; while Ritschl tracked out shades and *nuances* in early Christianity which Baur's over-logical method had missed.

"The years went on. With each the spirit of the time became more historical, more concrete. The forces generated by the great German historical school, by Ranke, and Mommsen, and Waitz, and by the offshoots of this school in France and England, made themselves felt more and more on theological ground. A new series of biographies of Jesus began. Strauss, after an abstinence of twenty years from theology, issued a new edition of the 'Leben Jesu,' largely modified by concessions to a more historical and positive spirit. Schenkel published his 'Charakterbild Jesu,' by which, in spite of what we should call its Broad Church orthodoxy, German clerical opinion was almost as violently exercised as it had been by Strauss thirty years before. Keim began his most interesting, most important, and most imperfect book, 'Jesus von Nazara,' and beyond the frontier Renan brought the results of two generations' labor within the reach of the whole educated world by the historical brilliance and acumen thrown into the successive volumes of the 'Origines.' In all this a generation has passed away since Baur died, and we are brought again to a point where we can provisionally strike a balance of results. Do you remember Harnack's article on the present state of critical theology in the 'Contemporary' two years or more ago? Harnack is a man of great ability and extraordinary industry, largely read in Germany and beginning to be largely read here. Well—as compared with the state of knowledge thirty years ago, when the Tübingen school was at its height, his verdict on the knowledge of to-day is simply this—'*richer in historical points of view.*' Harnack himself has carried opposition to some of the most characteristic Tübingen conclusions almost to extravagance; but here in this careful and fair-minded summary is not a word of disrespect to a famous school and 'a great master,' not a word of an 'attack' which has 'failed.' Because the person who is speaking knows better! Yet he draws with a firm hand the positive advances, the altered aspects of knowledge. Why have we come to know more of that problem of the rise of Catholicism, to which Baur devoted his life, than Baur could ever know? Simply because 'we have grown more realistic, more elastic, the historical temper has developed, we have acquired the power of transplanting ourselves into other times. Great historians—men like Ranke—have taught us this. Then we have realized that all history is one, that religion and church history is a mere section of the whole history of a period, and can not be understood except in relation to that whole.' And so on. My whole experience in Germany was an illustration of these words. As compared with my Oxford divinity training, it was like passing from a world of shadows to a world of living and breathing humanity. Each of my three professors on his own ground was grappling with the secret of the past, drawing it out with the spells of learning, sympathy, and imagination, working all the while perfectly freely, unhampered by subscription or articles, or the requirements of examinations. Our own theology can show nothing like it; the most elementary conditions of such work are lacking among us; it will take the effort of a generation to provide them.

"Two books in particular occur to me—if you are not weary of my disquisition!—as representing this most recent phase of development; Schürer's 'Geschichte des jüdischen Volkes im Zeitalter Jesu Christi,' and Hausrath's 'Neutestamentliche Zeitgeschichte.' In the first you have a minute study of all the social and intellectual elements in the life of Judea and Judaism generally, at the time of the appearance of Christianity. In the second you have the same materials, only handled in a more consecutive and artistic way, and as a setting first for the life of Jesus, and afterward for the history of the Apostles. If you compare them with Strauss, you see with startling clearness how far we have traveled in half a century. There, an empty background, an effaced personality, and in its stead the play of philosophical abstraction. Here, a landscape of extraordinary detail and realism, peopled with the town and country populations which belong to it; Pharisee and Essene, Sadducee and Hellenist, standing out with the dress and utterance and gesture native to each; and in their midst the figure which is at last becoming real, intelligible, human, as it has never yet been, and which in these latter days we are beginning again to see with something of the vision of those who first loved and obeyed!—The contrast sets us looking back with wonder over the long, long road. But there is no break in it, no serious deviation. From the beginning till now the driving impulse has been the same—the impulse to *understand*, the yearning toward a unified and rationalized knowledge. Each step has been necessary, and each step a development. A diluted and falsified history was first driven out by thought, which was then, as it were, left alone for a time on ground cleared by violence; now a juster thought has replaced the old losses by a truer history, a fuller and exacter range of conceptions.—An '*attack*' which has '*failed*.'—Could any description be more ludicrous than this common English label applied to a great and so far triumphant movement of thought? Looking back over the controversy, whether as to the Old Testament or the New, I see a similar orthodox judgment asserting itself again and again—generally as an immediate prelude to some fresh and imposing development of the critical process—and again and again routed by events. At the present moment it could only arise, like your quotation of Renan, if you will let me say so—and I mean no offense—in a country and amid minds for the most part willingly ignorant of the whole actual situation. Just as much as the criticism of Roman institutions and primitive Roman history has failed, just as much as the scientific investigation of Buddhism during the present century has failed, in the same degree has the critical investigation of Christianity failed—no more! In all three fields there has been the same alternation of hypothesis and verification, of speculative thought modified by controlling fact. But because some of Niebuhr's views as to the trustworthiness of Livy have been corrected here and there in a more conservative sense by his successors— because Sénart's speculations as to the mythical elements of Buddhism have been checked in certain directions by the conviction of a later school, that from the Páli texts now being brought to light a greater substratum of fact may be recovered for the life of Buddha and the primitive history of his order than was at one time suspected —because of these fluctuations of scholarship you do not point a hasty finger of scorn at the modern studies of Roman history or of Buddhism! Still less, I imagine, are you prepared to go back to an implicit belief in Rhea Sylvia, or to find the miracles of early Buddhism more historically convincing!"

Ronalds looked up quickly. "We do not admit your parallel for a moment! In the first place, the Christian phenomena are unique in the history of the world, and can not be profitably compared on equal terms with any other series of phenomena. In the second, the variations which do not substantially affect the credit of scholarship in matters stretching so far over time and place as Roman history or Buddhism are of vital consequence when it comes to Christianity. The period is so much narrower, the possibilities so much more limited. To throw back the Gospels from the second century, where Baur and Volkmar placed them, to the last thirty years of the first, is practically to surrender the bases of the rationalist theory. You give yourself no time for the play of legend, and, instead of idealizing followers writing mythical and hearsay accounts, the critic himself brings us back into the presence of either eye-witnesses, or at any rate the reporters of eye-witnesses. He has treated the testimony as he pleased, has subjected it to every harsh, irreverent test his ingenuity could suggest, and, instead of either getting rid of it wholesale or forcing it into the mold of his own arbitrary conceptions, he is obliged to put up with it, to acknowledge in it a power he can not overpass—the witness of truth to the living truth!'"

"'Obliged to put up with it'!" said Merriman with a smile, in which, however, there was a touch of deep melancholy. "How oddly such a phrase describes that patient, loving. investigation of every vestige and fragment of Christian antiquity which has been the work of the critical school, and to which the orthodox Church, little as she will acknowledge it, owes all the greater reasonableness and livingness of her own modern Christianity! On the contrary, Ronalds, men like Harnack and Hausrath have no quarrel with Christian testimony, no antipathy whatever to what it has to say. They have simply by long labor come to *understand* it, to be able to *translate* it. They, and a vast section of the thinking Christian world with them, have merely learned not to ask of that testimony more than it can give. They have come to recognize that it was conditioned by certain necessities of culture, certain laws of thought; that in a time which had no conception of history or of accurate historical reporting in our sense—a time which produced the allegorical interpretations of Alexandria, the Rabbinical interpretations of St. Paul and the Gospels, the historical method of Josephus, the superstitions of Justin and Papias, the childish criticism and information of Irenæus, and the mass of pseudepigraphical literature which meets us at every turn before, and in, and after the New Testament—it is useless to expect to find a history which is not largely legend, a tradition which is not largely delusion. Led by experience gathered not only from Christian history, but from all history, they expect beforehand what the Christian documents reveal. They see a sense of history so weak that, in preserving the tradition of the Lord, it can not keep clear and free from manifest contradiction even the most essential facts, not even the native place of his parents, the duration of his ministry, the date of his death, the place and time and order of the Resurrection appearances, the length of the mysterious period intervening between the Resurrection and the Ascension; and in preserving the tradition of the Apostles, it can not record with certainty for their disciples even the most essential facts as to their later lives, the scenes of their labors, the manner of their deaths. On all these points the documents show naïvely—as all early traditions do—the most irreconcilable discrepancies. The critical historian could have foretold them, finds them the most natural thing in the world. On the other hand, he grows familiar, as the inquiry grows deeper, with that fund of fancy and speculation, of superstitious belief or nationalist hope, in the mind of the first Christian period, the bulk of which he knows to be much older than the appearance of Jesus of Nazareth, and wherein he can trace the elements which conditioned the activity of the Master, and colored all the thoughts of his primitive followers about him. He measures the strength of these fantastic or poetical conceptions of nature and history by the absence or weakness, in the society producing them, of that controlling logical and scientific instinct which it has been the work of succeeding centuries, of the toil of later generations, to develop in mankind; and when he sees the passion of the Messianic hope, or the Persian and Parsee conceptions of an unseen world which the course of history had grafted on Judaism, or the Hellenistic speculation with which the Jewish Dispersion was everywhere penetrated, or the mere natural love of marvel which every populace possesses, and more especially an Eastern populace—when he watches these forces either shaping the consciousness of Jesus, or dictating the forms of belief and legend and dogma in which his followers cast the love and loyalty roused by a great personality—this also he could have foretold, this also is the most natural thing in the world. For to realize the necessity, the inevitableness, of these three features in the story of Christianity, he has only to look out on the general history of religions, of miracle, of sacred biography, of inspired books, to see the same forces and the same processes repeating themselves all over the religious field.

"So in the same way with the penetration and success of Christianity—the 'moral miracle,' which is to convince us of Christian dogma, when the appeal to physical miracle fails. To the historian there is no miracle, moral or physical, in the matter, any more than there is in the rise of Buddhism or of any other of those vast religious systems with which the soil of history is strewed. He sees the fuel of a great ethical and spiritual movement, long in preparation from many sides, kindled into flame by that spark of a great personality—a life of genius, a tragic death. He sees the movement shaping itself to the poetry, myth, and philosophy already existing when it began, he sees it producing a new literature, instinct with a new passion, simplicity, and feeling. He watches it, as time goes on, appropriating the strength of Roman institutions, the subtleties of Greek thought, and, although in every religious history, nay in every individual history, there remain puzzles and complexities which belong to the mysteries of the human organization, and which no critical process however sympathetic can ever completely fathom, still at the end the Christian problem is nearer a detailed solution for him than some others of the great religious problems of the world. How much harder for a European really to understand the vast spread and empire of Buddhism, its first rise, its tenacious hold on human life!

"But this relatively full understanding of the Christian problem is only reached *by a vigilant maintenance of that lookout over the whole religious field* of which I spoke just now. Only so can the historian keep his instinct sharp, his judgment clear. It is this constant use indeed of the comparative method which distinguishes him from the orthodox critic, which divides, say a German like Harnack or Hausrath from an Englishman like Westcott. The German is perpetually bringing into connection and relation; the Englishman, like Westcott, on the contrary, under the influence of Mansel's doctrine of 'affection,' works throughout from an isolation, from the perpetual assumption of a special case. The first method is throughout scientific. The second has nothing to do with science. It has its own justification, no doubt, but it must not assume a name that does not belong to it."

"Now I see, Merriman, how little you really understand the literature you profess to judge!" cried Ronalds; "as if Westcott, who knows everything, and is forever bringing Christianity into relation with the forces about it, can be accused of isolating it! A passage from the 'Gospel of the Resurrection' comes into my mind at the moment which is conclusive: 'Christianity is not an isolated system, but the result of a long preparation—Christianity can not be regarded alone and isolated from its antecedents. To attempt to separate Christianity from Judaism and Hellenism is not to interpret Christianity, but to construct a new religion '—and so on. What can be more clear?"

"I speak from a knowledge of Westcott's books," said Merriman, quietly. "The passages you quote concern the moral and philosophical phenomena of Christianity— I was speaking of the miraculous phenomena. No scholar of any eminence, whatever might have been the case fifty years ago, could at the present moment discuss the speculation and ethics of early Christendom without reference to surrounding conditions. So much the progress of knowledge has made impossible. But the procedure which the Christian apologist can not maintain in the field of ideas he still maintains in the field of miracle and event. Do you find Westcott seriously sifting and comparing the narratives of healing, of rising from the dead, of visions, and so on, which meet us in the New Testament, by the help of narratives of a similar kind to be found either in contemporary or later documents, of the materials offered by the history of other religions or of other periods of Christianity? And if the attempt is anywhere made, do you not feel all through that it is unreal, that the speaker's mind is made up, to begin with, under the influence of 'that affection which is part of insight,' and that he starts his history from an assumption which has nothing to do with history? No! Westcott is an eclectic, or a schoolman, of the most delicate, interesting, and attractive type possible; but his great learning is for him not an instrument and means of conviction, it is a mere adornment of it."

There was a long pause, which Ronalds at last broke, looking at his friend with emotion in every feature.

"And the result of it all, Merriman, for Germany and for yourself? Is Germany the better or the nobler for all her speculation? Are you the happier?"

Merriman thought awhile as he stood leaning over the fire; then he said: "Germany is in a religious state very difficult to understand, and the future of which is very difficult to forecast. To my mind, the chief evils of it come from that fierce reaction after '48, which prevented the convictions of liberal theology from mingling with the life and institutions of the people. Religion was for years made a question of politics and bureaucracy; and though the freedom of teaching was never seriously interfered with, the Church, which was for a long time the tool of political conservatism, organized itself against the liberal theological faculties, and the result has been a divorce between common life and speculative belief which affects the greater part of the cultivated class. The destructive forces of scientific theology have made them indifferent to dogma and formulæ, and reaction in Church and State has made it impossible for the new spiritual conceptions which belong to that theology to find new forms of religious action and expression."

"*Religious* action!" said Ronalds, bitterly. "What religion is possible to men who regard Christ as a good man with mistaken notions on many points, and God as an open question?"

"For me at the present moment," replied Merriman, with a singular gentleness, and showing in the whole expression of eye and feature, as he involuntarily moved nearer to his companion, a wish to soothe pain, a yearning to meet feeling with feeling, "that is not the point. The point is, What religion is possible to men, for whom God is the only reality, and Jesus that friend of God and man, in whom, through all human and necessary imperfection, they see the natural leader of their inmost life, the symbol of those religious forces in man which are primitive, essential, and universal?"

"What can a mere man, however good and eminent, matter to me," asked Ronalds, impatiently, "eighteen centuries after his death? The idea that Christianity can be reconstructed on any such basis is the merest dream."

"Then, if so, history is realizing a dream! For while you and those who think with you, Ronalds, are discussing whether a certain combination is possible, that combination is slowly and silently establishing itself in human life all about you! You dispute and debate—*solvitur ambulando*. All over the world, in quiet German towns, in Holland, in the circles which represent some of the best life of France, in large sections of Scotch and English life, and in large sections of American life, these ideas which you ridicule as chimerical, are being carried day by day into action, tried by all the tests which evil and pain can apply, and proving their power to help, inspire, and console human beings. All round us"—and the speaker drew himself up, an indescribable air of energy and hope pervading look and frame—"all round us I feel the New Reformation preparing, struggling into utterance and being! It is the product, the compromise of two forces, the scientific and the religious. In the English Reformed Church of the future, to which the Church of England and the Church of Scotland, the Presbyterians, the Congregationalists, the Independents, and the Unitarians will all contribute, and wherein the Liberal forces now rising in each body will ultimately coalesce, science will find the religion with which, as it has long since declared, through its wisest mouths, it has no rightful quarrel, and religion will find the science which belongs to it and which it needs. Ah! but when, *when?*"—and the tone changed to one of yearning and passion. "It is close upon us—it is prepared by all the forces of history and mind—its rise sooner or later is inevitable. But one has but the one life, and the years go by. Meanwhile the men whose hearts and heads are with us, who are our natural leaders, cling to systems which are for others, not for them, in which their faith is gone, and where their power is wasted, preaching a twofold doctrine—one for the *élite* and one for the multitude—and so ignoring all the teachings of history as to the sources and conditions of the religious life."

He stopped, a deep momentary depression stealing over the face and attitude, which ten minutes before had expressed such illimitable hope. Again Ronalds put up his hand and laid it lingeringly on the arm beside him.

"And yourself, Merriman?"

Merriman looked down into the anxious, friendly eyes, the moved countenance, and his own aspect gradually cleared. He spoke with a grave and mild solemnity as though making a confession of faith:

"I am content, Ronalds—inwardly more at rest than for years. This study of mine, which at first seemed to have swept away all, has given me back much. God—though I can find no names for Him—is more real, more present to me than ever before. And when, in the intervals of my law-work, I go back to my favorite books, it seems to me that I live with Jesus, beside Gennesareth, or in the streets of Jerusalem, as I never lived with him in the old days, when you and I were Anglicans together. I realize his historical limitations, and the more present

they are to me, the more my heart turns to him, the
more he means to me, and the more ready I am to go out
into that world of the poor and helpless he lost his life
for, with the thought of him warm within me. I do not
put him alone, on any non-natural pinnacle; but history,
led by the blind and yet divine instinct of the race, has
lifted this life from the mass of lives, and in it we Europeans see certain ethical and spiritual essentials concentrated and embodied, as we see the essentials of poetry
and art and knowledge concentrated and embodied in
other lives. And because ethical and spiritual things are
more vital to us than art and knowledge, this life is more
vital to us than those. Many others *may* have possessed
the qualities of Jesus, or of Buddha, but circumstance
and history have in each case decided as to the relative
worth of the particular story, the particular inspiration,
for the world in which it arose, in comparison with other
stories or other inspirations; and amid the difficulties of
existence, the modern European who persists in ignoring
the practical value of this exquisite Christian inheritance
of ours, or the Buddhist who should as yet look outside
his own faith for the materials of a more rational religious
development, is to my mind merely wasteful and impatient. We must submit to the education of God—the
revolt against miraculous belief is becoming now not so
much a revolt of reason as a revolt of conscience and faith
—but we must keep firm hold all the while of that vast
heritage of feeling which goes back, after all, through all
the overgrowths of dream and speculation, to that strongest of all the forces of human life—the love of man for
man, the trust of the lower soul in the higher, the hope
and the faith which the leader and the hero kindles amid
the masses!"

The two men remained silent awhile, Then Ronalds rose from his chair and grasped his companion's hand.

"We are nearer than we seemed half an hour ago," he said.

"And we shall come nearer yet," said Merriman, smiling.

Ronalds shook his head, stayed chatting awhile on indifferent subjects, and went.

THE END.

D. APPLETON & CO.'S PUBLICATIONS.

WHAT IS THE CHURCH? Or, PLAIN INSTRUCTION ABOUT THE CHURCH, ESPECIALLY IN ENGLAND; HER DOCTRINE, HER DISCIPLINE, HER OFFICE. By R. I. WOODHOUSE, M. A. With Notes and a Supplementary Chapter on the Protestant Episcopal Church in the United States, by J. A. SPENCER, S. T. D. 18mo. Paper, 40 cents.

In this convenient manual a great deal of information is crowded into a small space, and conveyed in a singularly clear and entertaining manner by the catechetical method.

A COMPREHENSIVE DICTIONARY OF THE BIBLE, MAINLY ABRIDGED FROM DR. WILLIAM SMITH'S DICTIONARY OF THE BIBLE. With Important Additions and Improvements. Edited by Rev. S. W. BARNUM, M. A. Embellished with many hundred Woodcuts, including Maps, Plans of Cities, Illustrations of Manners, Customs, etc. Complete in one vol. Large 8vo. Cloth, $5.00; sheep, $6.00; half morocco, $7.50.

Dr. Smith's Dictionary of the Bible, published in 1860-'63, and containing, in its three large octavo volumes, nearly 3,200 pages, is a work of acknowledged excellence; but its size, cost, and scholarly character, must prevent any extensive circulation of it among the great mass of those who desire and need a Dictionary of the Bible. The "Comprehensive Dictionary," on which nearly two years of editorial labor have already been expended, owes its origin to a settled conviction, on the part of the editor and publishers, of the need of such a modified abridgment of the original work as should make the results of Modern scholarship generally accessible.

STUDENT'S CONCORDANCE TO THE REVISED VERSION OF THE NEW TESTAMENT. Compiled upon an Original Plan, showing all the Changes in all Words referred to. With Appendices of the Chief Authorized Words and Passages omitted in the Revision, of Rare and Disused Words, and a List of Readings and Renderings preferred by the American Committee. Small 4to. Cloth, $2.50.

"A concordance of the revised version, to answer its end, should in a measure comprise both versions—to the extent, at least, of affording some clew to the changed words. This has been done in the present work, by giving under each word the words which in any text of the new version are substituted for the same word in the old."—*Extract from Preface.*

New York: D. APPLETON & CO., 1, 3, & 5 Bond Street.

D. APPLETON & CO.'S PUBLICATIONS.

THE LIFE AND WORDS OF CHRIST. By CUNNINGHAM GEIKIE, D. D. A new and cheap edition, printed from the same stereotype plates as the fine illustrated edition. Complete in one vol., 8vo, 1,258 pages. Cloth, $1.50.

This is the only cheap edition of Geikie's Life of Christ that contains the copious notes of the author, the marginal references, and an index.

"A work of the highest rank, breathing the spirit of true faith in Christ."—Dr. DELITZSCH, *the Commentator*.

"A most valuable addition to sacred literature."—A. N. LITTLEJOHN, D. D., *Bishop of Long Island*.

THE LIFE AND WORDS OF CHRIST. By CUNNINGHAM GEIKIE, D. D. New revised edition. In two vols., 12mo. Cloth, $2.50.

A new edition of this eminently popular Life of Christ, in a more convenient form and at a comparatively low price.

"We anticipate for it an extensive circulation, to which it is entitled for its substantial worth, its erudition, its brilliant style, and its fervent devotion."—The Rev. Dr. ADAMS, *President of Union Theological Seminary*.

"A great and noble work, rich in information, eloquent and scholarly in style, earnestly devout in feeling."—*London Literary World*.

"We think Dr. Geikie has caught a *new ray* from the 'Mountain of Light,' and has added a new page to our Christology which many will delight to read."—*Evangelist*.

EARLY CHRISTIAN LITERATURE PRIMERS. Now complete.

VOL. I. THE APOSTOLIC FATHERS AND THE APOLOGISTS OF THE SECOND CENTURY, A. D. 95-180. Cloth.
VOL. II. THE FATHERS OF THE THIRD CENTURY, A. D. 180-325. Cloth.
VOL. III. THE POST-NICENE GREEK FATHERS, A. D. 325-750. 18mo. Cloth.
VOL. IV. THE POST-NICENE LATIN FATHERS, A. D. 325-590.

By the Rev. GEORGE A. JACKSON. Edited by Professor GEORGE PARK FISHER, D. D. 18mo, cloth, 60 cents each; or put up in sets in box, $2.40.

The "Early Christian Literature Primers" embody, in a few small and inexpensive volumes, the substance of the characteristic works of the great Fathers of the Church. . . . Nearly every known author of the period is mentioned, and his place pointed out.

"The numbers of this series are so unpretentious that they might easily fail to receive the attention they deserve. They are done very well indeed, and really give a better introduction to the inner Christian life of the times and the real state of Christian opinion than could be obtained from a history."—*Independent*.

"The work shows a great amount of careful study, and excellent judgment and candor."—Professor E. C. SMYTH, D. D., *Andover Theological Seminary* (Congregational).

"I commend your plan heartily."—Professor T. W. COIT, *Berkeley Divinity School, Middletown* (Episcopal).

New York: D. APPLETON & CO., 1, 3, & 5 Bond Street.

D. APPLETON & CO.'S PUBLICATIONS.

Professor JOSEPH LE CONTE'S WORKS.

EVOLUTION AND ITS RELATION TO RELIGIOUS THOUGHT. By JOSEPH LE CONTE, LL. D., Professor of Geology and Natural History in the University of California. With numerous Illustrations. 12mo. Cloth, $1.50.

"Much, very much has been written, especially on the nature and the evidences of evolution, but the literature is so voluminous, much of it so fragmentary, and most of it so technical, that even very intelligent persons have still very vague ideas on the subject. I have attempted to give (1) a very concise account of what we mean by evolution, (2) an outline of the evidences of its truth drawn from many different sources, and (3) its relation to fundamental religious beliefs."—*Extract from Preface.*

ELEMENTS OF GEOLOGY. A Text-book for Colleges and for the General Reader. By JOSEPH LE CONTE, LL. D. With upward of 900 Illustrations. New and enlarged edition. 8vo. Cloth, $4.00.

"Besides preparing a comprehensive text-book, suited to present demands, Professor Le Conte has given us a volume of great value as an exposition of the subject, thoroughly up to date. The examples and applications of the work are almost entirely derived from this country, so that it may be properly considered an American geology. We can commend this work without qualification to all who desire an intelligent acquaintance with geological science, as fresh, lucid, full, authentic, the result of devoted study and of long experience in teaching."—*Popular Science Monthly.*

RELIGION AND SCIENCE. A Series of Sunday Lectures on the Relation of Natural and Revealed Religion, or the Truths revealed in Nature and Scripture. By JOSEPH LE CONTE, LL. D. 12mo. Cloth, $1.50.

"We commend the book cordially to the regard of all who are interested in whatever pertains to the discussion of these grave questions, and especially to those who desire to examine closely the strong foundations on which the Christian faith is reared."—*Boston Journal.*

SIGHT: An Exposition of the Principles of Monocular and Binocular Vision. By JOSEPH LE CONTE, LL. D. With Illustrations. 12mo. Cloth, $1.50.

"Professor Le Conte has long been known as an original investigator in this department; all that he gives us is treated with a master-hand. It is pleasant to find an American book that can rank with the very best of foreign books on this subject."—*The Nation.*

COMPEND OF GEOLOGY. By JOSEPH LE CONTE, LL. D. 12mo. Cloth, $1.40.

New York: D. APPLETON & CO., 1, 3, & 5 Bond Street.

D. APPLETON & CO.'S PUBLICATIONS.

THOMAS H. HUXLEY'S WORKS.

SCIENCE AND CULTURE, AND OTHER ESSAYS. 12mo. Cloth, $1.50.

THE CRAYFISH: AN INTRODUCTION TO THE STUDY OF ZOÖLOGY. With 82 Illustrations. 12mo. Cloth, $1.75.

SCIENCE PRIMERS: INTRODUCTORY. 18mo. Flexible cloth, 45 cents.

MAN'S PLACE IN NATURE. 12mo. Cloth, $1.25.

ON THE ORIGIN OF SPECIES. 12mo. Cloth, $1.00.

MORE CRITICISMS ON DARWIN, AND ADMINISTRATIVE NIHILISM. 12mo. Limp cloth, 50 cents.

MANUAL OF THE ANATOMY OF VERTEBRATED ANIMALS. Illustrated. 12mo. Cloth, $2.50.

MANUAL OF THE ANATOMY OF INVERTEBRATED ANIMALS. 12mo. Cloth, $2.50.

LAY SERMONS, ADDRESSES, AND REVIEWS. 12mo. Cloth, $1.75.

CRITIQUES AND ADDRESSES. 12mo. Cloth, $1.50.

AMERICAN ADDRESSES; WITH A LECTURE ON THE STUDY OF BIOLOGY. 12mo. Cloth, $1.25.

PHYSIOGRAPHY: AN INTRODUCTION TO THE STUDY OF NATURE. With Illustrations and Colored Plates. 12mo. Cloth, $2.50.

HUXLEY AND YOUMANS'S ELEMENTS OF PHYSIOLOGY AND HYGIENE. By T. H. HUXLEY and W. J. YOUMANS. 12mo. Cloth, $1.50.

New York: D. APPLETON & CO., 1, 3, & 5 Bond Street.

D. APPLETON & CO.'S PUBLICATIONS.

SIR JOHN LUBBOCK'S (Bart.) WORKS.

THE ORIGIN OF CIVILIZATION AND THE PRIMITIVE CONDITION OF MAN, MENTAL AND SOCIAL CONDITION OF SAVAGES. Fourth edition, with numerous Additions. With Illustrations. 8vo. Cloth, $5.00.

"This interesting work—for it is intensely so in its aim, scope, and the ability of its author—treats of what the scientists denominate *anthropology*, or the natural history of the human species; the complete science of man, body, and soul, including sex, temperament, race, civilization, etc."—*Providence Press.*

PREHISTORIC TIMES, AS ILLUSTRATED BY ANCIENT REMAINS AND THE MANNERS AND CUSTOMS OF MODERN SAVAGES. Illustrated. 8vo. Cloth, $5.00.

"This is, perhaps, the best summary of evidence now in our possession concerning the general character of prehistoric times. The Bronze Age, The Stone Age, The Tumuli, The Lake Inhabitants of Switzerland, The Shell Mounds, The Cave Man, and The Antiquity of Man, are the titles of the most important chapters."—*Dr. C. K. Adams's Manual of Historical Literature.*

ANTS, BEES, AND WASPS. A Record of Observations on the Habits of the Social Hymenoptera. With Colored Plates. 12mo. Cloth, $2.00.

"This volume contains the record of various experiments made with ants, bees, and wasps during the last ten years, with a view to test their mental condition and powers of sense. The author has carefully watched and marked particular insects, and has had their nests under observation for long periods—one of his ants' nests having been under constant inspection ever since 1874. His observations are made principally upon ants, because they show more power and flexibility of mind; and the value of his studies is that they belong to the department of original research."

ON THE SENSES, INSTINCTS, AND INTELLIGENCE OF ANIMALS, WITH SPECIAL REFERENCE TO INSECTS. "International Scientific Series." With over One Hundred Illustrations. 12mo. Cloth, $1.75.

The author has here collected some of his recent observations on the senses and intelligence of animals, and especially of insects, and has attempted to give, very briefly, some idea of the organs of sense, commencing in each case with those of man himself.

THE PLEASURES OF LIFE. 12mo. Cloth, 50 cents; paper, 25 cents.

CONTENTS.—THE DUTY OF HAPPINESS. THE HAPPINESS OF DUTY. A SONG OF BOOKS. THE CHOICE OF BOOKS. THE BLESSING OF FRIENDS. THE VALUE OF TIME. THE PLEASURES OF TRAVEL. THE PLEASURES OF HOME. SCIENCE. EDUCATION.

New York: D. APPLETON & CO., 1, 3, & 5 Bond Street.

D. APPLETON & CO.'S PUBLICATIONS.

ALEXANDER BAIN'S WORKS.

THE SENSES AND THE INTELLECT. By ALEXANDER BAIN, LL. D., Professor of Logic in the University of Aberdeen. 8vo. Cloth, $5.00.

The object of this treatise is to give a full and systematic account of two principal divisions of the science of mind—the senses and the intellect. The value of the third edition of the work is greatly enhanced by an account of the psychology of Aristotle, which has been contributed by Mr. Grote.

THE EMOTIONS AND THE WILL. By ALEXANDER BAIN, LL. D. 8vo. Cloth, $5.00.

The present publication is a sequel to the former one on "The Senses and the Intellect," and completes a systematic exposition of the human mind.

MENTAL SCIENCE. A Compendium of Psychology and the History of Philosophy. Designed as a Text-book for High-Schools and Colleges. By ALEXANDER BAIN, LL. D. 12mo. Cloth, leather back, $1.50.

The present volume is an abstract of two voluminous works, "The Senses and the Intellect" and "The Emotions and the Will," and presents in a compressed and lucid form the views which are there more extensively elaborated.

MORAL SCIENCE. A Compendium of Ethics. By ALEXANDER BAIN, LL. D. 12mo. Cloth, leather back, $1.50.

The present dissertation falls under two divisions. The first division, entitled The Theory of Ethics, gives an account of the questions or points brought into discussion, and handles at length the two of greatest prominence, the Ethical Standard and the Moral Faculty. The second division—on the Ethical Systems—is a full detail of all the systems, ancient and modern.

MIND AND BODY. Theories of their Relations. By ALEXANDER BAIN, LL. D. 12mo. Cloth, $1.50.

"A forcible statement of the connection between mind and body, studying their subtile interworkings by the light of the most recent physiological investigations."—*Christian Register.*

LOGIC, DEDUCTIVE AND INDUCTIVE. By ALEXANDER BAIN, LL. D. Revised edition. 12mo. Cloth, leather back, $2.00.

EDUCATION AS A SCIENCE. By ALEXANDER BAIN, LL. D. 12mo. Cloth, $1.75.

ENGLISH COMPOSITION AND RHETORIC. Enlarged edition. Part I. Intellectual Elements of Style. By ALEXANDER BAIN, LL. D., Emeritus Professor of Logic in the University of Aberdeen. 12mo. Cloth, leather back, $1.50.

ON TEACHING ENGLISH. With Detailed Examples and an Inquiry into the Definition of Poetry. By ALEXANDER BAIN, LL. D. 12mo. Cloth, $1.25.

PRACTICAL ESSAYS. By ALEXANDER BAIN, LL. D. 12mo. Cloth, $1.50.

New York: D. APPLETON & CO., 1, 3, & 5 Bond Street.

www.ingramcontent.com/pod-product-compliance
Lightning Source LLC
Chambersburg PA
CBHW021150230426
43667CB00006B/326